BLACK INDEX

CRITICAL STUDIES ON
BLACK LIFE AND CULTURE
(VOL. 4)

GARLAND REFERENCE LIBRARY
OF SOCIAL SCIENCE
(VOL. 65)

Volume 4

Critical Studies on Black Life and Culture

Advisory Editor
Professor Charles T. Davis, Chairman
Afro-American Studies, Yale University

Assistant Advisory Editor
Professor Henry-Louis Gates
Afro-American Studies, Yale University

BLACK INDEX

Afro-Americana in Selected Periodicals, 1907–1949

Richard Newman

GARLAND PUBLISHING, INC. • NEW YORK & LONDON
1981

Library of Congress Cataloging in Publication Data

Newman, Richard.
Black index.

(Garland reference library of social science ; v. 65)
(Critical studies on Black life and culture ; v. 4)
1. Afro-Americans—Periodicals—Indexes.
I. Title. II. Series: Critical studies on Black
life and culture ; v. 4.
Z1361. N39N58 [E185] 016.973′0496073 80-835
ISBN 0-8240-9513-8

Printed on acid-free, 250-year-life paper
Manufactured in the United States of America

For Nancy and
Randall K. Burkett

CONTENTS

Acknowledgments *ix*

Introduction *xi*

Periodicals indexed, listed alphabetically by symbol *xv*

Periodicals indexed, listed alphabetically by title *xxi*

Periodicals searched in which no Afro-Americana articles were located *xxvii*

The index *3*

ACKNOWLEDGMENTS

Over the years a number of friends have supported and encouraged by their interest my involvement in Black Studies. I am especially indebted to Robert A. Hill of UCLA; Malcolm McVey, formerly of the University of Nairobi; Dorothy Porter Wesley of Howard University; George Shepperson of the University of Edinburgh; and Harold Turner of the University of Aberdeen.

My debt to Nancy Burkett of the American Antiquarian Society and Randall K. Burkett of the College of the Holy Cross is only partially acknowledged by the dedication of this book to them.

In searching original articles it was a pleasure to be able to draw upon the extraordinary resources and generous and cooperative staffs of three great institutions: the Boston Athenaeum, the Boston Public Library, and The New York Public Library.

I am deeply grateful to my colleagues at Garland Publishing, Inc., for a great many reasons, not least of all to Ralph Carlson for wanting to publish this book and Barbara Bergeron for seeing it through production.

INTRODUCTION

This *Index* is an author and subject guide to over 1,000 articles on Afro-Americana in more than 350 periodicals published in the United States, Canada, and Great Britain during the first half of the twentieth century. The lists at the end of this introduction indicate the serials that are included and the time periods for which they were indexed.

This *Index* had its origin in the realization that a great amount of black material exists in little-known magazines and journals, particularly state historical publications, to which systematic access is often difficult. One source of access to some of these periodicals is the *Annual Magazine Subject Index* published from 1907 to 1949 by the F. W. Faxon Company.

The Faxon index performed an invaluable service by indexing periodicals which were, with very few exceptions, not indexed elsewhere. While strongest in state and local history, Faxon also drew heavily upon publications in art, current events, folklore, geography, political science, sociology, and religion.

Despite its uniqueness and usefulness, the Faxon index has several serious disadvantages. The primary one is that over the years it added and dropped journals (it was standard policy to eliminate journals as they were indexed elsewhere), and that journals were born and died. As a result, few periodicals are indexed continuously over their lifetimes, or, for that matter, over the life of Faxon's *Index*.

Other disadvantages are that Faxon provided no author access, and that for most articles there was only one subject listing. Also, over time, there were some inconsistencies in filing.

To create this present book, each of the 250,000 entries in Faxon was read and analyzed. An author card was made for each of the more than 1,000 articles dealing with an Afro-American subject. For each article, subject cards were made (ranging from one to eight in number, but averaging three for each), and these author and multiple subject cards were then interfiled.

The headings of author entries are printed in upper- and lower-case letters, while the headings of subject entries are printed in all capital letters.

Subject headings were also created for the form (e.g., letter, document, bibliography) as well as the content of certain articles. In addition, subject headings were made for historiography and certain sociological methodologies.

Of course, Black Studies as such was not a subject field when the Faxon index was being compiled. While there were many Afro-American titles filed by Faxon under "Negroes, United States" or "Slavery," there were many more that were filed under a variety of names, places, organizations, and events, often with no indication in the subject heading that this was in fact an aspect of Afro-American history. This *Index* identifies these Afro-American articles, brings them together in one place, and provides author as well as greatly expanded subject access.

The criterion for inclusion of articles in this *Index* was that the article be directly relevant to the study of the Afro-American experience. Limits had to be set, of course, and judgment exercised. African, West Indian, and Latin American topics were included only if they bore directly upon Afro-American life and history. This meant the exclusion, for example, of material on African animals and West Indian tourism. All articles dealing with the Abolitionist Movement and Reconstruction were included, but Civil War articles were only selectively included.

Book reviews were included, and each review is listed twice: once under the name of the reviewer, and once under the name of the author of the book.

A number of articles reflect the stereotypes of their day, and so their titles include value-laden words such as "primitive," "carpetbagger," "superstition," etc. Slave revolts may be called "conspiracies" or "massacres." However offensive, these terms have not been changed. For consistency, the word Negro has been silently capitalized whenever it appeared in lower case.

One major source of Afro-Americana, the *Journal of Negro History*, was indexed by Faxon from 1915 to 1949, including volumes 1 through 34. Those citations are not included in this *Index* since a separate index to the *Journal of Negro History* is readily available to researchers, and it seemed wise to limit this volume to those sources which are not so well known or easily accessible.

One should never use the titles listed here as formal bibliographic citations without checking the original articles. The Faxon indexers sometimes elaborated and expanded the titles to explain the contents of the articles. When a given title remained meaningless or included obscure references, the original article was examined in order to create appropriate subject headings. Factual errors of names, dates, spelling, etc., in the Faxon originals were silently corrected when found.

In spite of careful work and seemingly endless checking, this is the kind of project into which errors of various kinds are bound to have found their irksome way. I can only request that anyone finding errors communicate them to me ℅ Garland Publishing, Inc., 136 Madison Ave., New York 10016, so that they can be corrected in any subsequent editions.

Richard Newman

New York
February 1980

I. Periodicals indexed, listed alphabetically by symbol

AAA	Art and Archaeology, 1914–34
AAB	Architecture and Building, 1911–32, formerly Architects' and Builders' Magazine
ACA	Academy of Political Science. Proceedings, 1910–49
AFO	Architectural Forum, 1918–49, formerly Brickbuilder
AGS	American Geographical Society Bulletin, 1911–5, later Geographical Review
AHR	American Historical Review, 1914–49
AHS	Alabama Historical Society. Transactions, 1904–40
AIA	Art in America, 1913–49
AIR	American Irish Historical Society. Journal, 1915–41
AJH	American Jewish Historical Society. Proceedings and Publications, 1909–49 (vols. 18–39)
AJI	American Journal of International Law and Supplement, 1907–49 (vols. 1–43)
ALA	American Library Association Bulletin, 1918–49
AMA	American Magazine of Art, 1916–36, formerly Art and Progress; later Magazine of Art
AMC	American Catholic Historical Society. Records, 1907–49 (vols. 18–60)
AME	Americana, 1909–43, formerly American Historical Magazine
AMH	American Historical Magazine, 1906–9, later Americana
AMR	American Review, 1923–6, formerly School and Home Education
ANN	Annals of Iowa, 1907–15; 1920–49
APP	American Political Science Association. Proceedings, 1904–49
APS	American Political Science Review, 1906–49
ARA	Arkansas Historical Association. Publications, 1906–17
ARC	Architecture (New York), 1919–36
ARK	Arkansas Historical Quarterly, 1942–9
ART	The Arts, 1923–31
ASR	American Sociological Review, 1936–49 (vols. 1–14), successor to American Sociological Society. Publications
ASS	American Sociological Society. Proceedings and Publications, 1906–43

ATE	Atelier, 1931–2, later London Studio
BCH	British Columbia Historical Quarterly, 1937–49
BKL	Bookman (London), 1907–34
BKN	Book News Monthly, 1907–18
BSA	Bibliographical Society of America. Papers, 1911–49
BUB	Bulletin of Bibliography, 1897–1949
BUR	Burlington Magazine, 1903–49
CAF	Canadian Forum, 1945–9
CAL	California History Nugget, 1928–34
CAN	Canadian Historical Review, 1920–49
CHA	Chambers' Journal, 1913–31
CHR	Catholic Historical Review, 1915–49
CHS	Columbia Historical Society. Records, 1906–48
CJR	Contemporary Jewish Record, 1941–4
CNT	Connecticut Magazine, 1895–1908
COL	Colorado Magazine, 1923–49
COM	Commentary, 1945–9 (vols. 1–8)
CON	Connoisseur, 1901–32
COR	Cornhill Magazine, 1913–39; 1944–9
DAL	Dalhousie Review, 1921–49
DUB	Dublin Review, 1913–49
EBM	Educational Bi-Monthly, 1906–17
ENG	English Review, 1913–37
EXL	Ex Libris, 1923–5
FHS	Florida Historical Society. Publications, 1908–9; Quarterly, 1928–49
FLL	Folk-Lore (London), 1913–49
FOR	Foreign Affairs, 1922–33, formerly Journal of International Relations
FTE	Fortune, 1931–49
GEJ	Geographical Journal (London), 1911–49
GEO	Geographical Review, 1916–49, formerly American Geographical Society Bulletin
GHQ	Georgia Historical Quarterly, 1917–49
GOV	Government, 1907–8
GRA	Granite Monthly, 1906–29, later New Hampshire, the Granite Monthly
GSM	Granite State Magazine, 1906–11
HAH	Hispanic American Historical Review, 1918–22; 1926–49
HAM	Hampton's Magazine, 1909, formerly Broadway Magazine and Hampton's Broadway Magazine

HGM	Harvard Graduates Magazine, 1913–34
HIO	Historical Outlook, 1918–33, formerly History Teacher's Magazine; later The Social Studies
HIS	Historical Quarterly, 1926–9; Filson Club Historical Quarterly, 1930–49
HOL	Holiday, 1946–9
HOM	Homiletic Review, 1907–34
HTM	History Teacher's Magazine, 1911–8, later Historical Outlook
IAJ	Iowa Journal of History and Politics, 1903–49
IHC	Illinois State Historical Library. Collections, 1903–45
IHJ	Illinois State Historical Society. Journal, 1909–49
IHL	Illinois State Historical Library. Publications, 1905–37
INM	Indiana Magazine of History, 1905–49 (vols. 1–45)
INT	International Studio, 1914–31
IRM	International Review of Missions, 1916–48
JAF	Journal of American Folk-Lore, 1913–49
JAH	Journal of American History, 1907–35
JIR	Journal of International Relations, 1919–22, formerly Journal of Race Development; later Foreign Affairs
JMH	Journal of Mississippi History, 1939–49
JOB	Journal of Business, 1928–49
JRD	Journal of Race Development, 1910–9, later Journal of International Relations
JSH	Journal of Southern History, 1935–49 (vols. 1–15)
KAN	Kansas State Historical Society. Transactions (Historical Collections), 1906–8; Collections, 1910–28; Publications, 1920; 1930; later Kansas Historical Quarterly
KHQ	Kansas Historical Quarterly, 1931–49 (vols. 1–17), formerly Kansas State Historical Society. Publications
KID	Kindergarten Primary Magazine, 1907–33
KYR	Kentucky State Historical Society. Register, 1907–49 (vols. 5–47)
LHQ	Louisiana Historical Quarterly, 1917–49
LHS	Louisiana Historical Society. Publications, 1908–17
LON	London Mercury, 1919–39
LST	London Studio, 1932–9, formerly Atelier; later Studio
MAG	Magazine of History, 1911–22
MAR	Magazine of Art, 1937–49, formerly American Magazine of Art
MDH	Maryland Historical Magazine, 1906–49

MET	Metropolitan Magazine, 1907–11
MHM	Michigan History Magazine, 1917–49
MIV	Mississippi Valley Historical Association. Proceedings, 1907–24
MNN	Minnesota History, 1925–49, formerly Minnesota History Bulletin
MOD	Modern Music, 1924–46
MOH	Missouri Historical Review, 1906–49
MPC	Michigan Pioneer and Historical Society. Collections and Researches, 1904–20
MSS	Mississippi Historical Society. Publications, 1906–25
MUN	Munsey's Magazine, 1911–21
MUS	New Music Review, 1904–35
MVH	Mississippi Valley Historical Review, 1914–49
NAR	National Review (London), 1911–49
NAT	National Magazine, 1911–32
NCA	State Literary and Historical Association of North Carolina. Proceedings, 1914–21
NCH	North Carolina Historical Review, 1924–49
NDQ	University of North Dakota Quarterly Journal, 1919–33
NEQ	New England Quarterly, 1928–49
NEW	New Church Review, 1911–34
NGE	National Geographic Magazine, 1914–49
NHS	Nebraska State Historical Society. Collections, Proceedings, Publications, 1906–38
NIS	Journal of the National Institute of Social Sciences, 1915–34
NJS	New Jersey Historical Society. Proceedings, 1902–43 (vols. 3–16)
NMH	New Mexico Historical Review, 1926–49
NMQ	New Mexico Quarterly Review, 1948–9
NWH	New Hampshire, the Granite Monthly, 1929–30, formerly Granite Monthly; later Granite State Monthly
NYH	New York History, 1932–49, formerly New York State Historical Association Quarterly Journal
NYS	New York State Historical Association Quarterly Journal, 1919–31, later New York History
OAQ	Ohio State Archaeological and Historical Quarterly, 1887–1949 (vols. 9–41)
OHS	Ontario Historical Society. Papers and Records, 1906–47, later Ontario History
OKC	Chronicles of Oklahoma, 1938–49

ONW	Old Northwest Genealogical Quarterly, 1907–12
ORE	Oregon Historical Society Quarterly, 1900–49
OUT	Out West, 1911–7
PAH	Pennsylvania History, 1934–49 (vols. 1–16)
PAM	Pennsylvania Magazine of History and Biography, 1908–49
PBY	Presbyterian Historical Society. Journal, 1901–10, later Journal of the Department of History of the Presbyterian Church in the U.S.A., 1911–44
PCQ	Print Collectors' Quarterly, 1911–49
PEH	Protestant Episcopal Church. Historical Magazine, 1932–49
PHR	Pacific Historical Review, 1932–49 (vols. 2–18)
PLY	Public Libraries, 1918–9
PRI	Printing Art, 1907–24, later Printed Salesmanship
PRS	Pearson's Magazine, 1907–12
PUB	Public, 1911–8
QUE	Queen's Quarterly (Canada), 1908–49 (vols. 15–56)
RIH	Rhode Island History, 1942–9 (vols. 1–8), formerly Rhode Island Historical Society. Collections
ROR	Review of Religion, 1936–49 (vols. 1–14)
RSC	Royal Society of Canada. Proceedings and Transactions, 1906–42
SCH	School and Home Education, 1907–22, later American Review
SCI	Science Progress (London), 1906–39; 1946–9
SFQ	Southern Folklore Quarterly, 1937–49 (vols. 1–13)
SGM	Scottish Geographical Magazine, 1912–49
SHA	Southern History Association, 1907 (vol. 11)
SHS	Southern Historical Society. Papers, 1906–43
SJM	Sprague's Journal of Maine History, 1913–26
SOC	South Carolina Historical and Genealogical Magazine, 1907–49 (vols. 8–50)
SOS	The Social Studies, 1934–49, formerly Historical Outlook
SPM	Spirit of Missions, 1907–8
STR	Strand (London), 1911–8
SWH	Southwestern Historical Quarterly, 1912–49, formerly Texas State Historical Association Quarterly
TEC	Technical World, 1904–12
TEX	Texas Monthly, 1928–30, formerly Bunker's Monthly
THM	Tennessee Historical Magazine, 1915–35, later Tennessee Historical Quarterly

THQ	Tennessee Historical Quarterly, 1942–9 (vols. 1–8), formerly Tennessee Historical Magazine
TIM	Times Magazine, 1906–7
TRA	Travel, 1912–49
UNI	University Magazine, 1907–20
USC	United States Catholic Historical Society. Records and Studies, 1906–48
VAM	Virginia Magazine of History and Biography, 1893–1949 (vols. 1–57)
VHS	Vermont Historical Society. Proceedings, 1905–43
VQR	Virginia Quarterly Review, 1925–49
WAS	Washington Historical Quarterly (Seattle), 1906–35, later Pacific Northwest Quarterly
WDT	World Today (London), 1923–32, formerly World's Work
WHP	Wisconsin State Historical Society. Proceedings, Publications (Calendar Series), and Studies, 1906–19
WIM	Wisconsin Magazine of History, 1917–49
WLD	World Horizons, 1938–40
WMQ	William and Mary Quarterly, 1921–49
WOR	World Review (London), 1936–49, formerly Review of Reviews
WVA	West Virginia History, 1939–49 (vols. 1–10)
WWL	World's Work (London), 1902–23, later World Today
YHT	Yachting, 1938–44

II. Periodicals indexed, listed alphabetically by title

ACA	Academy of Political Science. Proceedings, 1910–49
AHS	Alabama Historical Society. Transactions, 1904–40
AMC	American Catholic Historical Society. Records, 1907–49 (vols. 18–60)
AGS	American Geographical Society Bulletin, 1911–5, later Geographical Review
AMH	American Historical Magazine, 1906–9, later Americana
AHR	American Historical Review, 1914–49
AIR	American Irish Historical Society. Journal, 1915–41
AJH	American Jewish Historical Society. Proceedings and Publications, 1909–49 (vols. 18–39)
AJI	American Journal of International Law and Supplement, 1907–49 (vols. 1–43)
ALA	American Library Association Bulletin, 1918–49
AMA	American Magazine of Art, 1916–36, formerly Art and Progress; later Magazine of Art
APP	American Political Science Association. Proceedings, 1904–49
APS	American Political Science Review, 1906–49
AMR	American Review, 1923–6, formerly School and Home Education
ASR	American Sociological Review, 1936–49 (vols. 1–14), successor to American Sociological Society. Publications
ASS	American Sociological Society. Proceedings and Publications, 1906–43
AME	Americana, 1909–43, formerly American Historical Magazine
ANN	Annals of Iowa, 1907–15; 1920–49
AFO	Architectural Forum, 1918–49, formerly Brickbuilder
ARC	Architecture (New York), 1919–36
AAB	Architecture and Building, 1911–32, formerly Architects' and Builders' Magazine
ARA	Arkansas Historical Association. Publications, 1906–17
ARK	Arkansas Historical Quarterly, 1942–9
AAA	Art and Archaeology, 1914–34
AIA	Art in America, 1913–49
ART	The Arts, 1923–31

ATE	Atelier, 1931–2, later London Studio
BSA	Bibliographical Society of America. Papers, 1911–49
BKN	Book News Monthly, 1907–18
BKL	Bookman (London), 1907–34
BCH	British Columbia Historical Quarterly, 1937–49
BUB	Bulletin of Bibliography, 1897–1949
BUR	Burlington Magazine, 1903–49
CAL	California History Nugget, 1928–34
CAF	Canadian Forum, 1945–9
CAN	Canadian Historical Review, 1920–49
CHR	Catholic Historical Review, 1915–49
CHA	Chambers' Journal, 1913–31
OKC	Chronicles of Oklahoma, 1938–49
COL	Colorado Magazine, 1923–49
CHS	Columbia Historical Society. Records, 1906–48
COM	Commentary, 1945–9 (vols. 1–8)
CNT	Connecticut Magazine, 1895–1908
CON	Connoisseur, 1901–32
CJR	Contemporary Jewish Record, 1941–4
COR	Cornhill Magazine, 1913–39; 1944–9
DAL	Dalhousie Review, 1921–49
DUB	Dublin Review, 1913–49
EBM	Educational Bi-Monthly, 1906–17
ENG	English Review, 1913–37
EXL	Ex Libris, 1923–5
FHS	Florida Historical Society. Publications, 1908–9; Quarterly, 1928–49
FLL	Folk-Lore (London), 1913–49
FOR	Foreign Affairs, 1922–33, formerly Journal of International Relations
FTE	Fortune, 1931–49
GEJ	Geographical Journal (London), 1911–49
GEO	Geographical Review, 1916–49, formerly American Geographical Society Bulletin
GHQ	Georgia Historical Quarterly, 1917–49
GOV	Government, 1907–8
GRA	Granite Monthly, 1906–29, later New Hampshire, the Granite Monthly
GSM	Granite State Magazine, 1906–11
HAM	Hampton's Magazine, 1909, formerly Broadway Magazine and Hampton's Broadway Magazine

HGM	Harvard Graduates Magazine, 1913–34
HAH	Hispanic American Historical Review, 1918–22; 1926–49
HIO	Historical Outlook, 1918–33, formerly History Teacher's Magazine; later The Social Studies
HIS	Historical Quarterly, 1926–9; Filson Club Historical Quarterly, 1930–49
HTM	History Teacher's Magazine, 1911–8, later Historical Outlook
HOL	Holiday, 1946–9
HOM	Homiletic Review, 1907–34
IHC	Illinois State Historical Library. Collections, 1903–45
IHL	Illinois State Historical Library. Publications, 1905–37
IHJ	Illinois State Historical Society. Journal, 1909–49
INM	Indiana Magazine of History, 1905–49 (vols. 1–45)
INM	Indiana Quarterly Magazine of History. See Indiana Magazine of History
IRM	International Review of Missions, 1916–48
INT	International Studio, 1914–31
IAJ	Iowa Journal of History and Politics, 1903–49
JAF	Journal of American Folk-Lore, 1913–49
JAH	Journal of American History, 1907–35
JOB	Journal of Business, 1928–49
JIR	Journal of International Relations, 1919–22, formerly Journal of Race Development; later Foreign Affairs
JMH	Journal of Mississippi History, 1939–49
JRD	Journal of Race Development, 1910–9, later Journal of International Relations
JSH	Journal of Southern History, 1935–49 (vols. 1–15)
NIS	Journal of the National Institute of Social Sciences, 1915–34
KHQ	Kansas Historical Quarterly, 1931–49 (vols. 1–17), formerly Kansas State Historical Society. Publications
KAN	Kansas State Historical Society. Transactions (Historical Collections), 1906–8; Collections, 1910–28; Publications, 1920; 1930; later Kansas Historical Quarterly
KYR	Kentucky State Historical Society. Register, 1907–49 (vols. 5–47)
KID	Kindergarten Primary Magazine, 1907–33
LON	London Mercury, 1919–39
LST	London Studio, 1932–9, formerly Atelier; later Studio
LHQ	Louisiana Historical Quarterly, 1917–49

LHS	Louisiana Historical Society. Publications, 1908–17
MAR	Magazine of Art, 1937–49, formerly American Magazine of Art
MAG	Magazine of History, 1911–22
MDH	Maryland Historical Magazine, 1906–49
MET	Metropolitan Magazine, 1907–11
MHM	Michigan History Magazine, 1917–49
MPC	Michigan Pioneer and Historical Society. Collections and Researches, 1904–20
MNN	Minnesota History, 1925–49, formerly Minnesota History Bulletin
MSS	Mississippi Historical Society. Publications, 1906–25
MIV	Mississippi Valley Historical Association. Proceedings, 1907–24
MVH	Mississippi Valley Historical Review, 1914–49
MOH	Missouri Historical Review, 1906–49
MOD	Modern Music, 1924–46
MUN	Munsey's Magazine, 1911–21
NGE	National Geographic Magazine, 1914–49
NAT	National Magazine, 1911–32
NAR	National Review (London), 1911–49
NHS	Nebraska State Historical Society. Collections, Proceedings, Publications, 1906–38
NEW	New Church Review, 1911–34
NEQ	New England Quarterly, 1928–49
NWH	New Hampshire, the Granite Monthly, 1929–30, formerly Granite Monthly; later Granite State Monthly
NJS	New Jersey Historical Society. Proceedings, 1902–43 (vols. 3–16)
NMH	New Mexico Historical Review, 1926–49
NMQ	New Mexico Quarterly Review, 1948–9
MUS	New Music Review, 1904–35
NYH	New York History, 1932–49, formerly New York State Historical Association Quarterly Journal
NYS	New York State Historical Association Quarterly Journal, 1919–31, later New York History
NCH	North Carolina Historical Review, 1924–49
OAQ	Ohio State Archaeological and Historical Quarterly, 1887–1949 (vols. 9–41)
ONW	Old Northwest Genealogical Quarterly, 1907–12

OHS	Ontario Historical Society. Papers and Records, 1906–47, later Ontario History
ORE	Oregon Historical Society Quarterly, 1900–49
OUT	Out West, 1911–7
PHR	Pacific Historical Review, 1932–49 (vols. 2–18)
PRS	Pearson's Magazine, 1907–12
PAH	Pennsylvania History, 1934–49 (vols. 1–16)
PAM	Pennsylvania Magazine of History, 1907–11, later Pennsylvania Magazine of History and Biography
PBY	Presbyterian Historical Society. Journal, 1901–10, later Journal of the Department of History of the Presbyterian Church in the U.S.A., 1911–44
PCQ	Print Collectors' Quarterly, 1911–49
PRI	Printing Art, 1907–24, later Printed Salesmanship
PEH	Protestant Episcopal Church. Historical Magazine, 1932–49
PUB	Public, 1911–8
PLY	Public Libraries, 1918–9
QUE	Queen's Quarterly (Canada), 1908–49 (vols. 15–56)
ROR	Review of Religion, 1936–49 (vols. 1–14)
RIH	Rhode Island History, 1942–9 (vols. 1–8), formerly Rhode Island Historical Society. Collections
RSC	Royal Society of Canada. Proceedings and Transactions, 1906–42
SCH	School and Home Education, 1907–22, later American Review
SCI	Science Progress (London), 1906–39; 1946–9
SGM	Scottish Geographical Magazine, 1912–49
SOS	The Social Studies, 1934–49, formerly Historical Outlook
SOC	South Carolina Historical and Genealogical Magazine, 1907–49 (vols. 8–50)
SFQ	Southern Folklore Quarterly, 1937–49 (vols. 1–13)
SHS	Southern Historical Society. Papers, 1906–43
SHA	Southern History Association, 1907 (vol. 11)
SWH	Southwestern Historical Quarterly, 1912–49, formerly Texas State Historical Association Quarterly
SPM	Spirit of Missions, 1907–8
SJM	Sprague's Journal of Maine History, 1913–26
NCA	State Literary and Historical Association of North Carolina. Proceedings, 1914–21
STR	Strand (London), 1911–8

TEC	Technical World, 1904–12
THM	Tennessee Historical Magazine, 1915–35, later Tennessee Historical Quarterly
THQ	Tennessee Historical Quarterly, 1942–9 (vols. 1–8), formerly Tennessee Historical Magazine
TEX	Texas Monthly, 1928–30, formerly Bunker's Monthly
TIM	Times Magazine, 1906–7
TRA	Travel, 1912–49
USC	United States Catholic Historical Society. Records and Studies, 1906–48
UNI	University Magazine, 1907–20
NDQ	University of North Dakota Quarterly Journal, 1919–33
VHS	Vermont Historical Society. Proceedings, 1905–43
VAM	Virginia Magazine of History and Biography, 1893–1949 (vols. 1–57)
VQR	Virginia Quarterly Review, 1925–49
WAS	Washington Historical Quarterly (Seattle), 1906–35, later Pacific Northwest Quarterly
WVA	West Virginia History, 1939–49 (vols. 1–10)
WMQ	William and Mary Quarterly, 1921–49
WIM	Wisconsin Magazine of History, 1917–49
WHP	Wisconsin State Historical Society. Proceedings, Publications (Calendar Series), and Studies, 1906–19
WLD	World Horizons, 1938–40
WOR	World Review (London), 1936–49, formerly Review of Reviews
WDT	World Today (London), 1923–32, formerly World's Work
WWL	World's Work (London), 1902–23, later World Today
YHT	Yachting, 1938–44

III. Periodicals searched in which no Afro-Americana articles were located

African Monthly, 1906–10
Alpina Americana, 1911, 1914
American Alpine Journal, 1911–34; 1940–9
American Catholic Historical Researches, 1908–12
American City, 1910 (vols. 2–3)
American Conservation, 1911–3
American Forestry, 1910–23, formerly Conservation; later American Forests and Forest Life
American Forests and Forest Life, 1924–49
American-German Review, 1945–9 (vols. 11/12–15/16)
American Homes and Gardens, 1905–8 (vols. 1–4)
American Labor Legislation Review, 1911–42
American Photography, 1915–49
American Planning and Civic Annual, 1935–49, formerly National Conference on City Planning
American Society for Municipal Improvements. Proceedings, 1907–29, later American Society of Municipal Engineers' Yearbook
American Society of International Law. Proceedings, 1907–49 (vols. 1–43)
American Society of Municipal Engineers' Yearbook, 1929–34, later Public Works Engineers' Yearbook
Annals of Wyoming, 1932–8
Appalachia, 1876–1949
The Architect, 1923–31
Architects' and Builders' Magazine, 1907–11, later Architecture and Building
Architectural Quarterly of Harvard University, 1912–4
Architecture (London), 1923–31, formerly Journal of the Society of Architects, London
Arizona Historical Review, 1928–36
Arizona Quarterly, 1945–9
Arkansas Historical Review, 1934
Art and Progress, 1912–5, later American Magazine of Art
Arts and Decoration, 1913–7
Association of American Geographers. Annals, 1911–49
Biblical Review, 1916–32
Bibliophile (London), 1908–9

Bird Lore, 1907–8 (vols. 9–10)
Brickbuilder, 1892–1916, later Architectural Forum
British Review, 1913–5
Broadway Magazine, 1907–8, later Hampton's Magazine
Bulletin. International Union of American Republics, 1909–10, later Bulletin of the Pan American Union
Bulletin of the Pan American Union, 1910, formerly Bulletin. International Union of American Republics
Bunker's Monthly, 1928, later Texas Monthly
Canadian Alpine Journal, 1907–49
Canadian Bookman, 1920–2
Canadian Forest and Outdoors, 1924–39, formerly Canadian Forestry Magazine; later Forest and Outdoors
Canadian Forestry Journal, 1910–20, later Canadian Forestry Magazine
Canadian Forestry Magazine, 1921–3, formerly Canadian Forestry Journal; later Canadian Forest and Outdoors
Canadian Geographical Journal, 1930–49
Celtic Review, 1912–6
Christian Art, 1907–8
Connecticut Historical Society. Collections, 1907–32
Conservation, 1908–9, formerly Forestry and Irrigation; later American Forestry
Countryside Magazine, 1914–7, formerly Suburban Life
Creative Art, 1927–33
Eastern Art, 1928–30
Economic Journal (London), 1915–49 (vols. 25–59)
Economic Review, 1913–4
Empire Forestry Journal, 1928–46, later Empire Forestry Review
Empire Forestry Review, 1947–9, formerly Empire Forestry Journal
English Historical Review, 1912–49
English Illustrated Magazine, 1912–3
Fine Arts Journal, 1912–9
Forest and Outdoors (Ottawa), 1932–49, formerly Canadian Forest and Outdoors
Forestry (London), 1927–49
Forestry and Irrigation, 1907, later Conservation
Forestry Quarterly, 1902–16, later Journal of Forestry
Geographical Society of Philadelphia. Bulletin, 1893–1938
Georgia Historical Society. Collections, 1904–16

Good Housekeeping, 1907–8
Granite State Monthly, 1930, formerly Granite Monthly
Graphic Arts, 1912–5
Harvard Theological Review, 1911–49
History Teacher's Magazine, 1911–8, later Historical Outlook
Home Geographic Monthly, 1931–2
House and Garden, 1907–27
House Beautiful, 1907–8
Illinois Catholic Historical Review, 1918–29, later Mid-America
Illinois State Historical Society. Occasional Publications, 1947–8
Illinois State Historical Society. Transactions, 1937–44
Indiana Historical Commission. Collections, 1922
Indiana Historical Society. Publications, 1906–49
Indoors and Out, 1905–7
Inland Architect, 1907–8
Inland Seas (Cleveland), 1945–9 (vols. 1–5)
International Studio, 1914–31
Jewish Center Worker, 1946
Jewish Quarterly Review, 1914–49
Jewish Review, 1943–8
Journal of Accountancy, 1911–49
Journal of Forestry, 1917–49, consolidation of Forestry Quarterly and Proceedings of American Society of Foresters
Journal of Geography, 1914–49
Journal of History, 1907–25
Journal of Pedagogy, 1907
Landscape Architecture, 1913–49
Leisure, 1933–8 (vols. 1–5)
The Library (London), 1920–49
Library Association Record (London), 1920–49
Library Journal, 1918–9
Maine Historical Society. Collections, 1906–13
Manual Training Magazine, 1899–1908
Massachusetts Magazine (Salem), 1908–17
Mazama, 1896–1949 (vols. 1–31)
Michigan Historical Commission. Collections, 1915
Mid-America, 1929–49, formerly Illinois Catholic Historical Review
Mind (London), 1913–49
Minnesota Historical Society. Collections, 1904–20
Minnesota History Bulletin, 1915–24, later Minnesota History
Montana Historical Society. Contributions, 1907–38

Moody's Monthly, 1905–17
Mountaineer, 1909–49
Musical Quarterly, 1915
National Conference on City Planning, 1910–34, later American Planning and Civic Annual
National Institute of Social Sciences, Proceedings, 1922
Nebraska History, 1938–49, formerly Nebraska History Magazine
Nebraska History Magazine, 1925–38, later Nebraska History
New Brunswick Historical Society. Collections, 1907–30
New Hampshire Historical Society. Proceedings, 1905–15
New Photo-Miniature, 1933–7, formerly Photo-Miniature
New York State Historical Association. Proceedings, 1906–18
Nomad, 1930–1
North Dakota Historical Quarterly, 1926–33, formerly North Dakota State Historical Society. Collections
North Dakota Magazine, 1906–11
North Dakota State Historical Society. Collections, 1906–25, later North Dakota Historical Quarterly
Northern Cordilleran, 1913
Nova Scotia Historical Society. Collections, 1908–47
Ohio Magazine, 1906–8
Ontario History, 1947–9, formerly Ontario Historical Society. Papers and Records
Oxford and Cambridge Review, 1907–12
Pacific Monthly, 1907–11, later Sunset
Pacific Northwest Quarterly, 1936–49, formerly Washington Historical Quarterly
Pall Mall Magazine, 1912–5 (Nash's and Pall Mall)
Pennsylvania Archaeologist, 1934–49
Photo-Era, 1911–4
Photo-Miniature, 1899–1932, later New Photo-Miniature
Popular Photography, 1915–6
Print, 1941–9, formerly Printing Art Quarterly
Print Connoisseur, 1920–34
Printed Salesmanship, 1925–35, formerly Printing Art, later Printing Art Quarterly
Printing Art Quarterly, 1936–9, formerly Printed Salesmanship; later Print
Public Works Engineers' Yearbook, 1936, formerly American Society of Municipal Engineers' Yearbook
Quarterly Journal of Forestry, 1907–49 (vols. 1–43)

Quarterly Journal of Public Speaking, 1915
Recreation, 1908–12
Review of Reviews, 1912–36, later World Review
Rhode Island Historical Society. Collections, 1902; 1918–41 (vols. 10–34), later Rhode Island History
Royal Historical Society. Transactions, 1907–49
Rudder, 1938–49
Scottish Historical Review, 1907–28
Sierra Club Bulletin, 1902–49
Sketch Book Magazine, 1930–2
Society of American Foresters. Proceedings, 1908–16
South Dakota Historical Review, 1935–7
South Dakota State Historical Society. Collections, 1906–49 (vols. 3–24)
Southwestern Lore, 1935–49 (vols. 1–15)
Studio (New York and London), 1939–43, formerly London Studio
Suburban Life, 1907–14, later Countryside Magazine
Sunset, 1907–12, merged with Pacific Monthly in 1912
System, 1912
Tequesta, 1941–9
Texas State Historical Association Quarterly, 1907–12, later Southwestern Historical Quarterly
Town Planning Review, 1912–39
Trail and Timberline, 1915–6
Twentieth Century Magazine, 1911–3
Unpopular Review, 1915
Utah Genealogical and Historical Magazine, 1918–40
Utah Historical Quarterly, 1930–3
Van Norden Magazine, 1908–10
Vermont Quarterly, 1944–9, formerly Vermont Historical Society. Proceedings
Village, 1906–8
Vocational Education, 1911–4
Washington State Historical Society. Publications, 1907–14; 1930
Western Architect, 1909–31
Windsor Magazine (London), 1895–1939
Wisconsin Archaeologist, 1907–49
Wisconsin State Historical Society. Biographies, 1936–40
Wisconsin State Historical Society. Collections, 1906–49
Wisconsin State Historical Society. Domesday Book, 1937
Wyoming State Historical Department. Collections and Proceedings, 1919–22

BLACK INDEX

Abbey, Kathryn T. History of El Destino and Chemonie (Fla.) plantations and documents pertaining thereto (1828-68). FHS 7:179-213, Jan. 1929 and following issues.

ABBOTT, LYMAN

Brown, I.V. American Freedmen's Union Commission--activities in Reconstruction under the direction of Lyman Abbott. JSH 15:22-38, Feb. 1949.

ABEL, ANNIE HELOISE

Landon, F. Review of Annie Heloise Abel and F.J. Klingberg, eds., A side-light on Anglo-American relations, 1839-58. CAN 9:72-3, Mar. 1928.

ABOLITION, BRAZILIAN

Hill, L.F. The abolition of the African slave trade to Brazil. HAH 11:169-97, May 1931.

Martin, P.A. Slavery and abolition in Brazil. HAH 13:151-96, May 1933.

"ABOLITION HOLES"

Koch, F.J. Marking the old "abolition holes" at Ripley. OAQ 22:308-18, Apr. 1913.

ABOLITIONIST MOVEMENT. See also ANTI-SLAVERY MOVEMENT, EMIGRANT AID MOVEMENT

Abolition and Henry Clay's visit to Richmond, Ind., 1842. INM 4:117-28, Sept. 1908.

Atherton, C.E. Daniel Howell Hise, abolitionist and reformer. MVH 26:343-58, Dec. 1939.

Clarke, C.M. "Uncle Tom's Cabin"--how it reached the British public. CHA 11:81-2, Jan. 8, 1921.

ABOLITIONIST MOVEMENT (cont'd)

Ellsworth, C.S. Ohio legislative attack upon abolition schools. MVH 21:379-86, Dec. 1934.

Ford, N.A. Henry David Thoreau's activities as an abolitionist. NEQ 19:359-71, Sept. 1946.

Galpin, W.F. Fugitive slave law of 1850. The Jerry Rescue precipitated a clash between the government and local abolitionists. NYH 26:19-33, Jan. 1945.

Giddings, F.H. Slavery and its abolition in the U.S. TIM 1:479-82, Mar. 1907.

Graham, A.A. Abolition colony in Ohio. OAQ 30-43, 1895.

Herriott, F.I. Parts played by German citizens of U.S. in abolition of slavery. IHL 35:101-91, 1928.

Hicks, Granville. Dr. Channing and the Creole case. AHR 37:516-25, Apr. 1932.

Hopkins, Geraldine. Editions of the "Liberty Minstrel," a rare abolitionist document. MVH 18:60-4, June 1931.

Koch, F.J. Marking the old "abolition holes" at Ripley. OAQ 22:308-18, Apr. 1913.

Muelder, H.R. Galesburg, Ill.; hot-bed of abolitionism. IHJ 35:216-35, Sept. 1942.

Quarles, Benjamin. Sources of abolitionist income. MVH 32:63-76, June 1945.

Riddell, W.R. Method of abolition of slavery in England, Scotland and Upper Canada compared. OHS 27: 511-3, 1931.

Sheppard, T.J. Putnam, Ohio, as an abolition centre. OAQ 19:266-9, July 1910.

Sherwin, O. The abolitionists and their fight against slavery. NEQ 18:70-82, Mar. 1945.

Simms, H.H. Abolition literature, 1830-40, a critical analysis. JSH 6:368-82, Aug. 1940.

Smither, Harriet. Effect of English abolitionism on annexation of Texas. SWH 32:193-205, Jan. 1929.

Staiger, C.B. Abolitionism and the Presbyterian schism of 1837-8. MVH 36:391-414, Dec. 1949.

Turner, E.R. Abolition of slavery in Pennsylvania. PAM 36:129-42, Apr. 1912.

Turner, E.R. First abolition society. PAM 36:92-109, Jan. 1912.

Wick, B.L. Delia Webster--her part in the underground railroad movement in Iowa. ANN 3d s. 18:228-31, Jan. 1932.

Williams, Ora. Story of underground railway signals. ANN 27:297-303, Apr. 1946.

ABOLITIONISTS

Emerson, O.B. Frances Wright and her Nashoba experiment. THQ 6:291-341, Dec. 1947.

Ford, N.A. Henry David Thoreau's activities as an abolitionist. NEQ 19:359-71, Sept. 1946.

Granville Sharp, abolitionist. PCQ 16:22, Jan. 1929.

Grim, P.R. Rev. John Rankin: His ancestry and early career. OAQ 46:215-56, July 1937.

Guiness, R.B. Daniel Howell Hise, abolitionist and reformer. SOS 36:297-300, Nov. 1945.

Haseltine, G.C. Biographical sketch of William Wilberforce. ENG 57:59-65, July 1933.

Higginson, Thomas W. John Greenleaf Whittier as abolitionist. BKN 26:259-62, Dec. 1907.

Hillis, N.D. Harriet Beecher Stowe and the Beecher family. MUN 46:191-201, Nov. 1911.

Laack, J.A. Biographical sketch of Jonathan Walker. WIM 32:312-20, Mar. 1949.

McDowell, Tremaine. Webster's words on abolitionists. NEQ 7:315, June 1934.

Nye, R.B. Marius Racine Robinson, his activities in the Ohio anti-slavery movement. OAQ 55:138-54, Apr.-June 1946.

Official reports of the killing of Rev. Elijah P. Lovejoy. IHJ 4:499-503, Jan. 1912.

Parks, E.W. Frances Wright--founder of the emancipating labor society, Nashoba, Tenn. THM 2d s. 2:74-86, Jan. 1932.

Pillsbury, A.E. Sketch of Parker Pillsbury. GRA 54:73-6, Mar. 1922.

Swing, J.B. Thomas Morris, Ohio pioneer. OAQ 10:352-60, Jan. 1902.

ABOLITIONISTS (cont'd)

Wick, B.L. Delia Webster--her part in the underground railroad movement in Iowa. ANN 3d s. 18:228-31, Jan. 1932.

Young, J.H. Anna Elizabeth Dickinson--a woman abolitionist views the South in 1875. GHQ 32:241-51, Dec. 1948.

Young, J.H. Anna Elizabeth Dickinson--her campaign during the Civil War period for and against Lincoln. MVH 31: 59-80, June 1944.

ABRAHAM

Porter, K.W. The Negro Abraham; his life among the Seminole Indians. FHS 25:1-43, July 1946.

Abrams, C. Homes for Aryans only: Restrictive covenant spreads legal racism in America. COM 3:421-7, May 1947.

ABSENTEE OWNERSHIP

Sitterson, J.C. The William J. Minor plantations: A study in ante-bellum absentee ownership. JSH 9:59-74, Feb. 1943.

ADAMIC, LOUIS

Knopland, P. Review of Louis Adamic, A nation of nations. WIM 29:457-60, June 1946.

Stephenson, G.M. Review of Louis Adamic, A nation of nations. MVH 32:598-9, Mar. 1946.

Adams, Fannie L.G. A childhood spent at Hayfield plantation near Fredericksburg, Va., during the Civil War. WMQ 2d s. 23:292-7, July 1948.

Adams, J.T. Disfranchisement of Negroes in New England. AHR 30:543-7, Apr. 1925.

ADAMS, JOHN QUINCY

John Q. Adams and secession, 1842. MAG 25:96-9, Sept.-Oct. 1917.

Addams, Jane. Race problems of a democracy. ASS 14:206-15, 1919.

AFRICA. See also names of specific countries

Condenhove, H. Certain facets of Negro mentality in Central Africa. COR n.s. 55:207-21, Aug. 1923.

Davis, J. The South and British Africa. VQR 13:362-75, Summer 1937.

DuBois, W.E.B. Political and social status in European possessions in Africa. FOR 3:423-44, Apr. 1925.

Edmiston, Dorothy. A ballet of the African Negro to be performed in Dallas, Texas. TEX 4:458-64, Nov. 1940.

Georgia and the African slave trade. GHQ 2:87-113, June 1918.

Herron, Stella. The African apprentice bill, 1858. MIV 8:135-45, 1914-5.

Locke, Alain. Exhibition of African art at Museum of Modern Art. AMA 28:270-8, May 1935.

Stopford, P.G. An African coast experience. CHA 7th s. 7:301-3, Apr. 7, 1917.

AFRICAN APPRENTICE BILL

Herron, Stella. The African apprentice bill, 1858. MIV 8:135-45, 1914-5.

AFRICANISMS

Kennedy, Stetson. Nanigo in Florida. SFQ 4:153-6, Sept. 1940.

Parsons, Elsie. Ashanti influence in Negro folktales and customs in Jamaica. JAF 47:391-5, Oct.-Dec. 1934.

AFRICANS

Middleton, A.P. The strange story of Job Ben Solomon, the African, 1750. WMQ 3d s. 5:342-50, July 1948.

AGRARIAN POLITICS

Woodward, C.V. Tom Watson and the Negro in agrarian politics. JSH 4:14-33, Feb. 1938.

AGRICULTURE

Gibson, B.D. Negro agricultural extension work in U.S. IRM 10:385-95, July 1921.

Aiken, Martha D. The underground railroad. MHM 6:597-610, no. 4, 1922.

ALABAMA

Bethel, Elizabeth. The Freedmen's Bureau in Alabama, 1865. JSH 14:49-92, Feb. 1948.

Fauset, A.H. Folk-tales from Alabama, Mississippi and Louisiana. JAF 40:214-303, June-Sept. 1927.

ALABAMA, BIRMINGHAM

Giddens, Lucia. Birmingham's Negro quarter. TRA 53:40-1, July 1941.

ALABAMA, TUSKEGEE

Park, R.M. Tuskegee international conference on the Negro. JRD 3:117-20, July 1912.

Wright, John C. Teaching English at Tuskegee Institute. EBM 3:26-30, Oct. 1908.

Aldrich, O.W. Illinois slavery. IHL 22:89-99, 1916.

Aldrich, O.W. Slavery or involuntary servitude in Illinois prior to and after admission as a state. IHJ 9:119-32, July 1916.

Alexander, R.J. Fair employment practices legislation in the U.S. CAF 28:31-2, May 1948.

Alexander, T.B. Kukluxism in Tennessee, 1865-69: A technique for the overthrow of radical Reconstruction. THQ 8: 195-219, Sept. 1949.

Alilunas, Leo. Fugitive slave cases in Ohio prior to 1850. OAQ 49:160-84, Apr.-June 1940.

Allen, C.E. The slavery question in Catholic newspapers, 1850-65. USC 26:99-169, 1936.

Allen, John W. Slavery and Negro servitude in Pope County, Illinois. IHJ 42:411-23, Dec. 1949.

Alpert, H. Review of R. Weaver, The Negro ghetto. ASR 13: 779-80, Dec. 1948.

ALSTON, REV. P.P.

Rev. P.P. Alston's story of his rise up from slavery. SPM 73:375-8, May 1907.

ALTOONA CONFERENCE

Hesseltine, W.B., and Hazel C. Wolf. The Emancipation Proclamation and the Altoona conference. PAM 71:195-205, July 1947.

AMAZON RIVER

Bell, W.J., Jr. Relation of Herndon and Gibbon's exploration of the Amazon to North American slavery, 1850-5. HAH 19:494-503, Nov. 1939.

AMERICAN COLONIZATION SOCIETY

Keith, E. Jean. Joseph Rogers Underwood of Kentucky and the American Colonization Society for the free people of color. HIS 22:117-32, Apr. 1938.

Sherwood, H.N. Paul Cuffe and his contribution to the American Colonization Society. MVH 6:370-402, 1913.

AMERICAN COTTON PLANTERS' ASSOCIATION

Wilkins, Mary, ed. The American Cotton Planters' Ass'n: Papers, 1865-6. THQ 7:335-61, Dec. 1948 and following issue.

AMERICAN FREEDMEN'S UNION COMMISSION

Brown, I.V. American Freedmen's Union Commission--activities in Reconstruction under the direction of Lyman Abbott. JSH 15:22-38, Feb. 1949.

AMERICAN INDIANS

Creer, L.H. Spanish-American slave trade in the Great Basin, 1800-1853. NMH 24:171-83, July 1949.

Forbes, G. Part played by Indian slavery in removal of tribes to Oklahoma. OKC 16:163-70, June 1938.

Hunt, H.F. Slavery among the Indians of Northwestern America. WAS 9:277-83, Oct. 1918.

Pennington, E.L. Work of Rev. Francis Le Jau in colonial South Carolina among Indians and Negro slaves. JSH 1:442-58, Nov. 1935.

Porter, K.W. The Creek Indian-Negro tradition. The Hawkins Negroes go to Mexico. OKC 24:55-8, Spring 1946.

Porter, K.W. The Negro Abraham; his life among the Seminole Indians. FHS 25:1-43, July 1946.

AMERICAN INDIANS (cont'd)

Porter, K.W. Negroes and Indians on the Texas frontier, 1834-74. SWH 53:151-63, Oct. 1949.

Porter, K.W. Notes on Seminole Negroes in the Bahamas. FHS 24:56-60, July 1945.

AMERICAN MISSIONARY ASSOCIATION

Landon, F. The work of the American Missionary Association among the Negro refugees in Canada West, 1848-64. OHS 21:198-205, 1924.

AMERICAN REVOLUTION

Miller, William. Effects of the American Revolution on indentured servitude. PAH 7:131-41, July 1940.

Phillips, D.E. Slaves who fought in the Revolution. JAH 5:143-6, Jan.-Mar. 1911.

Smith, M.H. Connecticut slaves in Revolutionary times. CNT 9:145-53, Jan. 1905.

Ames, R. Art in Negro folksong. JAF 56:241-54, Oct.-Dec. 1943.

AMISTAD CASE

Lewis, A.N. Amistad slave case, 1840. CNT 11:125-8, Jan. 1907.

AMNESTY

Dorris, J.T. Pardon and amnesty during the Civil War and Reconstruction: Excerpt from a forthcoming book. NCH 23:360-401, July 1946.

Anderson, Judith. Anna Elizabeth Dickinson, anti-slavery radical. PAH 3:147-63, July 1936.

Andrews, Rena M. Andrew Johnson, his plan of restoration of the South to the Union in relation to that of Lincoln. THM n.s. 1:165-81, Apr. 1931.

ANNIVERSARIES

Studley, Marian H. An August First anti-slavery picnic. NEQ 16:567-77, Dec. 1943.

ANTI-ABOLITIONIST MOVEMENT. See also PRO-SLAVERY MOVEMENT

Coleman, C.H. Three Vallandigham letters, 1865. OAQ 43:461-4, Oct. 1934.

McDowell, Tremaine. Webster's words on abolitionists. NEQ 7:315, June 1934.

Price, R. Anti-abolition disturbances of 1836 in Granville, Ohio. OAQ 45:365-8, Oct. 1936.

ANTI-ABOLITIONISTS

Van Fossan, W.H. Biography of Clement L. Vallandigham. OAQ 23:256-67, July 1914.

ANTI-CATHOLICISM

Russ, W.A., Jr. Anti-Catholic agitation. AMC 45:312-21, Dec. 1934.

ANTI-SLAVERY MOVEMENT. See also EMIGRANT AID MOVEMENT, ABOLITIONIST MOVEMENT

Anderson, Judith. Anna Elizabeth Dickinson, anti-slavery radical. PAH 3:147-63, July 1936.

Binder-Johnson, Hildegard. Germantown (Pa.) protest of 1688 against Negro slavery. PAM 65:145-56, Apr. 1941.

Bowers, A.L. Anti-slavery convention in Alton, Ill., in 1837. IHJ 20:329-56, Oct. 1927.

Clarke, Grace J. Anti-slavery letter of Daniel Worth to George W. Julian, and other documents. INM 26:152-7, June 1930.

Correspondence of Gov. Edward Coles with Rev. Thomas Lippincott. IHJ 3:59-63, Jan. 1911.

Emerson, O.B. Frances Wright and her Nashoba experiment. THQ 6:291-314, Dec. 1947.

Galbreath, C.B. Anti-slavery movement in Ohio. OAQ 30: 355-95, Oct. 1921.

Geiser, K.F. Anti-slavery movement, 1840-60, in the Western Reserve. MIV 5:73-98, 1912.

Gibbons, V.E., ed. Letters on the war in Kansas in 1856. KHQ 10:369-79, Nov. 1941.

Harlow, R.V. Rise and fall of emigrant aid movement in Kansas. AHR 41:1-25, Oct. 1935.

ANTI-SLAVERY MOVEMENT (cont'd)

Harrington, F.H. Nathaniel Banks. A study in anti-slavery politics. NEQ 9:626-54, Dec. 1936.

Harrison, L. Cassius M. Clay's anti-slavery newspaper, the "True American": Opposition in Kentucky to his struggle for emancipation of the Negro. HIS 22:30-49, Jan. 1948.

Jackson, Mrs. F.N. Anti-slavery relics. CON 77:9-17, Jan. 1927.

Johnson, S.A. The Emigrant Aid Company in Kansas. KHQ 1:429-41, Nov. 1932.

Johnson, S.A. The Emigrant Aid Company in the Kansas conflict. KHQ 6:21-33, Feb. 1937.

The Kansas fight against slavery. KAN 10:120-48+, 1908.

Landon, F. The Canadian anti-slavery group before the Civil War. UNI 17:540-7, Dec. 1918.

Lemen, Joseph B. The Jefferson-Lemen anti-slavery pact. IHL 13:74-84, 1908.

Lynch, W.O. Antislavery tendencies of the Democratic party in the Northwest, 1848-50. MVH 11:319-31, Dec. 1924.

Malin, J.C. John Brown and the Manes incident. KHQ 7:376-8, Nov. 1938.

Martin, A.E. Anti-slavery activities in the Methodist Church. THM 2:98-109, June 1916.

Martin, A.E. Anti-slavery press. MVH 2:509-28, Mar. 1916.

Martin, A.E. Tennessee anti-slavery societies. THM 1:261-81, Dec. 1915.

Nye, R.B. Marius Racine Robinson, his activities in the Ohio anti-slavery movement. OAQ 55:138-54, Apr.-June 1946.

Price, R. The Ohio Anti-Slavery Society's convention of 1836. OAQ 45:173-88, Apr. 1936.

Rammelkamp, C.H. Anti-slavery movement and Illinois College. IHL 13:192-203, 1909.

Rayback, J.G. The Liberty party leaders of Ohio: Exponents of anti-slavery coalition. OAQ 57:165-78, Apr. 1948.

Rodabaugh, J.H. Miami University, Calvinism and the anti-slavery movement. OAQ 48:66-73, Jan. 1939.

Ryan, J.H. Illinois anti-slavery struggle and its effect on the Methodist Church. IHL 19:67-76, 1913.

Stevens, Wayne E. Shaw-Hensen election contest. IHJ 7:389-401, Jan. 1915.

Studley, Marian H. An August First anti-slavery picnic. NEQ 16:567-77, Dec. 1943.

"Uncle Tom's Cabin" written in Brunswick, Me. SJM 5:160, Aug.-Oct. 1917.

Walsh, Anetta C. Three anti-slavery newspapers published in Ohio prior to 1823. OAQ 31:171-212, Apr. 1922.

Ward, Aileen. Rev. Josiah Henson, the original Tom of "Uncle Tom's Cabin"; his story. DAL 20:335-8, Oct. 1940.

Wayland, Francis F. Slavebreeding in America: The Stevenson-O'Connell imbroglio of 1838. VAM 50:47-54, Jan. 1942.

Wilkinson, N.B. The Philadelphia free produce attack on slavery. PAM 66:294-313, July 1942.

Apple, J.A. The carpetbaggers as some Southerners saw them, and its influence in the U.S. today. SOS 35:220-5, May 1949.

Aptheker, Herbert. Review of J.H. Franklin, From slavery to freedom. PAM 72:294, July 1948.

Aptheker, Herbert. Review of F. Tannenbaum, Slave and citizen: The Negro in the Americas. AHR 52:755-7, July 1947.

APTHEKER, HERBERT

Curti, M. Review of Herbert Aptheker, American Negro slave revolts. CHR 30:76-8, Apr. 1944.

Klingberg, F.J. Review of Herbert Aptheker, Essays in the history of the American Negro. JSH 12:280-1, May 1946.

Stavisky, L. Review of Herbert Aptheker, To be free: Studies in American Negro history. SOS 40:41, Jan. 1949.

Wharton, V.L. Review of Herbert Aptheker, Essays in the history of the American Negro. MVH 34:673-4, Mar. 1948.

AQUILLA, WILLIAM

Gittings, Victoria. What William saw; experiences of William Aquilla with the supernatural. JAF 58:135-7, Apr.-June 1945.

ARCHER, WILLIAM

Review of William Archer, Through Afro-America: An English reading of the race problem. APS 4:607-9, Nov. 1910.

ARCHITECTURE

Hampton Normal and Agricultural Institute, Hampton, Va. AAB 51:64+, Aug. 1914.

Hotel Theresa, New York City. AAB 45:465-7, Nov. 1913.

Housing problems for Negroes in New York City. Paul Laurence Dunbar apartments. ARC 59:5-12, Jan. 1929.

Laughlin, C.J. Plantation architecture in Louisiana. MAR 41:210-3, Oct. 1948.

Ardery, Julia S. Will of Richard "King" Harrison of Calvert Co., Md., granting freedom to his serving woman Kate Booth. KYR 46:637-46, Oct. 1958.

ARKANSAS

Carmichael, Maude. Federal experiments with Negro labor on abandoned plantations in Arkansas. ARK 1:101-16, June 1942.

Chester, S.H. African slavery as I knew it in Southern Arkansas. THM 9:178-84, Oct. 1925.

Driggs, O.T., Jr. Arkansas politics: The essence of the Powell Clayton regime, 1868-1871. ARK 8:1-75, Spring 1949.

Mitchell, J.B. An analysis of population by race, nativity and residence. ARK 8:115-32, Summer 1949.

Reynolds, John H. Presidential Reconstruction in Arkansas. ARA 1:352-61, 1906.

Robinson, J.T. History of suffrage in Arkansas. ARA 3:167-74, 1911.

Trieber, J. Legal status of Negroes in Arkansas before the Civil War. ARA 3:175-83, 1911.

ARMED SERVICES

Davis, P.C. The Negro in the armed services. VQR 24: 499-520, Autumn 1948.

ARMFIELD, JOHN

Howell, Isabel. Story of John Armfield, slave-trader. THQ 2:3-29, Mar. 1943.

Armour, A.W. Review of W.P.A. Writers' Program, The Negro in Virginia. WMQ 2d s. 21:70-4, Jan. 1941.

ARMSTRONG, SAMUEL

Dickinson, C.H. Samuel Armstrong's contribution to Christian missions. IRM 10:509-24, Oct. 1921.

Shillito, E. Samuel Chapman Armstrong. IRM 8:357-65, July 1919.

ARMY, U.S.

Carroll, H.B. Nolan's "lost nigger" expedition of 1877. SWH 44:55-75, July 1940.

Davies, W.E. The problem of race segregation in the Grand Army of the Republic. JSH 13:354-72, Aug. 1947.

Hay, T.R. The question of arming the slaves. MVH 6: 34-73, June 1919.

Spraggins, T.L. Mobilization of Negro labor for the Department of Virginia and North Carolina, 1861-5. NCH 24:160-97, Apr. 1947.

ART

Ames, R. Art in Negro folksong. JAF 56:241-54, Oct.-Dec. 1943.

Barnes, A.C. Negro art and America. EXL 1:323-7, May 1924.

Carline, R. The dating and provenance of Negro art. BUR 77:115-23, Oct. 1940.

Crite, Alan R. Why I illustrate spirituals. WLD 1:44-5+, May 1938.

Culin, S. Negro art. ART 3:346-50, May 1923.

de Zayas, M. Negro art. ART 3:198-205, Mar. 1923.

Evans, W. Three new paintings from the heart of the black belt. FTE 38:89+, Aug. 1948.

ART (cont'd)

Fletcher, R.S. Ransom's painting of John Brown on his way to execution. KHQ 9:343-6, Nov. 1946.

Locke, Alain. Exhibition of African art at Museum of Modern Art. AMA 28:270-8, May 1935.

McCausland, Elizabeth. Jacob Lawrence, the man and his work. MAR 38:251-4, Nov. 1945.

Porter, James A. Versatile interests of the early Negro artist: A neglected chapter of American art history. AIA 24:16-27, Jan. 1936.

Salmon, Andre. Negro art. BUR 36:164-72, Apr. 1920.

Sevier, M. Negro art. ATE 2:116-21, Aug. 1931.

Szecsi, L. Negro sculpture in interior decoration. LST 7:326-7, June 1933.

Szecsi, L. Tr. by A.S. Riggs. Primitive Negro art. AAA 34:130-6, May-June 1933.

ART HISTORY

Porter, James A. Versatile interests of the early Negro artist: A neglected chapter of American art history. AIA 24:16-27, Jan. 1936.

ARTISTS

Locke, Alain. The American Negro as artist. AMA 23:210-30, Sept. 1931.

McCausland, Elizabeth. Jacob Lawrence, the man and his work. MAR 38:251-4, Nov. 1945.

Porter, James A. Versatile interests of the early Negro artist: A neglected chapter of American art history. AIA 24:16-27, Jan. 1936.

ARTS

Lepage, P.C. Arts and crafts of Negroes. INT 78:577-80, Mar. 1924.

ASHANTI

Parsons, Elsie. Ashanti influence in Negro folktales and customs in Jamaica. JAF 47:391-5, Oct.-Dec. 1934.

Ashley-Montague, M.F. Review of W.A. Bonger, Race and crime. Tr. from the Dutch by Margaret Hurdyk. CJR 6:669-70, Dec. 1943.

Ashley-Montague, M.F. Review of G. Dahlberg, Race, reason and rubbish. CJR 6:670-1, Dec. 1943.

ASHLEY-MONTAGUE, M.F.

Werner, A. Review of M.F. Ashley-Montague, Man's most dangerous myth: The fallacy of race. COM 1:91-9, Apr. 1946.

ASSIMILATION

Park, R.E. Assimilation in secondary groups with particular reference to the Negro. ASS 8:66-83, 1913.

Weatherly, U.S. Racial elements in social assimilation. ASS 5:57-76, 1910.

ASSOCIATIONS

Wilkins, Mary, ed. The American Cotton Planters' Ass'n: Papers, 1865-6. THQ 7:335-61, Dec. 1948 and following issue.

ASTRONOMERS

Phillips, F.L. The life of Benjamin Banneker. CHS 20: 114-20, 1917.

Atherton, C.E. Daniel Howell Hise, abolitionist and reformer. MVH 26:343-58, Dec. 1939.

ATTITUDES

Cahnman, W.J. Attitudes of minority youth: A methodological introduction. ASR 14:543-8, Aug. 1949.

Lyons, John F. Attitude of Presbyterians in Ohio, Indiana and Illinois toward slavery. PBY 11:69-82, June 1921.

Schmidt, H. Slavery and attitudes toward slavery in Hunterdon Co., N.J. NJS 58:151-69, July 1940 and following issue.

Settle, E. Ophelia. Social attitudes during the slave regime: Household servants versus field hands. ASS 28:95-8, May 1934.

Williams, T.H. Reconstruction. An analysis of some attitudes. JSH 12:469-86, Nov. 1946.

Wilson, C.J. People's attitude toward the Negro in early Ohio. OAQ 39:717-68, Oct. 1930.

Auchampaugh, P. Buchanan, the Court, and the Dred Scott case. THM 9:231-40, Jan. 1926.

AUCTIONS

Slave auction, New Orleans. HTM 3:188, Oct. 1912.

BACKWARD RACES

Stoutemyer, J.H. Certain experiments with backward races. JRD 5:438-66, Apr. 1916.

BAHAMAS

Porter, K.W. Notes on Seminole Negroes in the Bahamas. FHS 24:56-60, July 1945.

Bailey, William S. The underground railroad in southern Chautauqua County, N.Y. NYH 16:53-63, Jan. 1935.

Bain, R. Review of C.S. Johnson, Growing up in the black belt: Negro youth in the rural South. ASR 6:424-6, June 1941.

Bain, R. Review of H.W. Odum and G.B. Johnson, The Negro and his songs. AMR 4:104-7, Jan.-Feb. 1926.

Baker, Emily V. Responsibility of the elementary teacher to overcome racial intolerance in future citizens. HIO 24:86-9, Feb. 1933.

Baker, Eugene C. The influence of slavery in the colonization of Texas. MVR 11:3-36, June 1924; and SWH 28:1-33, July 1924.

Baldwin, James. The Harlem ghetto: Jewish-Negro relations. COM 5:165-70, Feb. 1948.

BALLADS

Milling, C.J. "Delia Holmes," a neglected Negro ballad. SFQ 1:3-8, Dec. 1937.

BALLOWE, H.L.

Brewer, J.M. Review of H.L. Ballowe, The Lawd sayin' the same. SFQ 12:227-9, Sept. 1948.

Tison, Yvonne P. Review of H.L. Ballowe, The Lawd sayin' the same. LHQ 31:154-6, Jan. 1948.

BANKS, GEN. NATHANIEL PRENTISS

Harrington, F.H. Nathaniel Banks. A study in anti-slavery politics. NEQ 9:626-54, Dec. 1936.

Williams, H. General Banks and the radical Republicans in the Civil War. NEQ 12:268-80, June 1939.

BANNEKER, BENJAMIN

Phillips, F.L. The life of Benjamin Banneker. CHS 20: 114-20, 1917.

BAPTIST CHURCH

Todd, Willie G. North Carolina Baptists and slavery. NCH 24:135-59, Apr. 1947.

Barnes, A.C. Negro art and America. EXL 1:323-7, May 1924.

Barnes, Charles E. Battlecreek as a station on the underground railway. MPC 38:279-85, 1912.

BARNES, G.H.

Crittenden, C.C. Review of G.H. Barnes, The anti-slavery impulse. NCH 12:62-4, Jan. 1935.

Barnes, H.E. The struggle of races and social groups as a factor in development of political and social institutions. JRD 9:394-419, Apr. 1919.

Barnes, L. The Negro in the British Empire. VQR 10:78-93, Jan. 1934.

Barnett, S.A. Light on theories of race. WOR 33-9, July 1945.

Barnett, V.M. Review of Tom C. Clark and Philip B. Perlman, Prejudice and property: An historic brief against racial covenants; submitted to the Supreme Court. APS 42:819-20, Aug. 1948.

Barnhart, John D., ed. Letters on Reconstruction on the lower Mississippi, 1864-78. MVH 21:387-96, Dec. 1934.

Barr, Ruth B., and Modeste Hargis. Voluntary exile of free Negroes in Pensacola, Fla., 1857. FHS 17:3-14, July 1938.

Barry, Louise. The Emigrant Aid Company parties 1854-5. KHQ 12:115-55, May 1943 and following issue.

Bascom, W.R. Review of Georgia W.P.A. Writer's Project, Drums and shadows: Survival studies among the Georgia coastal Negroes. JAF 55:262-3, Oct.-Dec. 1942.

Bass, R.D. Negro songs from the Pedee country, South Carolina. JAF 44:418-36, Oct.-Dec. 1931.

Basset, T. Review of Naomi F. Goldstein, The roots of prejudice against the Negro in the U.S. MVH 35:684, Mar. 1949.

BASSETT, JOHN SPENCER

Stephenson, W.H. The Negro in the thinking and writing of John Spencer Bassett, 1867-1928. NCH 25:427-41, Oct. 1948.

Taylor, R.H. Review of John S. Bassett, The plantation overseer. NCH 3:506-8, July 1926.

Bates, Thelma. The legal status of the Negro in Florida. FHS 6:159-81, Jan. 1928.

Beale, H.K. On rewriting Reconstruction history. AHR 45: 807-27, July 1940.

Bean, W.G. Review of J.W. Coleman, Jr., Slavery times in Kentucky. VAM 48:381-2, Oct. 1940.

BEECHER FAMILY

Hillis, N.D. Harriet Beecher Stowe and the Beecher family. MUN 46:191-201, Nov. 1911.

BEHAVIOR

Glick, C.E. Collective behavior in race relations. ASR 13:287-94, June 1948.

BELIEFS

Stoddard, A.H. Origin, dialect, beliefs and characteristics of the Negroes of the South Carolina and Georgia coasts. GHQ 28:186-95, Sept. 1944.

Taylor, Helen L., ed. Negro beliefs and place legends from New Castle, Del. JAF 51:92-4, Jan.-Mar. 1938.

BELL, JOHN

Parks, J.H. John Bell and the Compromise of 1850. JSH 9:328-56, Aug. 1943.

Bell, W.J., Jr. Relation of Herndon and Gibbon's exploration of the Amazon to North American slavery, 1850-5. HAH 19:494-503, Nov. 1939.

Beltran, G.A. The slave trade in Mexico. HAH 24:412-31, Aug. 1944.

Bentley, G.R. Political activity of the Freedmen's Bureau in Florida, 1865-70. FHS 28:28-37, July 1949.

BEQUESTS

Sherwood, H.N. Colonization of manumitted slaves in Ohio. John Randolph's bequest. MVH 5:39-59, 1912.

Bergmann, Leola N. The Negro in Iowa: Before the Civil War to World War II. IAJ 46:3-90, Jan. 1948.

BERKLEY, SIR WILLIAM

Dimmick, J. Sir William Berkley's plantation at Green Spring, Va. WMQ 2d s. 9:129-30, Apr. 1929.

Bernanos, Georges. Nation against race. DUB 209:1-6, July 1941.

Bernstein, Adele. See Bernstein, David

Bernstein, D. Review of F. Tannenbaum, Slave and citizen: The Negro in the Americas. COM 3:399-400, Apr. 1947.

Bernstein, David, and Adele Bernstein. Washington (D.C.): Tarnished symbol. Our capitol's treason against America. COM 6:397-403, Nov. 1948.

Bethel, Elizabeth. The Freedmen's Bureau in Alabama, 1865. JSH 14:49-92, Feb. 1948.

Bettersworth, J.K., ed. Mississippi unionism: The case of Mr. Lyon. JMH 1:37-52, Jan. 1939.

Beyer, R.L. Slavery in colonial New York. JAH 23:102-8, 1929.

BIBLE

Griffis, W.E. Does the Bible throw light on the race question? HOM 70:94-9, Aug. 1915.

Strong, J. Race question from the Scriptural side. HOM 58:123-9, Aug. 1909.

BIBLIOGRAPHIES

Funkhouser, Myrtle, comp. Bibliography of folk-lore of the American Negro. BUB 16:28-9, Jan.-Apr. 1937 and following issues.

Galbreath, C.B. John Brown. Bibliography. OAQ 30:180-289, July 1921.

King, J.F. The Negro in continental Spanish America: A select bibliography. HAH 24:547-59, Aug. 1944.

Lash, J.S. The American Negro and American literature: A check list of significant commentaries. BUB 19: 33-6, Jan.-Apr. 1947 and previous issue.

Lawson, Holda J. The Negro in American drama: Bibliography. BUB 17:7-8, Jan.-Apr. 1940 and following issue.

Ovington, Mary W. Certain books on the Negro. EXL 2: 263-4, June 1925.

Porter, Dorothy B. Early American Negro writings: A bibliographical study with a preliminary check list of the published writings of American Negroes, 1760-1835. BSA 39:192-268, Third Quarter, 1945.

Sampson, F.A., and W.C. Breckenridge. Bibliography of slavery in Missouri. MOH 2:233-44, Apr. 1908.

Simms, H.H. Abolition literature, 1830-40, a critical analysis. JSH 6:368-82, Aug. 1940.

Biggert, Elizabeth. Review of Virginia Cunningham, Paul Dunbar and his song. OAQ 56:455-6, Oct. 1947.

BIGOTRY

Himelhoch, J. Is there a bigot personality? A report on some preliminary studies. COM 3:277-84, Mar. 1947.

Binder-Johnson, Hildegard. Germantown (Pa.) protest of 1688 against Negro slavery. PAM 65:145-56, Apr. 1941.

BIOLOGY

Hogden, L. Biology and modern race dogmas. CJR 4:3-12, Feb. 1941.

Kephart, W.M. Is the American Negro becoming lighter? An analysis of the sociological and biological trends. ASR 13:437-43, Aug. 1948.
Comment by J.T. Blue, Jr., ASR 13:766-7, Dec. 1948.

Birbeck, M. Slavery in the U.S. IHL 10:147-63, 1905.

BIRON

Trial and sentence of Biron, runaway Negro slave, 1728. LHQ 8:23-7, Jan. 1925.

Bishop, Shelton H. A history of St. Philip's Church: The first colored parish in the Diocese of New York. PEH 15:298-317, Dec. 1917.

Black, P.W. Lynching in Iowa. IAJ 10:151-254, Apr. 1912.

Black, Stephen. Black men and white women. ENG 29:352-7, Oct. 1919.

BLACK CODES

McLoughlin, James J. The black code. LHS 8:28-35, 1916; MIV 8:210-6, 1914-5.

Violette, E.M. Black code in Missouri. MIV 6:287-316, 1913.

Zornow, William F. Judicial modifications of the Maryland black code in the District of Columbia. MDH 44: 18-32, Mar. 1949.

BLACK FRANK

Rice, M.M. Black Frank, a lovable character. WDT 53: 434-6, Apr. 1929.

BLACK JOHN

Trueblood, Lillie D. The story of John Williams, colored. INM 30:149-52, June 1934.

BLACK LAW

Gridley, J.N. A case under Illinois black law in 1862. IHJ 4:401-25, Jan. 1912.

BLACK MAGIC. See also OBEAH, HOODOO, VODUN

Simms, Marion. Black magic in New Orleans yesterday and today. TRA 81:18-9, July 1943.

Blazer, D.N. Underground railroad in McDonough County, Ill. IHJ 15:579-91, Oct. 1922-Jan. 1923.

Blizzard, Sam W. Review of O.C. Cox, Caste, class and race: A study in social dynamics. ASR 13:357-8, June 1948.

Bloom, L.B., ed. Lt. John Bourke's description of a lynching in Tucson, N.M., in 1873. NMH 19:233-42, July 1944 and following issue.

Bloom, Leonard. Concerning ethnic research: With discussion. ASR 13:171-82, Apr. 1948.

Blue, J.T., Jr. See Kephart, W.M.

Bogle, Sarah C.N. Training for Negro librarians. ALA 25: 133, Apr. 1931.

BOND, F.W.

Simms, H.H. Review of F.W. Bond, The Negro and the drama. MVH 27:686, Mar. 1941.

BOND, HORACE M.

DuBois, W.E.B. Review of Horace M. Bond, Negro education in Alabama. AHR 45:669-70, Apr. 1940.

Bond, W.G. Race rivalry. ENG 43:74-9, July 1926.

BONDAGE

Morris, R.B. White bondage and compulsory labor in ante-bellum South Carolina. SOC 49:191-207, Oct. 1948.

BONGER, W.A.

Ashley-Montague, M.F. Review of W.A. Bonger, Race and crime. Tr. from the Dutch by Margaret Hurdyk. CJR 6: 669-70, Dec. 1943.

BOOK REVIEWS

Vance, R.B. Tragic dilemma: The Negro and the American dream. Review of recent books. VQR 20:435-45, Summer 1944.

BOOKS

Powdermaker, Hortense. Discussion of recent books on the race problem. CJR 6:203-4, Apr. 1943.

BOOTH, KATE

Ardery, Julia S. Will of Richard "King" Harrison of Calvert Co., Md., granting freedom to his serving woman Kate Booth. KYR 46:637-46, Oct. 1958.

BOOTH CASE

Schafer, W. Fugitive slave act. Decision of the Booth case. WIM 20:89-110, Sept. 1936.

BOOTLEGGERS

Winston, S. Negro bootleggers in Eastern North Carolina. ASR 8:692-7, Dec. 1943.

BOTKIN, B.A.

Brewer, J.M. Review of B.A. Botkin, ed., Lay my burden down: Autobiographical narratives of Negro ex-slaves. JAF 60:94-6, Jan.-Mar. 1947.

Morris, R.L. Review of B.A. Botkin, ed., Lay my burden down: A folk history of slavery. ARK 5:411-2, Winter 1946.

Review of B.A. Botkin, ed., Lay my burden down. GHQ 30: 262-3, Sept. 1946.

Boucher, C.S. That aggressive slavocracy. MVH 8:13-79, June-Sept. 1921.

BOURKE, LT. JOHN

Bloom, L.B., ed. Lt. John Bourke's description of a lynching in Tucson, N.M., in 1873. NMH 19:233-42, July 1944 and following issue.

Bowers, A.L. Anti-slavery convention in Alton, Ill., in 1837. IHJ 20:329-56, Oct. 1927.

Bradley, P. Psycho-analyzing the Ku Klux Klan. AMR 2:683-6, Nov.-Dec. 1924.

Bragg, George F., Jr. The Negro race and the Episcopal Church. PEH 4:47-52, Mar. 1935.

BRANDS

Linaker, R.H. A silver slave brand. CON 69:161-4, July 1924.

Braun, Robert. Man farthest down. PUB 16:152, Feb. 14, 1913.

BRAWLEY, B.

Review of B. Brawley, A social history of the American Negro. APS 17:137-8, Feb. 1923.

BRAY ASSOCIATES

Pennington, E.L. Philanthropic activities of the Bray Associates among the Negroes. PAM 58:1-25, Jan. 1934.

BRAZIL

Bell, W.J., Jr. Relation of Herndon and Gibbon's exploration of the Amazon to North American slavery, 1850-5. HAH 19:494-503, Nov. 1939.

Hill, L.F. The abolition of the African slave trade to Brazil. HAH 11:169-97, May 1931.

Martin, P.A. Slavery and abolition in Brazil. HAH 13: 151-96, May 1933.

Turner, L.D. Contrasts of Brazilian ex-slaves with Nigeria. VQR 27:55-67, Jan. 1942.

BRAZIL, BAHIA

Carneiro, E. The structure of African cults in Bahia, Brazil. JAF 53:271-8, Oct.-Dec. 1940.

Frazier, E. Franklin. The Negro family in Bahia, Brazil. ASR 7:465-78, Aug. 1942.

Pierson, D. The Negro in Bahia, Brazil. ASR 4:524-33, Aug. 1939.

Breckenridge, W.C. See Sampson, F.A.

BRECKINRIDGE, ROBERT J.

Tapp, H. Conflict between Robert Wickliffe and Robert J. Breckinridge prior to the Civil War. HIS 19:156-70, July 1945.

Brewer, J.M. Review of H.L. Ballowe, The Lawd sayin' the same. SFQ 12:227-9, Sept. 1948.

Brewer, J.M. Review of B.A. Botkin, ed., Lay my burden down: Autobiographical narratives of Negro ex-slaves. JAF 60:94-6, Jan.-Mar. 1947.

Brewer, W.M. Effects of the plantation system on the ante-bellum South. GHQ 11:250-73, Sept. 1927.

Brewer, W.M. Review of J.H. Franklin, From slavery to freedom. WMQ 3d s. 5:440-2, July 1948.

BRITISH COLUMBIA, VANCOUVER ISLAND

Howay, F.W. The Negro immigration into Vancouver Island in 1858. BCH 3:101-13, Apr. 1939.

Howay, F.W. Negro immigration into Vancouver Island in 1858. RSC 3d s. 29:145-56, sec. 2, May 1935.

BRITISH COLUMBIA, VICTORIA

Reid, R.L. How one slave became free: An episode in the old days of Victoria. BCH 6:251-6, Oct. 1942.

BRITISH EMPIRE

Barnes, L. The Negro in the British Empire. VQR 10:78-93, Jan. 1934.

Davis, J. The South and British Africa. VQR 13:362-75, Summer 1937.

Hoernle, R.F.A. Racial problems in the Empire. WOR 6:49-53, Feb. 1939.

Broderick, F.L. Review of Benjamin Quarles, Frederick Douglass. NEQ 21:551-2, Dec. 1948.

BRONZEVILLE

Drake, St. Clair, and H.R. Cayton. Bronzeville: Chicago's huge Negro community. HOL 2:34-8+, May 1947.

BROOKS, PRESTON S.

Campbell, J.E. Sumner--Brooks--Burlingame. The last of the great challenges. OAQ 34:435-73, Oct. 1925.

BROWN, G.G.

Welshans, Genevieve. Review of G.G. Brown, Law administration and Negro-white relations in Philadelphia; recreational facilities and Negro-white relations in Philadelphia. PAH 16:68-9, Jan. 1949.

Brown, I.V. American Freedmen's Union Commission--activities in Reconstruction under the direction of Lyman Abbott. JSH 15:22-38, Feb. 1949.

Brown, J.N. Lovejoy's influence on John Brown. MAG 23:97-102, Sept.-Oct. 1916.

BROWN, JOHN

Brown, J.N. Lovejoy's influence on John Brown. MAG 23:97-102, Sept.-Oct. 1916.

Brown, S. John Brown and sons in Kansas territory. INM 31:142-50, June 1935.

Caskie, G.E. Trial of John Brown. ANN 9:359-79, Apr. 1910.

Cavanagh, Catherine F. Last days of John Brown. AME 5:201-10, Feb. 1910.

Celebration of John Brown's day. AME 5:980, Sept.-Oct. 1910.

Donovan, S.K. John Brown at Harper's Ferry and Charlestown. OAQ 30:300-36, July 1921.

Draper, D.C. Legal phases of John Brown's trial. WVA 1:87-103, Jan. 1940.

England, G.A. Description of Harper's Ferry and incidents of John Brown's last days. TRA 50:28-32+, Mar. 1928.

Filler, L., ed. John Brown in Ohio: An interview with Charles S.S. Griffing. OAQ 58:213-8, Apr. 1949.

Fletcher, R.S. Ransom's painting of John Brown on his way to execution. KHQ 9:343-6, Nov. 1946.

Floyd, J.B. Official report of John Brown's raid upon Harper's Ferry. ORE 10:314-24, Sept. 1909.

Galbreath, C.B. John Brown. Bibliography. OAQ 30:180-289, July 1921.

Gee, C.S. John Brown's last letter, written to Lora Case. OAQ 40:185-9, Apr. 1931.

Gue, B.F. Iowa men in John Brown's raid. AMH 1:143-69, Mar. 1906.

Halsted, M. John Brown's execution. OAQ 30:290-9, July 1921.

Hamilton, James A. Life and work of John Brown. NYS 5:148-57, Apr. 1924.

Harlow, R.V. Gerrit Smith and the John Brown raid. AHR 38:32-60, Oct. 1932.

Huhner, L. Some Jewish associates of John Brown. AJH 23: 55-78, 1915.

Land, Mary. John Brown's Ohio environment. OAQ 57:24-47, Jan. 1948.

Letter from John Brown on the wool trade, 1849. MAG 16: 36-8, Jan. 1913.

Letter from Secretary of State concerning John Brown. MAG 20:184, Mar.-Apr. 1915.

Letters of John Brown. VAM 9:385-94, April 1902 and following issues.

Malin, J.C. Identification of the stranger at the Pottawatomie massacre. KHQ 9:3-12, Feb. 1940.

Malin, J.C. John Brown and the Manes incident. KHQ 7: 376-8, Nov. 1938.

Malin, J.C. The John Brown legend in pictures. KHQ 8: 339-41, Nov. 1939; 9:339-42, Nov. 1940.

Meader, J.R. Harper's Ferry raid. AME 7:29-36, Jan. 1912.

Miller, E.C. John Brown's ten years in Northwestern Pennsylvania. PAH 15:24-33, Jan. 1948.

Moody, Joel. Marais des Cygnes massacre. KAN 14:208-23, 1915-8.

Overturf, W. John Brown's cabin at Nebraska City. NHS 21:92-100, Apr.-June 1940.

Rex, Millicent B. John Brown's life and burial at Lake Placid. AME 25:141-9, Apr. 1931.

Stutler, B.B. The "originals" of John Brown's letter to the Rev. Luther Humphrey. WVA 9:1-25, Oct. 1947.

Swayze, L.E. "Ossawattomie Brown," an old play on John Brown. KHQ 6:34-59, Feb. 1937.

Tannar, A.H. Marais des Cygnes and rescue of Ben Rice. KAN 14:224-34, 1915-8.

Teakle, T. Rendition of Barclay Coppoc. IAJ 10:503-66, Oct. 1912.

Thurston, Mrs. C.B. Letter of 1859. News of the John Brown raid on Harper's Ferry. MDH 39:162-3, June 1944.

Brown, S. John Brown and sons in Kansas territory. INM 31: 142-50, June 1935.

Brownell, R. Review of Capt. T. Canot, Adventures of an African slaver. TRA 51:39-41, 46-7, Aug. 1928.

BROWNSVILLE, TEXAS, AFFAIR

Paine, A.B. Truth about the Brownsville, Texas, affair, by Capt. "Bill" McDonald. PRS 20:221-35, Sept. 1908.

Bruce, Kathleen. Slave labor in Virginia iron industry. WMQ 2d s. 6:289-302, Oct. 1932 and following issues.

Bruce, W.C. A plantation retrospect of the Reconstruction period after the Civil War. VQR 7:546-61, Oct. 1931.

BUCHANAN, JAMES

Auchampaugh, P. Buchanan, the Court, and the Dred Scott case. THM 9:231-40, Jan. 1926.

Harmon, G.D. Buchanan's attitude toward the admission of Kansas on the slavery question. PAM 53:51-91, Jan. 1929.

Ranck, J.B. The attitude of James Buchanan towards slavery. PAM 51:126-42, Apr. 1927.

Buck, D.H. Poor whites of the ante-bellum South. AHR 31: 41-54, Oct. 1925.

Buell, R.L. Conditions of slavery in Liberia. VQR 7:161-71, Apr. 1931.

BUFORD EXPEDITION

Fleming, W.L. Kansas territory and the Buford expedition of 1856. AHS 4:167-92, 1904.

BURLINGAME, ANSON B.

Campbell, J.E. Sumner--Brooks--Burlingame. The last of the great challenges. OAQ 34:435-73, Oct. 1925.

Burma, J.H. Humor as a technique in race conflict. ASR 11: 710-5, Dec. 1946.

Burma, J.H. Racial minorities in wartime. SOS 35:157-8. Apr. 1944.

BURNS, ANTHONY

Landon, F. Anthony Burns in Canada. OHS 22:162-6, 1925.

Sherwin, O. Boston: The case of Anthony Burns, Negro. NEQ 19:212-23, June 1946.

Burns, F.P. White supremacy in the South. The battle for constitutional government, 1866. LHQ 18:581-616, July 1935.

Burroughs, W.G. Oberlin's part in the slavery conflict. OAQ 20:269-334, Apr.-July 1911.

BUSH NEGROES

Kirke, D.B. Bush Negroes of Dutch Guiana. CHA 7th s. 15:549-52, Aug. 1, 1925.

BUSINESSMEN

Negro businessmen of New Orleans. FTE 40:112+, Nov. 1949.

Butler, M. See Winston, S.

Butsch, J. Negro Catholics in U.S. CHR 3:33-51, Apr. 1917.

Cahnman, W.J. Attitudes of minority youth: A methodological introduction. ASR 14:543-8, Aug. 1949.

CALIFORNIA

How Thomas Starr King saved California to the Union during the slavery discussion. CAL 3:10-5, Oct.-Nov. 1929.

Callaway, A. Review of Sarah G. Millin, God's step-children. IRM 18:612-5, Oct. 1929.

CALLCOTT, W.H.

Parks, E.T. Review of W.H. Callcott, The Caribbean policy of the U.S. JSH 9:430-2, Aug. 1943.

CALVINISM

Rodabaugh, J.H. Miami University, Calvinism and the anti-slavery movement. OAQ 48:66-73, Jan. 1939.

Campbell, J.E. Sumner--Brooks--Burlingame. The last of the great challenges. OAQ 34:435-73, Oct. 1925.

CANADA

Cooley, Verna. Illinois and the underground railroad to Canada. IHL 23:76-98, 1917.

Grey, F.W. Race questions in Canada. UNI 7:212-30, Apr. 1908.

Landon, F. Anthony Burns in Canada. OHS 22:162-6, 1925.

Landon, F. Canada's part in freeing the slaves. OHS 17: 74-84, 1919.

Landon, F. The Canadian anti-slavery group beforc the Civil War. UNI 17:540-7, Dec. 1918.

Landon, F. The fugitive slave in Canada before the American Civil War. UNI 18:270-9, Apr. 1919.

Landon, F. Negro colonization schemes in Upper Canada before 1860. RSC 3d s. 23:73+, sec. 2, May 1929.

Landon, F. Social conditions among the Negroes in Upper Canada before 1865. OHS 22:144-61, 1925.

Landon, F. The work of the American Missionary Association among the Negro refugees in Canada West, 1848-64. OHS 21:198-205, 1924.

Paquet, L.A. Slaves and slavery in Canada. RSC 3d s. 7: 139-49, sec. 1, 1913.

Riddell, W.R. International complications between Illinois and Canada arising out of slavery. IHJ 25:123-6, Apr.-July 1932.

Riddell, W.R. Method of abolition of slavery in England, Scotland, and Upper Canada compared. OHS 27: 511-3, 1931.

Riddell, W.R. A Negro slave in Canadian Detroit, 1795. MHM 18:48-52, Winter 1934.

Riddell, W.R. An official record of slavery in Upper Canada. OHS 25:393-7, 1929.

CANADA, ONTARIO

Green, Ernest. Upper Canada's black defenders. OHS 27:365-91, 1931.

Landon, F. Refugee Negroes from the United States in Ontario. DAL 5:523-31, Jan. 1926.

CANADA, SASKATCHEWAN

Activities of Ku Klux Klan in Saskatchewan. QUE 35:592-609, Autumn 1928.

Candler, M.A. Beginnings of slavery in Georgia. MAG 14:342-51, July 1911.

CANOT, CAPT. T.

Brownell, R. Review of Capt. T. Canot, Adventures of an African slaver. TRA 51:39-41, 46-7, Aug. 1928.

CAPABILITY

Negro capability. PUB 15:1059, Nov. 8, 1912.

CAPITALISM

Handlin, Oscar. Prejudice and capitalist exploitation: Does economics explain racism? COM 6:79-85, July 1948.

Cardozo, M. Review of F. Tannenbaum, Slave and citizen: The Negro in the Americas. CHR 33:66-7, Apr. 1947.

CARIBBEAN. See also WEST INDIES

Commercial interest in the Caribbean. ACA 7:383-91, July 1917.

Slaughter, J.W. Our Caribbean policy. PUB 20:850-3, June 8, 1917.

Thomas, K. Caribbean--America's "Mare Nostrum." JIR 11:406-24, Jan. 1921.

Carline, R. The dating and provenance of Negro art. BUR 77: 115-23, Oct. 1940.

Carmichael, Maude. Federal experiments with Negro labor on abandoned plantations in Arkansas. ARK 1:101-16, June 1942.

Carneiro, E. The structure of African cults in Bahia, Brazil. JAF 53:271-8, Oct.-Dec. 1940.

Carnegie, A. Negroes in U.S. GOV 3:131-49, June 1908.

CARPETBAGGERS

Apple, J.A. The carpetbaggers as some Southerners saw them, and its influence in the U.S. today. SOS 35: 220-5, May 1949.

Smith, G.W. Carpetbag imperialism in Florida, 1862-8. FHS 27:99-130, Oct. 1948 and following issue.

Carroll, H.B. Nolan's "lost nigger" expedition of 1877. SWH 44:55-75, July 1940.

Carsel, W. The slaveholders' indictment of Northern wage slavery. JSH 6:504-20, Nov. 1940.

Carter, K. "The Cruz": An incident of the slave trade. CHA 7th s. 19:177-80, Feb. 16, 1929 and following issue.

Catterall, Helen T. Antecedents of the Dred Scott case. AHR 30:56-71, Oct. 1924.

CARVER, GEORGE WASHINGTON

MHR 38:470-1, July 1944.

TEC 17:266, May 1912.

Reed, C.D. Tribute to George Washington Carver. ANN 3d s. 24:248-53, Jan. 1943.

CASE, LORA

Gee, C.S. John Brown's last letter, written to Lora Case. OAQ 40:185-9, Apr. 1931.

Caskie, G.E. Trial of John Brown. ANN 9:359-79, Apr. 1910.

Cason, C.E. Review of C.S. Johnson, et al., The Negro in American civilization. VQR 6:594-600, Oct. 1930.

Cason, C.E. Review of Louise V. Kennedy, The Negro peasant turns cityward. VQR 6:594-600, Oct. 1930.

CASTE

Grossman, M. Caste or democracy? An American dilemma. CJR 7:475-86, Oct. 1944.

CATHOLIC CHURCH. See ROMAN CATHOLIC CHURCH

Cavanagh, Catherine F. Last days of John Brown. AME 5:201-10, Feb. 1910.

Cayton, H.R. See Drake, St. Clair

CENSUS

Gibb, H.L. Slaves in old Detroit, from a census of 1782. MHM 18:143-6, Spring 1934.

CENTRAL UNITED STATES

Phelan, R.V. Slavery in central United States. WHP 1905:252-64.

CEREMONIES

Seale, Lee, and Marianna Seale. A Louisiana Negro ceremony: Easter Rock. JAF 212-8, Oct.-Dec. 1942.

Simpson, George E. Four specialized ceremonies of the vodun cult in Northern Haiti. JAF 59:154-67, Apr.-June 1946.

Simpson, George E. Two vodun-related ceremonies from Haiti. JAF 61:49-52, Jan.-Mar. 1948.

Chamberlain, A.F. Contributions of Negroes to human civilization. JRD 1:482-502, Apr. 1911.

Chamberlain, A.F. Review of Mary W. Ovington, Half a man. JRD 2:345-6, Jan. 1912.

Chamberlain, A.F. Universal Races Congress: Papers and proceedings. JRD 2:494-7, Apr. 1912.

CHAMPION, S.G.

Jente, R. Review of S.G. Champion, Racial proverbs. JAF 53:279-80, Oct.-Dec. 1940.

CHANNING, WILLIAM ELLERY

Hicks, Granville. Dr. Channing and the Creole case. AHR 37:516-25, Apr. 1932.

Letters to Dr. William E. Channing on slavery and the annexation of Texas. NEQ 5:587-601, July 1932.

Chapple, J.M. Tuskegee Institute and its new work. NAT 33:617-24, Mar. 1911.

CHARACTER

Puckett, N.N. Negro character as revealed in folk lore. ASS 28:12-23, May 1934.

CHASE, SALMON P.

Letters of S.P. Chase, Henry Clay, Henry George. INM 7:123-32, Sept. 1911.

CHAVIS, JOHN

Knight, E.W. Notes on career of John Chavis, Negro Presbyterian preacher and teacher, 1763(?)- , as a teacher of Southern white children and of his ministry. NCH 7: 326-45, July 1930.

CHECKLISTS

Lash, J.S. The American Negro and American literature: A check list of significant commentaries. BUB 19:33-6, Jan.-Apr. 1947 and previous issue.

Porter, Dorothy B. Early American Negro writings: A bibliographical study with a preliminary check list of the published writings of American Negroes, 1760-1835. BSA 39:192-268, Third Quarter, 1945.

Chester, S.H. African slavery as I knew it in Southern Arkansas. THM 9:178-84, Oct. 1925.

CHICAGO

Drake, St. Clair, and H.R. Cayton. Bronzeville: Chicago's huge Negro community. HOL 2:34-8+, May 1947.

CHILDREN

Dickins, Dorothy, and R.N. Ford. Geophagy among Negro school children. ASR 7:59-65, Feb. 1942.

Emery, Julia C. How the church helps Southern Negro children. SPM 72:113-5, Feb. 1907.

Johnson, C.S. The problem of Negro child education. ASR 1:264-72, Apr. 1936.

Knight, E.W. Notes on career of John Chavis, Negro Presbyterian preacher and teacher, 1763(?)- , as a teacher of Southern white children and of his ministry. NCH 7:326-45, July 1930.

Nebbit, L. Letter of a colored child of the Sacred Heart. AMC 24:179-81, June 1913.

Perkins, A.E., comp. Riddles from Negro school children in New Orleans, La. JAF 35:105-15, Apr.-June 1922.

Seeman, M. Skin color values in three all-Negro school classes. ASR 11:315-21, June 1946.

Chisholm, G.C. Review of E. Huntington, Character of races. SGM 41:299-302, Sept. 15, 1925.

CHRISTIANITY

Goodwin, Mary F. Christianizing and educating the Negro in colonial Virginia. PEH 1:143-52, Sept. 1932.

CHURCH MUSIC

Work, John W. Changing patterns in Negro folk songs. JAF 62:136-44, Apr.-June 1949.

CHURCH OF ENGLAND

Klingberg, F.J. Missionary activity of the S.P.G. among the African immigrants of colonial Pennsylvania and Delaware. PEH 11:126-53, June 1942.

Klingberg, F.J. The Society for the Propagation of the Gospel program for Negroes in colonial New York. PEH 8:306-71, Dec. 1939.

CHURCHES. See also particular bodies, e.g., BAPTIST CHURCH, ROMAN CATHOLIC CHURCH

Emery, Julia C. How the church helps Southern Negro children. SPM 72:113-5, Feb. 1907.

Taylor, A.W. The church and the color line. HOM 92:479-81, Dec. 1926.

CIVIL RIGHTS

McElfresh, Mona H. President's Committee on Civil Rights. ALA 42:74-5, Feb. 1948.

Stone, A.H. A Mississippian's view of civil rights, states rights, and the Reconstruction background. JMH 10:181-239, July 1948.

Wechsler, James A., and Nancy F. Wechsler. Report of President's Committee on Civil Rights: One year later. COM 6:297-304, Oct. 1948.

CIVIL WAR

Adams, Fannie L.G. A childhood spent at Hayfield plantation near Fredericksburg, Va., during the Civil War. WMQ 2d s. 23:292-7, July 1948.

Davies, W.E. The problem of race segregation in the Grand Army of the Republic. JSH 13:354-72, Aug. 1947.

Dorris, J.T. Pardon and amnesty during the Civil War and Reconstruction: Excerpt from a forthcoming book. NCH 23:360-401, July 1946.

CIVIL WAR (cont'd)

Harlow. R.V. Rise and fall of emigrant aid movement in Kansas. AHR 41:1-25, Oct. 1935.

Hawley, C.A. Historical background of the Jasper Colony attitude toward slavery and the Civil War. IAJ 34: 172-97, Apr. 1936.

Hay, T.R. The question of arming the slaves. MVH 6:34-73, June 1919.

House, A.V., Jr., ed. Deterioration of a Georgia rice plantation during the Civil War. JSH 9:98-113, Feb. 1943.

Nelson, B.H. Aspects of Negro life in North Carolina during the Civil War. NCH 25:143-66, Apr. 1948.

Nelson, B.H. Legislative control of the Southern free Negro, 1861-65. CHR 32:28-46, Apr. 1946.

Spraggins, T.L. Mobilization of Negro labor for the Department of Virginia and North Carolina, 1861-5. NCH 24:160-97, Apr. 1947.

Trexler, H.A. The opposition of planters to employment of slaves as laborers by the Confederacy. MVH 27: 211-24, Sept. 1940.

Whittington, G.P., ed. Facts concerning the loyalty of slaves in Northern Louisiana in 1863 as shown in the letters of J.H. Ransdell to Gov. T.O. Moore. LHQ 14: 487-502, Oct. 1931.

Williams, H. General Banks and the radical Republicans in the Civil War. NEQ 12:268-80, June 1939.

Young, J.H. Anna Elizabeth Dickinson--her campaign during the Civil War period for and against Lincoln. MVH 31:59-80, June 1944.

CIVILIZATION

Chamberlain, A.F. Contributions of Negroes to human civilization. JRD 1:482-502, Apr. 1911.

Sparendam, W.F. The fraud of white civilization; a Negro's opinion. WOR 1:38-40, June 1936.

Clark, J.H. West Indian superstitions. CHA 8:603-5, Aug. 17, 1918.

Clark, K.B. Negro-Jewish relations: A complex social problem. COM 1:8-14, Feb. 1946.

Clark, R.D. Bishop Matthew Simpson and the Emancipation Proclamation. MVH 35:263-71, Sept. 1948.

Clark, T.D. Slave trade between Kentucky and the cotton kingdom. MVH 21:331-42, Dec. 1934.

Clark, T.D. The slavery background of Foster's "My Old Kentucky Home." HIS 10:1-17, Jan. 1936.

CLARK, TOM C.

Barnett, V.M. Review of Tom C. Clark and Philip B. Perlman, Prejudice and property: An historic brief against racial covenants; submitted to the Supreme Court. APS 42:819-20, Aug. 1948.

Clarke, C.M. "Uncle Tom's Cabin"--how it reached the British public. CHA 7th s. 11:81-2, Jan. 8, 1921.

Clarke, Grace J. Anti-slavery letter of Daniel Worth to George W. Julian, and other documents. INM 26:152-7, June 1930.

Clarke, T.W. The Negro plot in New York City of 1741. NYH 25:167-81, Apr. 1944.

CLAY, CASSIUS M.

Craig, D.M. An old letter concerning Cassius M. Clay and the "True American," 1845, presented to the Filson Club. HIS 22:197-8, July 1948.

Harrison, L. Cassius M. Clay's anti-slavery newspaper, the "True American": Opposition in Kentucky to his struggle for emancipation of the Negro. HIS 22:30-49, Jan. 1948.

Rothert, O.A. Two letters by Cassius Clay, 1862 and 1869. HIS 12:162-9, July 1938.

CLAY, HENRY

Abolition and Henry Clay's visit to Richmond, Ind., 1842. INM 4:117-28, Sept. 1908.

Letters of S.P. Chase, Henry Clay, Henry George. INM 7:123-32, Sept. 1911.

Simpson, Lucretia C. Henry Clay and Liberia. JAH 16:237-45, July-Sept. 1922.

CLAYTON, POWELL

Driggs, O.T., Jr. Arkansas politics: The essence of the Powell Clayton regime, 1868-1871. ARK 8:1-75, Spring 1949.

Clemence, Stella R. Deed and notes covering emancipation of a Negro slave woman in 1585. HAH 10:51-7, Feb. 1930.

CLEMENT ATTACHMENT

Herring, Harriet L. The Clement attachment: An episode in Reconstruction industrial history. JSH 4:185-98, May 1938.

Cleven, N.A.N. Ministerial order of José de Galvez establishing a uniform duty on the importation of Negro slaves into the Indies. HAH 4:266-76, May 1921.

CLIMATE

Huntington, E. Climate, a neglected factor in race development. JRD 6:167-84, Oct. 1915.

Taylor, E.G.R. Ideas current between 1580 and 1650 on influence of climate on racial characteristics. SGM 51:1-6, Jan. 1935.

Warner, C.D. Race and climate. OUT 44:38-9, Feb. 1917.

Cocke, R.H. Sir Joseph de Courcy Laffan's views on slavery. WMQ 2d s. 19:42-8, Jan. 1939.

Coffin, N.E. Case of Archie P. Webb. ANN 3rd s. 11:200-14, July-Oct. 1913.

Cohen, F.S. FEPC fight initiates a new epoch. COM 1:17-22, Mar. 1946.

Cole, A.C. Lincoln's election an immediate menace to slavery in the states? AHR 36:740-67, July 1931.

Coleman, C.H. Three Vallandigham letters, 1865. OAQ 43: 461-4, Oct. 1934.

Coleman, C.H. Use of the term "Copperhead." MVH 25:263-4, Sept. 1938.

COLEMAN, E.M.

Klingberg, F.J. Review of E.M. Coleman, ed., Creole Voices: Poems in French by free men of color. PEH 12: 396-8, Dec. 1943.

Coleman, J.W., Jr. Delia Webster and Calvin Fairbanks, underground railroad agents. HIS 17:129-42, July 1943.

Coleman, J.W., Jr. Lexington, Ky., slave dealers and their Southern trade. HIS 12:1-23, Jan. 1938.

COLEMAN, J.W., JR.

Bean, W.G. Review of J.W. Coleman, Jr., Slavery times in Kentucky. VAM 48:381-2, Oct. 1940.

Eaton, C. Review of J.W. Coleman, Jr., Slavery times in Kentucky. JSH 7:106-7, Feb. 1941.

COLES, GOV. EDWARD

Correspondence of Gov. Edward Coles with Rev. Thomas Lippincott. IHJ 3:59-63, Jan. 1911.

Edward Coles, the man who saved Illinois from slavery. JAH 16:153-7, Apr.-June 1922.

Washburne, E.B. Sketch of Edward Coles, second governor of Illinois and of the slavery struggle of 1823-4. IHC 15:1-135, 1920.

Coles, H.L., Jr. Slaveownership and landownership in Louisiana, 1850-1860. JSH 9:381-94, Aug. 1943.

COLFAX, SCHUYLER

Smith, W.H. Schuyler Colfax: His role in the development of Reconstruction policy. INM 39:323-44, Dec. 1943.

COLLEGES

Johnson, C.S. Racial attitudes of college students. ASS 28:24-31, May 1934.

Rammelkamp, C.H. Anti-slavery movement and Illinois College. IHL 13:192-203, 1909.

Rammelkamp, C.H. Reverberations of the slavery conflict in Illinois College. MVH 14:447-61, Mar. 1928.

COLONIES

DuBois, W.E.B. Political and social status in European possessions in Africa. FOR 3:423-44, Apr. 1925.

Goodwin, Mary F. Liberia--America's only foreign colonial settlement. VAM 55:338+, Oct. 1947.

Graham, A.A. Abolition colony in Ohio. OAQ 30-43, 1895.

COLONIES (cont'd)

Jernegan, M.W. Slavery and the beginnings of industrialization in the colonies. AHR 25:220-40, Jan. 1920.

COLONIZATION

Baker, Eugene C. The influence of slavery in the colonization of Texas. MVR 11:3-36, June 1924; and SWH 28:1-33, July 1924.

Dyer, B. Persistence of the idea of Negro colonization. PHR 12:53-65, Mar. 1943.

Landon, F. Negro colonization schemes in Upper Canada before 1860. RSC 3d s. 23:73+, sec. 2, May 1929.

Lynch, W.O. Colonization of Kansas, 1854-1860. MIV 9:380-2, 1919.

Mowry, D. Negro colonization. AME 5:975-6, Sept.-Oct. 1910.

Sherwood, H.N. Colonization of manumitted slaves in Ohio. John Randolph's bequest. MVH 5:39-59, 1912.

Sherwood, H.N. Paul Cuffe and his contribution to the American Colonization Society. MVH 6:370-402, 1913.

Shunk, E.W. "Ohio in Africa," a plan for a colony of Ohio free-Negro emigrants in Liberia, c. 1850. OAQ 51:70-87, Apr.-June 1942.

COLOR

Kephart, W.M. Is the American Negro becoming lighter? An analysis of the sociological and biological trends. ASR 13:437-43, Aug. 1948.
Comment by J.T. Blue, Jr., ASR 13:766-7, Dec. 1948.

Seeman, M. Skin color values in three all-Negro school classes. ASR 11:315-21, June 1946.

Weale, B.L.P. How color divides the world. WWL 14:598-604, Nov. 1909.

COLOR BAR

Noble, P. Influence of screen portrayal of the Negro upon the colour bar in America. WOR 53-6, June 1944.

COLORADO

Harvey, J.R. Pioneer Negroes in Colorado. COL 26:165-76, July 1949.

COMMUNITIES

Harn, Julia E. Life and customs on plantations and in small communities of the ante-bellum South. GHQ 16: 47-55, Mar. 1932 and previous and following issues.

COMPETITION, RACIAL

Barnes, H.E. The struggle of races and social groups as a factor in development of political and social institutions. JRD 9:394-419, Apr. 1919.

COMPROMISE OF 1850

Harmon, G.D. Stephen A. Douglas--his leadership in Compromise of 1850, regarding government and question of slavery in territory acquired from Mexico. IHJ 21: 452-90, Jan. 1929.

Hearon, C. Mississippi Compromise of 1850. MSS 14:7-230, 1914.

Hodder, F.H. Authorship of the Compromise of 1850. MVH 22:525-36, Mar. 1936.

Parks, J.H. John Bell and the Compromise of 1850. JSH 9:328-56, Aug. 1943.

Sharpe, Esther E. Slavery in the territories under the Compromise of 1850. HIO 18:107-9, Mar. 1927.

Sioussat, St. G.L. The Compromise of 1850 and the Nashville convention. THM 4:215-47, Dec. 1918.

Condenhove, H. Certain facets of Negro mentality in Central Africa. COR n.s. 55:207-21, Aug. 1923.

CONFEDERACY

Coulter, E.M. Planters' wants in the days of the Confederacy. GHQ 12:38-52, Mar. 1928.

McClendon, R. Earl. Status of the ex-Confederate states as seen in the readmission of U.S. senators. AHR 41: 702-9, July 1936.

Trexler, H.A. The opposition of planters to employment of slaves as laborers by the Confederacy. MVH 27:211-24, Sept. 1940.

CONGRESS

Lerche, C.O., Jr. Congressional interpretation of the guarantee of a republican form of government during Reconstruction. JSH 15:192-211, May 1949.

CONGRESS (cont'd)

Ross, M. The 80th Congress and job discrimination: The outlook for a new F.E.P.C. COM 3:301-8, Apr. 1947.

CONGRESSES

Chamberlain, A.F. Universal Races Congress: Papers and proceedings. JRD 2:494-7, Apr. 1912.

Conklin, Julia S. Underground railroad in Indiana. INM 6: 63-74, June 1910.

CONNECTICUT

Norton, F.C. Negro slaves in Connecticut. CNT 5:320-8, June 1899.

Smith, M.H. Connecticut slave days. CNT 9:753-63, Oct. 1905.

Smith, M.H. Connecticut slaves in Revolutionary times. CNT 9:145-53, Jan. 1905.

Smith, M.H. Old slave days in Connecticut. CNT 10:113-28, Jan.-Mar. 1906 and following issue.

CONNECTICUT, CANTERBURY

Small, E.W., and Miriam H. Small. Prudence Crandall, her efforts to promote Negro education, 1833-4. NEQ 17: 506-29, Dec. 1944.

Connelley, W.E., and A. Morrall. Proslavery activity in Kansas. KAN 14:123-42, 1915-8.

Connolly, J.C. Slavery and the causes operating against its extension in colonial New Jersey. NJS n.s. 14:181-202, Apr. 1929.

CONRAD, E.

Klingberg, F.J. Review of E. Conrad, Harriet Tubman: Story of a Maryland slave. PEH 12:396-7, Dec. 1943.

Review of Harriet Tubman: Story of a Maryland slave. GHQ 29:120-1, June 1945.

CONSCIOUSNESS

Jones, L. Negro consciousness and democracy. PUB 15: 820-2, Aug. 30, 1912.

CONSPIRACIES

Taylor, R.H. Slave conspiracies in North Carolina. NCH 5:20-34, June 1928.

CONSTITUTION

Lerche, C.O., Jr. Congressional interpretation of the guarantee of a republican form of government during Reconstruction. JSH 15:192-211, May 1949.

Leslie, W.R. The constitutional significance of Indiana's statute of 1824 on fugitives from labor. JSH 13:338-53, Aug. 1947.

Rose, J.C. Suffrage: Constitutional point of view. APS 1:17-43, Nov. 1906.

Way, R.B. Was the fugitive slave clause in the constitution necessary? IAJ 5:326-36, July 1907.

CONSTITUTIONAL CONVENTIONS

Gregory, J.P., Jr. The question of slavery in the Kentucky constitutional convention of 1849. HIS 23: 89-110, Apr. 1949.

Cooley, S. Civic backsliding. PUB 18:753-4, Aug. 6, 1915.

Cooley, S. Negro emigration. PUB 20:450-1, May 11, 1917.

Cooley, S. Progress of Negroes. PUB 18:875, Sept. 10, 1915.

Cooley, S. Storing up trouble for their children. PUB 19: 150, Feb. 18, 1916.

Cooley, Verna. Illinois and the underground railroad to Canada. IHL 23:76-98, 1917.

Cooper, F. Reconstruction in Scott Co., Miss. MSS 13:99-222, 1913.

COOPER, JAMES FENIMORE

Spiller, R.E. Fenimore Cooper's defense of slaveowning America. AHR 35:575-82, Apr. 1930.

CO-OPERATIONISM

Shugg, R.W. A Louisiana co-operationist protest against secession. LHQ 19:199-203, Jan. 1936.

Copeland, F. The New Orleans press and the Reconstruction. LHQ 30:149-337, Jan. 1947.

COPPERHEADS

Coleman, C.H. Use of the term "Copperhead." MVH 25: 263-4, Sept. 1938.

COPPOC, BARCLAY

Teakle, T. Rendition of Barclay Coppoc. IAJ 10:503-66, Oct. 1912.

Corbitt, D.C. Notes on Saco's History of Negro slavery. HAH 24:452-7, Aug. 1944.

Corbitt, D.C. Shipments of slaves from the U.S. to Cuba, 1789-1807. JSH 7:540-9, Nov. 1949.

"CORNER STONE" RESOLUTION

Mowry, Duane. New York Democratic convention's "corner stone" resolution, 1847. IHJ 3:88-90, Oct. 1910.

CORRESPONDENCE

Correspondence of Gov. Coles and Rev. T. Lippincott. IHJ 3:59-63, Jan. 1911.

Slavery and Reconstruction. J.R. Doolittle correspondence, 1848-65. SHA 11:94-105, Mar. 1907.

Corry, J.P. Racial elements in colonial Georgia. GHQ 20: 30-40, Mar. 1936.

Corwin, C.E. Efforts of Dutch colonial pastors for the conversion of the Negroes. PBY 12:425-35, Apr. 1927.

CORWIN, THOMAS

Pendergraft, D. The political career of Thomas Corwin and the conservative Republican reaction, 1858-61. OAQ 57: 1-23, Jan. 1948.

COTTON

Wilkins, Mary, ed. The American Cotton Planters' Ass'n: Papers, 1865-6. THQ 7:335-61, Dec. 1948 and following issue.

COTTON KINGDOM

Clark, T.D. Slave trade between Kentucky and the cotton kingdom. MVH 21:331-42, Dec. 1934.

COTTON MANUFACTURE

Herring, Harriet L. The Clement attachment: An episode in Reconstruction industrial history. JSH 4:185-98, May 1938.

Coulter, E.M. Avondale and Deerbrook, Ga., plantation documents. GHQ 17:150-9, June 1933 and following issues.

Coulter, E.M. History of a century on a Georgia plantation. MVH 16:334-46, Dec. 1929.

Coulter, E.M. Planters' wants in the days of the Confederacy. GHQ 12:38-52, Mar. 1928.

COULTER, E.M.

Dargan, M. Review of E.M. Coulter, The South during Reconstruction. NMQ 18:360-1, Autumn 1948.

Eaton, C. Review of E.M. Coulter, The South during Reconstruction. CHR 34:73-4, Apr. 1948.

Eckenrode, H.J. Review of E.M. Coulter, The South during Reconstruction. VAM 56:214-5, Apr. 1948.

Goodall, Elizabeth J. Review of E.M. Coulter, The South during Reconstruction. WVA 9:300-1, Apr. 1948.

Hamilton, J.G. DeR. Review of E.M. Coulter, The South during Reconstruction. JSH 14:134-6, Feb. 1948.

Isely, J.A. Review of E.M. Coulter, The South during Reconstruction. MDH 43:146, June 1948.

Lissfelt, Mildred B. Review of E.M. Coulter, The South during Reconstruction. SOS 39:133-4, Mar. 1948.

Mabry, W.A. Review of E.M. Coulter, The South during Reconstruction. NCH 25:522-4, Oct. 1948.

Mooney, C.C. Review of E.M. Coulter, The South during Reconstruction. INM 44:110-2, Mar. 1948.

Nixon, H.C. Review of E.M. Coulter, The South during Reconstruction. VQR 24:454-5, Summer 1948.

Ousley, F.L. Review of E.M. Coulter, The South during Reconstruction. SWH 52:248-50, Oct. 1948.

Pearce, H.J., Jr. Review of E.M. Coulter, The South during Reconstruction. GHQ 32:71-2, Mar. 1948.

Pritchard, W. Review of E.M. Coulter, The South during Reconstruction. LHQ 31:150-4, Jan. 1948.

COULTER, E.M. (cont'd)

Wharton, V.L. Review of E.M. Coulter, The South during Reconstruction. JMH 9:271-2, Oct. 1948.

Zorn, R.C. Review of E.M. Coulter, The South during Reconstruction. ARK 7:153-4, Summer 1948.

COURTS

Danziger, S. Courts and minority rights. PUB 16:866, Sept. 12, 1913.

Coward, H. "Jazzery," why the white races should ban it. NAR 90:395-400, Nov. 1927.

Cox, J.H. Negro tales from West Virginia. JAF 47:341-57, Oct.-Dec. 1934.

Cox, O.C. Sex ratio and marital status among Negroes. ASR 5:937-47, Dec. 1940.

COX, O.C.

Blizzard, Sam W. Review of O.C. Cox, Caste, class and race: A study in social dynamics. ASR 13:357-8, June 1948.

Johnson, G.B. Review of O.C. Cox, Caste, class and race: A study in social dynamics. VQR 24:455-9, Summer 1948.

CRAFTMANSHIP

Stavisky, L. Negro craftmanship in early America. AHR 54:315-25, Jan. 1949.

CRAFTS

Lepage, P.C. Arts and crafts of Negroes. INT 78: 577-80, Mar. 1924.

Craig, D.M. An old letter concerning Cassius M. Clay and the "True American," 1845, presented to the Filson Club. HIS 22:197-8, July 1948.

CRANDALL, PRUDENCE

McCarron, Anna T. Prudence Crandall's trial. CNT 12: 225-32, Apr.-June 1908.

Small, E.W., and Miriam H. Small. Prudence Crandall, her efforts to promote Negro education, 1833-4. NEQ 17: 506-29, Dec. 1944.

Tisler, C.C. Story of Prudence Crandall. IHJ 33:203-6, June 1940.

Crane, V.W. Benjamin Franklin on slavery and American liberties. PAM 62:1-11, Jan. 1938.

Crawford, Myrtle B. Instructions for producing pageant for Negro History Week. SOS 32:27-31, Jan. 1941.

CREEK INDIANS

Porter, K.W. The Creek Indian-Negro tradition. The Hawkins Negroes go to Mexico. OKC 24:55-8, Spring 1946.

Creer, L.H. Spanish-American slave trade in the Great Basin, 1800-1853. NMH 24:171-83, July 1949.

Crenshaw, O. Review of L.J. Greene, The Negro in colonial New England. VAM 52:157-8, Apr. 1944.

CRENSHAW, O.

Roseboom, E.H. Review of O. Crenshaw, The slave states in the presidential election of 1860. MVH 34:307+, Sept. 1947.

Stampp, K.M. Review of O. Crenshaw, The slave states in the presidential election of 1860. JSH 13:116-7, Feb. 1947.

CREOLES

Durel, L.C. Donaldsville, La., Creole civilization, 1850, according to the newspaper "Le Vigilant." LHQ 31:981-94, Oct. 1948.

Smelser, M. Housing in Creole St. Louis, 1764-1821: An example of cultural change. LHQ 21:337-48, Apr. 1938.

CRIME

Moses, E.R. Differentials in crime rates between Negroes and whites, based on comparisons of four socio-economically equated areas. ASR 12:411-20, Aug. 1947.

CRIMINALS

Letter regarding Negro criminal. PUB 14:843-4, Aug. 18, 1911.

Crite, Alan R. Why I illustrate spirituals. WLD 1:44-5+, May 1938.

CRITICAL ANALYSES

Simms, H.H. Abolition literature, 1830-40, a critical analysis. JSH 6:368-82, Aug. 1940.

Crittenden, C.C. Review of G.H. Barnes, The anti-slavery impulse. NCH 12:62-4, Jan. 1935.

Cross, Cora M. Early days in Texas. Reminiscences by an old-time darky. TEX 4:380-93, Oct. 1929.

CRUM, H.

Dyer, J.P. Review of H. Crum, Gullah: Negro life in the Caroline Sea Islands. JSH 7:108-9, Feb. 1941.

Herskovitz, M.J. Review of H. Crum, Gullah: Negro life in the Caroline Sea Islands. ASR 6:423-4, June 1941.

Patton, J.W. Review of H. Crum, Gullah: Negro life in the Caroline Sea Islands. MVH 28:300, Sept. 1941.

Wiley, B.I. Review of H. Crum, Gullah: Negro life in the Caroline Sea Islands. AHR 46:933-4, July 1941.

"CRUSADER IN CRINOLINE." See STOWE, HARRIET BEECHER

"THE CRUZ"

Carter, K. "The Cruz": An incident of the slave trade. CHA 7th s. 19:177-80, Feb. 16, 1929 and following issue.

CUBA

Corbitt, D.C. Shipments of slaves from the U.S. to Cuba, 1789-1807. JSH 7:540-9, Nov. 1949.

Kennedy, Stetson. Nanigo in Florida. SFQ 4:153-6, Sept. 1940.

Negro insurrection in Cuba. PUB 15:514-5, May 31, 1912; PUB 15:566, June 14, 1912.

CUFFE, PAUL

Sherwood, H.N. Paul Cuffe and his contribution to the American Colonization Society. MVH 6:370-402, 1913.

Culin, S. Negro art. ART 3:346-50, May 1923.

CULTS, AFRICAN

Carneiro, E. The structure of African cults in Bahia, Brazil. JAF 53:271-8, Oct.-Dec. 1940.

CULTURAL CHANGE

Smelser, M. Housing in Creole St. Louis, 1764-1821: An example of cultural change. LHQ 21:337-48, Apr. 1938.

CULTURE

DuBois, W.E.B. Culture of white folk. JRD 7:434-47, Apr. 1917.

Oliver, W.P. Cultural progress of the Negro in Nova Scotia. DAL 29:203-300, Oct. 1949.

Taylor, G. Evolution and distribution of race, culture and language. GEO 11:54-119, Jan. 1921.

Wolfe, B. Uncle Remus and the malevolent rabbit: The Negro in popular American culture. COM 8:31-41, July 1949.

CUNNINGHAM, VIRGINIA

Biggert, Elizabeth. Review of Virginia Cunningham, Paul Dunbar and his song. OAQ 56:455-6, Oct. 1947.

Current, R.N. Love, hate and Thaddeus Stevens. PAH 14:259-72, Oct. 1947.

Curti, M. Review of Herbert Aptheker, American Negro slave revolts. CHR 30:76-8, Apr. 1944.

Curtis, Agnes B. A strange story of a Negro and his white deliverer. JAH 18:349-55, Oct.-Dec. 1924.

Dabney, V. Review of L.P. Jackson, Free Negro labor and property holding in Virginia, 1830-60. VAM 51:212-3, Apr. 1913.

DAHLBERG, G.

Ashley-Montague, M.F. Review of G. Dahlberg, Race, reason and rubbish. CJR 6:670-1, Dec. 1943.

DAMAGES

Suit for damages for personal injuries to a slave, 1764. LHQ 5:58-62, Jan. 1922.

Damon, S.F. The Negro in early American songsters. BSA 28:132-63, 1934.

DANCE

Edmiston, Dorothy. A ballet of the African Negro to be performed in Dallas, Texas. TEX 4:458-64, Nov. 1940.

Dancy, J.C. The Negro people in Michigan. MHM 24:221-40, Spring 1940.

Danziger, S. Courts and minority rights. PUB 16:866, Sept. 12, 1913.

Danziger, S. Segregation and land monopoly. PUB 19:891-2, Sept. 22, 1916.

Dargan, M. Review of E.M. Coulter, The South during Reconstruction. NMQ 18:360-1, Autumn 1948.

Dart, H.P., ed. See Sanders, A.G., tr.

Davenport, T.W. Slavery in Oregon. ORE 9:309-73, Dec. 1908.

Davenport, T.W., and G.H. Williams. Oregon agitation up to 1801. ORE 8:189-273, Sept. 1908.

Davies, W.E. The problem of race segregation in the Grand Army of the Republic. JSH 13:354-72, Aug. 1947.

Davis, H.C. Folk-lore in South Carolina. JAF 27:241-54, July-Sept. 1914.

Davis, J. The South and British Africa. VQR 13:362-75. Summer 1937.

DAVIS, JEFFERSON

Murphee, D. Hurricane and Brierfield, the Jefferson Davis plantations on Palmyra Island, Miss. JMH 9:98-107, Apr. 1947.

Davis, P.C. The Negro in the armed services. VQR 24:499-520, Autumn 1948.

DE AYARZA, JOSÉ PONSEANO

A document (in Spanish) on the Negro in higher education in Spanish America: Case of José Ponseano de Ayarza, 1794-98. HAH 24:432-51, Aug. 1944.

DEBTOR RELIEF

St. Clair, K.E. Debtor relief in North Carolina during Reconstruction, 1865. NCH 18:215-35, July 1941.

DEFOREST, J.W.

Ferguson, J.S. Review of J.W. DeForest, A Union officer in the Reconstruction. JMH 10:175-7, Apr. 1948.

Harmon, D. Review of J.W. DeForest, A Union officer in the Reconstruction. PAM 72:432-3, Oct. 1948.

Klement, F. Review of J.W. DeForest, A Union officer in the Reconstruction. WIM 32:225-6, Dec. 1948.

Miller, P. Review of J.W. DeForest, A Union officer in the Reconstruction. NEQ 21:392-4, Sept. 1948.

Williams, T.H. Review of J.W. DeForest, A Union officer in the Reconstruction. JSH 14:560-1, Nov. 1948.

de GALVEZ, JOSÉ

Cleven, N.A.N. Ministerial order of José de Galvez establishing a uniform duty on the importation of Negro slaves into the Indies. HAH 4:266-76, May 1921.

DELAWARE

Klingberg, F.J. Missionary activity of the S.P.G. among the African immigrants of colonial Pennsylvania and Delaware. PEH 11:126-53, June 1942.

DELAWARE, NEW CASTLE

Taylor, Helen L., ed. Negro beliefs and place legends from New Castle, Del. JAF 51:92-4, Jan.-Mar. 1938.

"DELIA HOLMES"

Milling, C.J. "Delia Holmes," a neglected Negro ballad. SFQ 1:3-8, Dec. 1937.

DELINQUENT BEHAVIOR

Robison, Sophia M. Effects of the factors of race and nationality on the registration of behavior as delinquent in New York City in 1930. ASS 28:37-44, May 1934.

DEMOCRACY

Addams, Jane. Race problems of a democracy. ASS 14:206-15, 1919.

Dowd, J. Race segregation in a democracy. ASS 14:189-205, 1919.

Ellis, G.W. The Negro and the war for democracy. JRD 8:439-53, Apr. 1918.

DEMOCRACY (cont'd)

Ellis, G.W. Negroes in the new democracy. JRD 7:82-3, July 1916.

Grossman, M. Caste or democracy? An American dilemma. CJR 7:475-86, Oct. 1944.

Humphrey, N.D. Race can work toward democracy. SOS 35: 246-8, Oct. 1944.

Jones, L. Negro consciousness and democracy. PUB 15: 820-2, Aug. 30, 1912.

Means, P.A. Race appreciation and democracy. JRD 9: 180-8, Oct. 1918.

Mecklin, J.M. Ku Klux Klan and the democratic tradition. AMR 2:241-51, May-June 1924.

DEMOCRATIC PARTY

Lynch, W.O. Antislavery tendencies of the Democratic party in the Northwest, 1848-50. MVH 11:319-31, Dec. 1924.

Mowry, Duane. New York Democratic convention's "corner stone" resolution, 1847. IHJ 3:88-90, Oct. 1910.

DEPARTMENT OF VIRGINIA AND NORTH CAROLINA

Spraggins, T.L. Mobilization of Negro labor for the Department of Virginia and North Carolina, 1861-5. NCH 24:160-97, Apr. 1947.

DEPORTATION

Fleming, W.H. Historic attempts to solve the race problem in America by deportation. JAH 4:197-213, Apr. 1910.

Sherwood, H.N. Deportation projects. MVH 2:484-508, Mar. 1916.

Sherwood, H.N. Indiana and Negro deportation, 1817. MVH 9:414-21, 1919.

de Rivera, B. How women can halt "the great black plague." PRS 23:417-20, Mar. 1910.

DETERIORATION

Dickson, Harris. Deterioration of the race. HAM 23: 497-505, Oct. 1909.

DEVELOPMENT

Pratt, L.R. Development of Negroes in the U.S. AME 6: 529-34, June 1911.

Woodruff, C.E. Laws of racial and intellectual development. JRD 3:156-75, Oct. 1912.

Dexter, R.C. Review of J.E. Johnson, comp., The Negro problem. JIR 12:587-9, Apr. 1922.

Deye, A.H. Review of Madeleine H. Rice, American Catholic opinions in the slavery controversy. CHR 30:180-1, July 1944.

de Zayas, M. Negro art. ART 3:198-205, Mar. 1923.

DIALECTS

Stoddard, A.H. Origin, dialect, beliefs and characteristics of the Negroes of the South Carolina and Georgia coasts. GHQ 28:186-95, Sept. 1944.

Dickins, Dorothy, and R.N. Ford. Geophagy among Negro school children. ASR 7:59-65, Feb. 1942.

DICKINSON, ANNA ELIZABETH

Anderson, Judith. Anna Elizabeth Dickinson, anti-slavery radical. PAH 3:147-63, July 1936.

Young, J.H. Anna Elizabeth Dickinson--a woman abolitionist views the South in 1875. GHQ 32:241-51, Dec. 1948.

Young, J.H. Anna Elizabeth Dickinson--her campaign during the Civil War period for and against Lincoln. MVH 31: 59-80, June 1944.

Dickinson, C.H. Samuel Armstrong's contribution to Christian missions. IRM 10:509-24, Oct. 1921.

Dickson, Harris. Deterioration of the race. HAM 23:497-505, Oct. 1909.

Dickson, Harris. The Negro in politics. HAM 23:225-36, Aug. 1909.

Dickson, Harris. The unknowable Negro. HAM 22:728-42, June 1909 and following issues.

Dimmick, J. Sir William Berkley's plantation at Green Spring, Va. WMQ 2d s. 9:129-30, Apr. 1929.

Dinkins, J. Negroes as slaves. SHS 35:60-8, Jan.-Dec. 1907.

DIPLOMATS

Sears, L.M. Frederick Douglass: His career as U.S. minister to Haiti, 1889-91. HAH 21:222-38, May 1941.

DISCIPLES OF CHRIST

Haynes, N.S. Disciples of Christ and their attitude toward slavery. IHL 19:52-9, 1913.

DISCRIMINATION

Graves, John T. The Southern Negro and the war crisis. VQR 18:500-17, Autumn 1942.

Northrup, H.R. Race discrimination in trade unions. COM 2:124-31, Aug. 1946.

Ross, M. The 80th Congress and job discrimination: The outlook for a new F.E.P.C. COM 3:301-8, Apr. 1947.

Zornow, William F. Judicial modifications of the Maryland black code in the District of Columbia. MDH 44:18-32, Mar. 1949.

DISFRANCHISEMENT

Adams, J.T. Disfranchisement of Negroes in New England. AHR 30:543-7, Apr. 1925.

Grantham, D.W., Jr. Politics and the disfranchisement of the Negro. GHQ 32:1-21, Mar. 1948.

Russ, W.A., Jr. Disfranchisement in Louisiana, 1862-70. LHQ 18:557-80, July 1935.

Russ, W.A., Jr. Disfranchisement in Maryland, 1861-7. MDH 28:309-28, Dec. 1933.

Russ, W.A., Jr. Radical disfranchisement in Georgia, 1867-71. GHQ 19:175-209, Sept. 1935.

Russ, W.A., Jr. Radical disfranchisement in North Carolina, 1867-8. NCH 11:271-83, Oct. 1934.

Russ, W.A., Jr. Radical disfranchisement in Texas, 1867-70. SWH 38:40-52, July 1934.

Russ, W.A., Jr. Registration and disfranchisement under radical Reconstruction. MVH 21:163-80, Sept. 1931.

Tindall, George B. The campaign for the disfranchisement of Negroes in South Carolina. JSH 15:212-34, May 1949.

DISTRICT OF COLUMBIA

Milburn, P. Emancipation of slaves in the District of Columbia. CHS 16:96-119, 1913.

Zornow, William F. Judicial modifications of the Maryland black code in the District of Columbia. MDH 44:18-32, Mar. 1949.

DISTRICT OF COLUMBIA, WASHINGTON

Bernstein, David, and Adele Bernstein. Washington (D.C.): Tarnished symbol. Our capitol's treason against America. COM 6:397-403, Nov. 1948.

The Negroes in Washington, D.C. FTE 19:132+, Dec. 1934.

Riggs, J.B. Early Maryland landowners in the vicinity of Washington. CHS 48:249-63, 1949.

DIXON, R.B.

Starr, F. Review of R.B. Dixon, The racial history of mankind. APS 17:675-7, Nov. 1923.

DOCUMENTS

Hopkins, Geraldine. Editions of the "Liberty Minstrel," a rare abolitionist document. MVH 18:60-4, June 1931.

Sanders, A.G., tr. H.P. Dart, ed. Documents covering the beginning of the African slave trade in Louisiana, 1718. LHQ 14:103-77, Apr. 1931.

Dodd, Dorothy. The schooner "Emperor" in the illegal slave trade in Florida. FHS 13:117-28, Jan. 1935.

Dodd, William E. Review of Elizabeth Dounan, Documents illustrative of the history of the slave trade in America. NEQ 8:592-4, Dec. 1935.

Dodd, William E. Review of W.E.B. DuBois, Black reconstruction. VQR 12:138-41, Jan. 1936.

DOLLARD, JOHN

Lewinson, P. Review of John Dollard, Class and caste in a Southern town. AHR 43:428-9, Jan. 1938.

Donald, D.H. The role of the scalawag in Mississippi Reconstruction. JSH 10:447-60, Nov. 1944.

Donovan, S.K. John Brown at Harper's Ferry and Charlestown. OAQ 30:300-36, July 1921.

DOOLITTLE, SEN. JAMES R.

Marshall, Ruth. Duane Mowry, ed. Property in Negroes: A Southern slaveholding woman's plea to Sen. J.R. Doolittle. AME 8:530-2, June 1913.

Mowry, Duane. New York Democratic convention's "corner stone" resolution, 1847. IHJ 3:88-90, Oct. 1910.

Slavery and Reconstruction. J.R. Doolittle correspondence, 1848-65. SHA 11:94-105, Mar. 1907.

Dorris, J.T. Pardon and amnesty during the Civil War and Reconstruction: Excerpt from a forthcoming book. NCH 23:360-401, July 1946.

DOUGLAS, STEPHEN A.

Harmon, G.D. Stephen A. Douglas--his leadership in Compromise of 1850, regarding government and question of slavery in territory acquired from Mexico. IHJ 21:452-90, Jan. 1929.

Hubbart, H.C. Revisionist interpretations of Douglas and his doctrine of popular sovereignty. SOS 25:103-7, Mar. 1934.

Stephen A. Douglas and his attempt to settle the slavery question in the territories, 1850-60. WAS 2:209-32, Apr. 1908 and following issues.

DOUGLASS, FREDERICK

Sears, L.M. Frederick Douglass: His career as U.S. minister to Haiti, 1889-91. HAH 21:222-38, May 1941.

Dounan, Elizabeth. The New England slave trade after the Revolution. NEQ 3:251-78, Apr. 1930.

Dounan, Elizabeth. Slave trade in South Carolina before the Revolution. AHR 33:804-28, July 1928.

DOUNAN, ELIZABETH

Dodd, William E. Review of Elizabeth Dounan, Documents illustrative of the history of the slave trade in America. NEQ 8:592-4, Dec. 1935.

Dowd, J. Race segregation in a democracy. ASS 14:189-205, 1919.

DOWD, J.

Work, M.N. Review of J. Dowd, The Negro in American life. IRM 16:298-9, Apr. 1927.

Drake, St. Clair, and H.R. Cayton. Bronzeville: Chicago's huge Negro community. HOL 2:34-8+, May 1947.

DRAKE, ST. CLAIR

Review of St. Clair Drake and H.R. Cayton, Black metropolis: A study of Negro life in a Northern city. AFO 84:150, Feb. 1946.

Strong, S.M. Review of St. Clair Drake and H.R. Cayton, Black metropolis: A study of Negro life in a Northern city. ASR 11:240-1, Apr. 1946.

DRAMA

Lawson, Holda J. The Negro in American drama: Bibliography. BUB 17:7-8, Jan.-Apr. 1940 and following issue.

Draper, D.C. Legal phases of John Brown's trial. WVA 1:87-103, Jan. 1940.

DRED SCOTT CASE

Auchampaugh, P. Buchanan, the Court, and the Dred Scott case. THM 9:231-40, Jan. 1926.

Catterall, Helen T. Antecedents of the Dred Scott case. AHR 30:56-71, Oct. 1924.

Hodder, F.H. Some phases of the Dred Scott case. MVH 16:3-22, June 1929.

Lee, T.Z. Chief Justice Taney and the Dred Scott decision. AIR 22:142-4, 1923.

McCormac, E.I., and R.R. Stenberg. The Dred Scott case, 1857. MVH 19:565-77, Mar. 1933.

Synder, C.E. Dred Scott and his owner, Dr. John Emerson. ANN 3d s. 21:440-61, Oct. 1938.

Driggs, O.T., Jr. Arkansas politics: The essence of the Powell Clayton regime, 1868-1871. ARK 8:1-75, Spring 1949.

DuBois, W.E.B. Culture of white folk. JRD 7:434-47, Apr. 1917.

DuBois, W.E.B. Liberia, the League and the United States. FOR 11:682-95, July 1933.

DuBois, W.E.B. The Negro as a national asset. HOM 86:52-8, July 1923.

DuBois, W.E.B. Political and social status in European possessions in Africa. FOR 3:423-44, Apr. 1925.

DuBois, W.E.B. Review of Horace M. Bond, Negro education in Alabama. AHR 45:669-70, Apr. 1940.

DUBOIS, W.E.B.

Dodd, William E. Review of W.E.B. DuBois, Black Reconstruction. VQR 12:138-41, Jan. 1936.

Lewonson, P. Review of W.E.B. DuBois, Black folk then and now. MVH 26:580-1, Mar. 1940.

Lorain, C.T. Review of W.E.B. DuBois, Black folk then and now. AHR 46:95-6, Oct. 1940.

Duffus, R.L. Salesmen of hate. WWL 42:461-9, Oct. 1923 and following issue.

DUMOND, D.

Owsley, F.L. Review of D. Dumond, Antislavery origins of the Civil War in the U.S. NCH 17:186-8, Apr. 1940.

DUNBAR, PAUL LAWRENCE

Appreciation. OUT n.s. 8:35-7, July 1914.

Dunbar, R. Status of American Negroes. WOR 61-4, Mar. 1942.

Dunn, J.P. Indiana's part in "Uncle Tom's Cabin." INM 7:112-8, Sept. 1911.

Durel, L.C. Donaldsonville, La., Creole civilization, 1850, according to the newspaper "Le Vigilant." LHQ 31:981-94, Oct. 1948.

DUTCH GUIANA

Kirke, D.B. Bush Negroes of Dutch Guiana. CHA 7th s. 15:549-52, Aug. 1, 1925.

DUTCH REFORMED CHURCH

Corwin, C.E. Efforts of Dutch colonial pastors for the conversion of the Negroes. PBY 12:425-35, Apr. 1927.

"THE DUTY OF THE FREE STATES"

Hicks, Granville. Dr. Channing and the Creole case. AHR 37:516-25, Apr. 1932.

Dyer, B. Persistence of the idea of Negro colonization. PHR 12:53-65, Mar. 1943.

Dyer, J.P. Review of H. Crum, Gullah: Negro life in the Caroline Sea Islands. JSH 7:108-9, Feb. 1941.

EAST FLORIDA

Siebert, W.H. History of slavery in East Florida, 1776-1785. FHS 10:139-62, Jan. 1932 and previous issue.

Siebert, W.H. Slavery and white servitude in East Florida, 1726 to 1776. FHS 10:3-23, July 1931.

EASTER ROCK

Seale, Lee, and Marianna Seale. A Louisiana Negro ceremony: Easter Rock. JAF 55:212-8, Oct.-Dec. 1942.

Easterby, J.H. Review of F.S. Simkins, and R.H. Woody, South Carolina during Reconstruction. NCH 10:85-7, Jan. 1933.

Eastin, L.J. Notes on a proslavery march against Lawrence, Kan. KHQ 11:45-64, Feb. 1942.

Eaton, C. Review of J.W. Coleman, Jr., Slavery times in Kentucky. JSH 7:106-7, Feb. 1941.

Eaton, C. Review of E.M. Coulter, The South during Reconstruction. CHR 34:73-4, Apr. 1948.

Eaton, C. Review of J.H. Franklin, The free Negro in North Carolina, 1790-1860. NCH 20:371-2, Oct. 1943.

Eaton, C., ed. Minutes and resolutions of a Kentucky emancipation meeting in 1849. JSH 14:511-5, Nov. 1948.

Eckenrode, H.J. Negroes in Richmond, Va., in 1864. VAM 46:193-200, July 1938.

Eckenrode, H.J. Review of E.M. Coulter, The South during Reconstruction. VAM 56:214-5, Apr. 1948.

ECONOMICS

Franklin, J.H. The free Negro in the economic life of ante-bellum North Carolina. NCH 19:239-59, July 1942 and following issue.

Handlin, Oscar. Prejudice and capitalist exploitation: Does economics explain racism? COM 6:79-85, July 1948.

Hartwell, E.C. Economics of slavery. HTM 4:50, Feb. 1913.

Letters pertaining to economic and social life of plantations in 1833-36. GHQ 14:150-73, June 1930.

Reiller, E.C. Politico-economic considerations in Western Reserve's early slavery controversy. OAQ 52:141-57, Apr.-June 1943.

Russell, R.R. The general effects of slavery upon Southern economic progress. JSH 4:34-54, Feb. 1938.

Edmiston, Dorothy. A ballet of the African Negro to be performed in Dallas, Texas. TEX 4:458-64, Nov. 1940.

EDUCATION

Garrison, C.W., ed. Letters of Atticus G. Haygood to Rutherford B. Hayes regarding the education of Negroes of the South. JSH 5:223-45, May 1939.

Goodwin, Mary F. Christianizing and educating the Negro in colonial Virginia. PEH 1:143-52, Sept. 1932.

Hollingsworth, R.R. Education and the Reconstruction in Georgia. GHQ 19:112-33, June 1935 and following issue.

Humphrey, G.D. Public education for whites. JMH 3:26-36, Jan. 1941.

Jenkins, Frances. Education adapted to meet racial needs. SCH 37:126-8, Feb. 1918.

Johnson, C.S. The problem of Negro child education. ASR 1:264-72, Apr. 1936.

Johnson, W.H. Lincoln University, the pioneer institution in the world for the education of the Negro. PBY 14:142-3, Sept. 1930.

King, Emma. Some aspects of the work of the Society of Friends for Negro education in North Carolina. NCH 1:403-11, Oct. 1924.

Lawrence, J.B. Religious education of Negroes in the colony of Georgia. GHQ 14:41-57, Mar. 1930.

Phillips, Edna. A plan for cooperation between evening school teachers and librarians in the educational development of racial groups. ALA 26:29-30, Jan. 1932.

Porter, Betty. The history of Negro education in Louisiana. LHQ 25:728-831, July 1942.

Small, E.W., and Miriam H. Small. Prudence Crandall, her efforts to promote Negro education, 1833-4. NEQ 17:506-29, Dec. 1944.

Swint, H.L., ed. Reports from educational agents of Freedmen's Bureau in Tennessee, 1865-70. THQ 1:51-80, Mar. 1942 and following issue.

Timberlake, Elsie. Did the Reconstruction give Mississippi new schools? MSS 12:72-93, 1912.

Tisler, C.C. Story of Prudence Crandall. IHJ 33:203-6, June 1940.

Wells, L.G. Story of Myrtilla Miner. NYH 24:358-75, July 1943.

West Virginia Colored Institute. NAT 39:528-30, Dec. 1913.

Williams, Mildred, and W.L. Van Loan. Education for racial equality. SOS 34:308-11, Nov. 1943.

Wright, John C. Teaching English at Tuskegee Institute. EBM 3:26-30, Oct. 1908.

EDUCATION, ELEMENTARY

Baker, Emily V. Responsibility of the elementary teacher to overcome racial intolerance in future citizens. HIO 24:86-9, Feb. 1933.

Riley, H.M. History of Negro elementary education in Indianapolis. INM 26:280-305, Sept. 1930.

EDUCATION, HIGHER

A document (in Spanish) on the Negro in higher education in Spanish America: Case of José Ponseano de Ayarza, 1794-98. HAH 24:432-51, Aug. 1944.

EDUCATION, LIBRARY SCIENCE

Bogle, Sarah C.N. Training for Negro librarians. ALA 25:133, Apr. 1931.

EDUCATORS

Wells, L.G. Story of Myrtilla Miner. NYH 24:358-75, July 1943.

ELECTIONS

Hamilton, J.G. DeR. Lincoln's election an immediate menace to slavery in the states. AHR 37:700-11, July 1932.

Ryle, W.H. Slavery and party realignment in the Missouri state election of 1856. MOH 39:320-32, Apr. 1945.

Stevens, Wayne E. Shaw-Hensen election contest. IHJ 7:389-401, Jan. 1915.

Weeks, O.D. The white primary: 1944-48. APS 42:500-10, June 1948.

ELEMENTARY EDUCATION. See EDUCATION, ELEMENTARY

ELLINGTON, EDWARD KENNEDY "DUKE"

The Harlem rendezvous and his Negro jazz orchestra. Edward Kennedy "Duke" Ellington. FTE 8:47+, Aug. 1933.

Elliott, Helen. Frances Wright's experiment with Negro emancipation. INM 35:141-57, June 1939.

Ellis, G.W. The Negro and the war for democracy. JRD 8:439-53, Apr. 1918.

Ellis, G.W. Negroes in the new democracy. JRD 7:82-3, July 1916.

Ellis, G.W. The new slavery in the South. JRD 7:467-88, Apr. 1917.

Ellis, G.W. Psychology of American race prejudice. JRD 5:297-315, Jan. 1915.

Ellsworth, C.S. Ohio legislative attack upon abolition schools. MVH 21:379-86, Dec. 1934.

EMANCIPATING LABOR SOCIETY

Parks, E.W. Frances Wright--founder of the Emancipating Labor Society, Nashoba, Tenn. THM 2d s. 2:74-86, Jan. 1932.

EMANCIPATION. See also MANUMISSION

Eaton, C., ed. Minutes and resolutions of a Kentucky emancipation meeting in 1849. JSH 14:511-5, Nov. 1948.

Elliott, Helen. Frances Wright's experiment with Negro emancipation. INM 35:141-57, June 1939.

Gardner, D.H. The emancipation of slaves in New Jersey. NJS 9:1-21, Jan. 1924.

Gilmer, A.H. Boston and emancipation, 1863. MAG 16: 141-7, Apr. 1913.

Landon, F. Canada's part in freeing the slaves. OHS 17:74-84, 1919.

McCain, William D. The emancipation of Indiana Osborne. JMH 8:97-8, Apr. 1946.

McGroarty, W.B. Settlement by colonies of emancipated Negroes in Brown Co., Ohio, 1818-46. WMQ 2d s. 21: 208-26, July 1941.

Milburn, P. Emancipation of slaves in the District of Columbia. CHS 16:96-119, 1913.

Studley, Marian H. An August First anti-slavery picnic. NEQ 16:567-77, Dec. 1943.

Traube, C.C. Voluntary emancipation of slaves in Tennessee. THM 4:50-68, Mar. 1918.

EMANCIPATION PROCLAMATION

Clark, R.D. Bishop Matthew Simpson and the Emancipation Proclamation. MVH 35:263-71, Sept. 1948.

Hesseltine, W.B., and Hazel C. Wolf. The Emancipation Proclamation and the Altoona conference. PAM 71:195-205, July 1947.

Emerson, F.V. Geographical influences in the distribution of slaves and slavery. AGS 43:13-26, June 1911 and following issues.

EMERSON, DR. JOHN

Synder, C.E. Dred Scott and his owner, Dr. John Emerson. ANN 3d s. 21:440-61, Oct. 1938.

Emerson, O.B. Frances Wright and her Nashoba experiment. THQ 6:291-314, Dec. 1947.

Emery, Julia C. How the church helps Southern Negro children. SPM 72:113-5, Feb. 1907.

EMIGRANT AID COMPANY

Barry, Louise. The Emigrant Aid Company parties of 1854-5. KHQ 12:115-55, May 1943 and following issue.

Johnson, S.A. The Emigrant Aid Company in Kansas. KHQ 1:429-41, Nov. 1932.

Johnson, S.A. The Emigrant Aid Company in the Kansas conflict. KHQ 6:21-33, Feb. 1937.

Langsdorf, Edgar. Samuel Clarke Pomeroy and the New England Emigrant Aid Company, 1854-8. KHQ 7:227-45, Aug. 1938 and following issue.

EMIGRANT AID MOVEMENT

Harlow, R.V. Rise and fall of emigrant aid movement in Kansas. AHR 41:1-25, Oct. 1935.

EMIGRATION

Cooley, S. Negro emigration. PUB 20:450-1, May 11, 1917.

Keith, E. Jean. Joseph Rogers Underwood of Kentucky and the American Colonization Society for the free people of color. HIS 22:117-32, Apr. 1938.

Shunk, E.W. "Ohio in Africa," a plan for a colony of Ohio free-Negro emigrants in Liberia, c. 1850. OAQ 51: 70-87, Apr.-June 1942.

"EMPEROR"

Dodd, Dorothy. The schooner "Emperor" in the illegal slave trade in Florida. FHS 13:117-28, Jan. 1935.

EMPLOYERS

Wilson, L., and H. Gilmore. White employers and Negro workers. ASR 8:698-705, Dec. 1943.

EMPLOYMENT

Alexander, R.J. Fair employment practices legislation in the U.S. CAF 28:31-2, May 1948.

ENFORCEMENT ACT

McNeilly, J.S. Enforcement act of 1871 and Ku Klux Klan in Mississippi. MSS 9:109-71, 1906.

Engelsman, J.C. Work of the Freedmen's Bureau in Louisiana. LHQ 32:145-224, Jan. 1949.

England, G.A. Description of Harper's Ferry and incidents of John Brown's last days. TRA 50:28-32+, Mar. 1928.

England, J.M. The free Negro in ante-bellum Tennessee. JSH 9:37-58, Feb. 1943.

ENGLAND

Riddell, W.R. Method of abolition of slavery in England, Scotland and Upper Canada compared. OHS 27:511-3, 1931.

ENGLISH

Wright, John C. Teaching English at Tuskegee Institute. EBM 3:26-30, Oct. 1908.

Eno, J.N. Race in relation to solidarity, government. AME 27:179-85, Apr. 1933.

EPISCOPAL CHURCH. See PROTESTANT EPISCOPAL CHURCH

EPPES, MRS. N.W.

Robertson, J.A. Review of Mrs. N.W. Eppes, The Negro in the old South. NCH 3:380-3, Apr. 1926.

Epstein, S. Thaddeus Stevens. NYH 29:72-4, Jan. 1948.

EQUAL RIGHTS

Sillen, S. The Negro's struggle for equal rights. WOR 6:57-9, Feb. 1939.

EQUALITY

Williams, Mildred, and W.L. Van Loan. Education for racial equality. SOS 34:308-11, Nov. 1943.

ERLICH, L.

Lindsay, P. Review of L. Erlich, God's angry man. BKL 85:240-1, Dec. 1933.

ERWIN, JOSEPH

White, Alice P. The plantation experience of Joseph and Lavinia Erwin, 1807-36: Records and papers. LHQ 27:343-478, Apr. 1944.

ERWIN, LAVINIA

White, Alice P. The plantation experience of Joseph and Lavinia Erwin, 1807-36: Records and papers. LHQ 27:343-478, Apr. 1944.

ETHNIC RELATIONS

Hughes, E.C. Queries concerning industry and society growing out of a study of ethnic relations in industry. ASR 14:211-30, Apr. 1949.

ETHNICITY STUDIES

Merton, R.K. Fact and factitiousness in ethnic opinionnaires. ASR 5:13-28, Feb. 1940.

ETHIOPIA

Lees, G.F. Ras Tafari and his people. WDT 44:121-9, July 1924.

EUROPE

European Catholic opinions on slavery (reprint of an old and rare pamphlet). AMC 25:18-29, Mar. 1914.

EVANGELISM

Corwin, C.E. Efforts of Dutch colonial pastors for the conversion of the Negroes. PBY 12:425-35, Apr. 1927.

Evans, W. Three new paintings from the heart of the black belt. FTE 38:89+, Aug. 1948.

EVOLUTION

Taylor, G. Evolution and distribution of race, culture and language. GEO 11:54-119, Jan. 1921.

Ewing, C.A.M. Two Reconstruction impeachments. NCH 15:204-30, July 1938.

EXILE

Barr, Ruth B., and Modeste Hargis. Voluntary exile of free Negroes in Pensacola, Fla., 1857. FHS 17:3-14, July 1938.

EXPERIMENTS

Stoutemyer, J.H. Certain experiments with backward races. JRD 5:438-66, Apr. 1916.

EXPLOITATION

Handlin, Oscar. Prejudice and capitalist exploitation: Does economics explain racism? COM 6:79-85, July 1948.

EX-SLAVES

Turner, L.D. Contrasts of Brazilian ex-slaves with Nigeria. VQR 27:55-67, Jan. 1942.

F.E.P.C. See also FAIR EMPLOYMENT PRACTICES

Cohen, F.S. FEPC fight initiates a new epoch. COM 1:17-22, Mar. 1946.

FAIR EMPLOYMENT PRACTICES

Alexander, R.J. Fair employment practices legislation in the U.S. CAF 28:31-2, May 1948.

Northrup, H.R. Proving ground for fair employment: Some lessons from New York State's experience. COM 4:552-6, Dec. 1947.

Ross, M. The 80th Congress and job discrimination: The outlook for a new F.E.P.C. COM 3:301-8, Apr. 1947.

FAIRBANKS, CALVIN

Coleman, J.W., Jr. Delia Webster and Calvin Fairbanks, underground railroad agents. HIS 17:129-42, July 1943.

Wick, B.L. Delia Webster--her part in the underground railroad movement in Iowa. ANN 3d s. 18:228-31, Jan. 1932.

FAIRCHILD, H.P.

Handlin, Oscar. Review of H.P. Fairchild, Race and nationality as factors in American life. COM 5:476-7, May 1948.

FAMILY

Frazier, E. Franklin. The Negro family in Bahia, Brazil. ASR 7:465-78, Aug. 1942.

FAMILY LIFE

Frazier, E. Franklin. Impact of urban civilization on Negro family life. ASR 2:609-18, Oct. 1937.

Farnsworth, P.R. Review of O. Klineberg, Characteristics of the American Negro. ASR 9:589-90, Oct. 1944.

Farrison, W.E. Negro population of Guilford Co., N.C., before the Civil War. NCH 21:319-29, Oct. 1944.

Faulkner, W.J. Review of R.I. McKinney, Religion in higher education among Negroes. IRM 36:408-9, July 1947.

Fauset, A.H. Folk-tales from Alabama, Mississippi and Louisiana. JAF 40:214-303, June-Sept. 1927.

FAUSET, A.H.

Herskovits, M.J. Review of A.H. Fauset, Black gods of the metropolis: The cult practices of five Negro religious groups in Philadelphia. ROR 9:186-9, Jan. 1945.

FEDERAL GOVERNMENT

Walter, D.O. Proposals for a federal anti-lynching law. APS 28:436-42, June 1934.

Ferguson, J.S. Review of J.W. DeForest, A Union officer in the Reconstruction. JMH 10:175-7, Apr. 1948.

FIELD, DAVID DUDLEY

Mowry, Duane. New York Democratic convention's "corner stone" resolution, 1847. IHJ 3:88-90, Oct. 1910.

FIELD HANDS

Settle, E. Ophelia. Social attitudes during the slave regime: Household servants versus field hands. ASS 28:95-8, May 1934.

Filler, L. Review of R.B. Nye, Fettered freedom: Civil liberties and the slavery controversy. AHR 55:162-4, Oct. 1949.

Filler, L., ed. John Brown in Ohio: An interview with Charles S.S. Griffing. OAQ 58:213-8, Apr. 1949.

Filler, L., ed. Parker Pillsbury: Biographical sketch. NEQ 19:315-37, Sept. 1946.

FILMS

Noble, P. Influence of screen portrayal of the Negro upon the colour bar in America. WOR 53-6, June 1944.

FILSON CLUB

Craig, D.M. An old letter concerning Cassius M. Clay and the "True American," 1845, presented to the Filson Club. HIS 22:197-8, July 1948.

FINANCES

Randall, J.G. Part played by Sen. John Sherman in financial legislation during Reconstruction. MVH 19:382-93, Dec. 1932.

Sitterson, J.C. Financing and marketing the sugar crop of the old South. JSH 10:188-99, May 1944.

Finley, Mrs. H.R. Measures against the American slave trade. AME 18:252-7, July 1924.

FISHER, W. ARMS

Review of Negro spirituals. MUS 25:378, Nov. 1926.

Flanders, R.B. The free Negro in ante-bellum Georgia. NCH 9:250-72, July 1932.

Flanders, R.B. Planters' problems in ante-bellum Georgia. GHQ 14:17-40, Mar. 1930.

Flanders, R.B. Review of W.T. Jordan, Hugh Davis and his Alabama plantation. JSH 15:112-3, Feb. 1949.

Fleming, W.H. Historic attempts to solve the race problem in America by deportation. JAH 4:197-213, Apr. 1910.

Fleming, W.L. Kansas territory and the Buford expedition of 1856. AHS 4:167-92, 1904.

Fleming, W.L. Moses of the colored exodus. AME 7:936-44, Oct. 1912.

Fleming, W.L. Plantation life in the South. JAH 3:233-46, Apr.-June 1909.

FLEMING, WALTER LYNWOOD

Green, F.M. Writings of Walter Lynwood Fleming. JSH 2: 497-521, Nov. 1936.

Fletcher, R.S. Ransom's painting of John Brown on his way to execution. KHQ 9:343-6, Nov. 1946.

Florant, L.C. Negro internal migration. ASR 7:782-91, Dec. 1942.

FLORIDA

Abbey, Kathryn T. History of El Destino and Chemonie (Fla.) plantations and documents pertaining thereto (1828-68). FHS 7:179-213, Jan. 1929 and following issues.

Bates, Thelma. The legal status of the Negro in Florida. FHS 6:159-81, Jan. 1928.

Bentley, G.R. Political activity of the Freedmen's Bureau in Florida, 1865-70. FHS 28:28-37, July 1949.

Dodd, Dorothy. The schooner "Emperor" in the illegal slave trade in Florida. FHS 13:117-28, Jan. 1935.

Granberry, E. Primitive Negroes in Florida's turpentine forests. TRA 58:32-5, Apr. 1932.

Greene, C.R. Florida folk songs: Negro tunes and words. FLQ 9:103-5, June 1945.

Kennedy, Stetson. Nanigo in Florida. SFQ 4:153-6, Sept. 1940.

Siebert, W.H. History of slavery in East Florida, 1776-1785. FHS 10:139-62, Jan. 1932 and previous issue.

Siebert, W.H. Slavery and white servitude in East Florida, 1726 to 1776. FHS 10:3-23, July 1931.

Smith, G.W. Carpetbag imperialism in Florida, 1862-8. FHS 27:99-130, Oct. 1948 amd following issue.

Smith, R.M. Racial strains in Florida. FHS 11:16-32, July 1932.

Williams, E.L., Jr. Negro slavery in Florida. FHS 28: 93-110, Oct. 1949 and following issue.

FLORIDA, PENSACOLA

Barr, Ruth B., and Modeste Hargis. Voluntary exile of free Negroes in Pensacola, Fla., 1857. FHS 17:3-14, July 1938.

Floyd, J.B. Official report of John Brown's raid upon Harper's Ferry. ORE 10:314-24, Sept. 1909.

FOLKLORE

Davis, H.C. Folk-lore in South Carolina. JAF 27:241-54, July-Sept. 1914.

Funkhouser, Myrtle, comp. Bibliography of folk-lore of the American Negro. BUB 16:28-9, Jan.-Apr. 1937 and following issues.

Halpert, H. Some Negro riddles collected in New Jersey. JAF 56:200-2, July-Sept. 1943.

Herskovits, M.J. Future steps in the study of Negro folklore. JAF 56:1-7, Jan.-Mar. 1943.

Puckett, N.N. Negro character as revealed in folk lore. ASS 28:12-23, May 1934.

Webb, J.W. Irwin Russell and Negro folk literature. SFQ 12:137-49, June 1948.

FOLK SONGS. See also MUSIC, SONGS, SPIRITUALS

Ames, R. Art in Negro folksong. JAF 56:241-54, Oct.-Dec. 1943.

Bass, R.D. Negro songs from the Pedee country, South Carolina. JAF 44:418-36, Oct.-Dec. 1931.

Greene, C.R. Florida folk songs: Negro tunes and words. FLQ 9:103-5, June 1945.

Longini, Muriel D. Folk-songs of Chicago Negroes. JAF 52:96-111, Jan.-Mar. 1939.

Odum, Anna K. Folk-songs from Tennessee. JAF 27:255-65, July-Sept. 1914.

Work, John W. Changing patterns in Negro folk songs. JAF 62:136-44, Apr.-June 1949.

FOLKTALES

Cox, J.H. Negro tales from West Virginia. JAF 47:341-57, Oct.-Dec. 1934.

Fauset, A.H. Folk-tales from Alabama, Mississippi and Louisiana. JAF 40:214-303, June-Sept. 1927.

Folk-tales by Tuskegee students. JAF 32:397-401, July-Sept. 1919.

Kirgan, Sadie E. Tales the darkies tell of ghosts that walk in Freestone County, Texas. TEX 5:385-91, May 1930.

FOLKTALES (cont'd)

Parsons, Elsie. Ashanti influence in Negro folktales and customs in Jamaica. JAF 47:391-5, Oct.-Dec. 1934.

Parsons, Elsie. Folk-tales of Negroes. FLL 28:408-14, Dec. 1917.

Wolfe, B. Uncle Remus and the malevolent rabbit: The Negro in popular American culture. COM 8:31-41, July 1949.

Folmsbee, Stanley J. The origin of the first "Jim Crow" law. JSH 15:235-47, May 1949.

Folsom, J.F. A slave indenture of colonial days. NJS 3d s. 10:111-5, July-Oct. 1915.

Forbes, G. Part played by Indian slavery in removal of tribes to Oklahoma. OKC 16:163-70, June 1938.

Forbes, R.H. The black man's industries. GEO 23:230-47, Apr. 1933.

Ford, N.A. Henry David Thoreau's activities as an abolitionist. NEQ 19:359-71, Sept. 1946.

FORD, NATHANIEL

The case of Robin Holmes vs. Nathaniel Ford. ORE 23:111-37, June 1922.

Ford, R.N. Study of white-Negro contacts. Scaling experience by a multiple response technique. ASR 6:9-23, Feb. 1941.

Ford, R.N. See also Dickins, Dorothy

FOREIGN POLICY

Treaty with the U.S. regarding the finances, economic development and tranquility of Haiti. (Text.) AJI Supp. 10:234-8, Oct. 1916.

What U.S. is doing for Santo Domingo, Nicaragua and Haiti. NGE 30:143-77, Aug. 1916.

Foreman, P.B. Negro lifeways in the rural South: A typological approach to social differentiation. ASR 13: 409-18, Aug. 1948.

FOSTER, STEPHEN

Clark, T.D. The slavery background of Foster's "My Old Kentucky Home." HIS 10:1-17, Jan. 1936.

FRAMES OF REFERENCE

Seeman, M. Moral judgment: A study in racial frames of reference. ASR 12:404-11, Aug. 1947.

FRANCHISE

Kemmerer, D.L. The suffrage franchise in colonial New Jersey. NJS 52:166-73, July 1934.

FRANKLIN, BENJAMIN

Crane, V.W. Benjamin Franklin on slavery and American liberties. PAM 62:1-11, Jan. 1938.

Franklin, John H. The free Negro in the economic life of ante-bellum North Carolina. NCH 19:239-59, July 1942 and following issue.

Franklin, John H. Negro members of the Protestant Episcopal Church in ante-bellum North Carolina. PEH 13:216-34, Sept. 1944.

Franklin, John H. Review of James A. Porter, Modern Negro art. NCH 21:172-3, Apr. 1944.

Franklin, John H. Review of Benjamin Quarles, Frederick Douglass. MVH 35:515-6, Dec. 1948.

Franklin, John H. Review of F. Tannenbaum, Slave and citizen: The Negro in the Americas. WMQ 3d s. 4:544-5, Oct. 1947.

FRANKLIN, JOHN H.

Aptheker, Herbert. Review of J.H. Franklin, From slavery to freedom. PAM 72:294, July 1948.

Brewer, W.M. Review of J.H. Franklin, From slavery to freedom. WMQ 3d s. 5:440-2, July 1948.

Eaton, C. Review of J.H. Franklin, The free Negro in North Carolina, 1790-1860. NCH 20:371-2, Oct. 1943.

Hesseltine, W.B. Review of J.H. Franklin, From slavery to freedom. AHR 54:155-6, Oct. 1948.

FRANKLIN, JOHN H. (cont'd)

Hogan, P.E. Review of J.H. Franklin, From slavery to freedom. CHR 34:343-4, Oct. 1948.

Johnson, C.S. Review of J.H. Franklin, From slavery to freedom. NYH 29:215-8, Apr. 1948.

Lissfelt, Mildred B. Review of J.H. Franklin, From slavery to freedom. SOS 39:134, Mar. 1948.

Randall, J.G. Review of J.H. Franklin, From slavery to freedom. MVH 35:288-9, Sept. 1948.

Smith, R.W. Review of J.H. Franklin, From slavery to freedom. PHR 17:502-3, Nov. 1948.

Wiley, B.I. Review of J.H. Franklin, From slavery to freedom. JSH 14:264-5, May 1948.

FRAUD

Sparendam, W.F. The fraud of white civilization; a Negro's opinion. WOR 1:38-40, June 1936.

Frazier, E. Franklin. Impact of urban civilization on Negro family life. ASR 2:609-18, Oct. 1937.

Frazier, E. Franklin. The Negro family in Bahia, Brazil. ASR 7:465-78, Aug. 1942.

Frazier, E. Franklin. Negro-white contacts from the standpoint of the social structure of the Negro world. ASR 14: 1-11, Feb. 1949.

Frazier, E. Franklin. Sociological theory and race relations. ASR 12:261-71, June 1947.

FRAZIER, E. FRANKLIN

Herskovits, M.J. Review of E. Franklin Frazier, The Negro family in Bahia, Brazil. ASR 8:394-404, Aug. 1943.

Mooney, C.C. Review of E. Franklin Frazier, The Negro in the U.S. JSH 15:543-5, Nov. 1949.

Thompson, E.T. Review of E. Franklin Frazier, The Negro in the U.S. ASR 14:813-4, Dec. 1949.

Vance, R.B. Review of E. Franklin Frazier, The Negro in the U.S. VQR 25:620-3, Autumn 1949.

FREE NEGROES

Barr, Ruth B., and Modeste Hargis. Voluntary exile of free Negroes in Pensacola, Fla., 1857. FHS 17:3-14, July 1938.

England, J.M. The free Negro in ante-bellum Tennessee. JSH 9:37-58, Feb. 1943.

Flanders, R.B. The free Negro in ante-bellum Georgia. NCH 9:250-72, July 1932.

Franklin, J.H. The free Negro in the economic life of ante-bellum North Carolina. NCH 19:239-59, July 1942 and following issue.

Hamer, Philip M. Great Britain, the United States, and the Negro seamen acts, 1822-48. JSH 1:3-28, Feb. 1935 and following issue, which covers 1850-60.

Herron, Stella. The African apprentice bill, 1858. MIV 8:135-45, 1914-5.

Keith, E. Jean. Joseph Rogers Underwood of Kentucky and the American Colonization Society for the free people of color. HIS 22:117-32, Apr. 1938.

Muir, A.F. The free Negro in Harris Co., Texas. SWH 46:214-38, Jan. 1943.

Nelson, B.H. Legislative control of the Southern free Negro, 1861-65. CHR 32:28-46, Apr. 1946.

Rogers, W.M. Free Negro legislation in Georgia before 1865. GHQ 16:27-37, Mar. 1932.

Schoen, H. The free Negro in the Republic of Texas. SWH 39:292-308, Apr. 1936 and following issues.

Shunk, E.W. "Ohio in Africa," a plan for a colony of Ohio free-Negro emigrants in Liberia, c. 1850. OAQ 51:70-87, Apr.-June 1942.

Sydnor, C.S. The free Negro in Mississippi before the Civil War. AHR 32:769-88, July 1927.

FREEDMEN

Buried at master's feet. AME 6:814-5, Aug. 1911.

Pantle, Alberta, ed. Larry Lapsley, 1840-97. Story of a Kansas freedman. KHQ 11:341-69, Nov. 1942.

FREEDMEN'S BUREAU

Bentley, G.R. Political activity of the Freedmen's Bureau in Florida, 1865-70. FHS 28:28-37, July 1949.

Bethel, Elizabeth. The Freedmen's Bureau in Alabama, 1865. JSH 14:49-92, Feb. 1948.

Engelsman, J.C. Work of the Freedmen's Bureau in Louisiana. LHQ 32:145-224, Jan. 1949.

Swint, H.L., ed. Reports from educational agents of Freedmen's Bureau in Tennessee, 1865-70. THQ 1:51-80, Mar. 1942 and following issue.

Thompson, C. Mildred. The Freedmen's Bureau in Georgia in 1865-6. GHQ 5:40-9, Mar. 1921.

FREEDOM

Westermann, W.L. Between slavery and freedom. AHR 50: 213-27, Jan. 1945.

FREEPORT QUESTION

Montgomery, Horace. A Georgia precedent for the Freeport question. JSH 10:200-7, May 1944.

Freidel, F. Francis Lieber, Charles Sumner, and slavery. JSH 9:75-93, Feb. 1943.

FUGITIVE SLAVE LAW

Caspar Hanway and the fugitive slave law. MAG 21:148-50, Oct. 1915.

Galbreath, C.B. The fugitive slave law, 1839. OAQ 34: 216-40, Apr. 1925.

Galpin, W.F. Fugitive slave law of 1850. The Jerry Rescue precipitated a clash between the government and local abolitionists. NYH 26:19-33, Jan. 1945.

Money, C.H. Fugitive slave law of 1850. Indiana cases. INM 17:159-98, June 1921 and following issue.

Ohio fugitive slave law of 1839. ONW 13:69-72, Apr.-Oct. 1910.

Schafer, W. Fugitive slave act. Decision of the Booth case. WIM 20:89-110, Sept. 1936.

Speech delivered by John Hossack upon his conviction for violating the fugitive slave act, 1860. IHJ 41:67-74, Mar. 1948.

FUGITIVE SLAVES. See also SLAVES

Alilunas, Leo. Fugitive slave cases in Ohio prior to 1850. OAQ 49:160-84, Apr.-June 1940.

Fugitive or rescue case of 1857 in Ohio. OAQ 16:292-309, July 1907.

Fugitive slave case. INM 7:23-4, Mar. 1911.

Landon, F. The fugitive slave in Canada before the American Civil War. UNI 18:270-9, Apr. 1919.

Leslie, W.R. The constitutional significance of Indiana's statute of 1824 on fugitives from labor. JSH 13:338-53, Aug. 1947.

Way, R.B. Was the fugitive slave clause in the constitution necessary? IAJ 5:326-36, July 1907.

Fuller, J.D.P. Effect of the slavery issue on the movement to annex Mexico, 1846-48. MVH 21:31-48, June 1934.

Fuller, J.D.P. Slavery propaganda during the Mexican War. SWH 38:235-45, Apr. 1935.

Funkhouser, Myrtle, comp. Bibliography of folk-lore of the American Negro. BUB 16:28-9, Jan.-Apr. 1937 and following issues.

FUR TRADE

Varied parts played by Negroes in the American fur trade. MNN 15:421-33, Dec. 1934.

FUSION RULE

Mabry, W.A. Negro suffrage and fusion rule in North Carolina. NCH 12:79-102, Apr. 1935.

Galbreath, C.B. Anti-slavery movement in Ohio. OAQ 30:355-95, Oct. 1921.

Galbreath, C.B. The fugitive slave law, 1839. OAQ 34:216-40, Apr. 1925.

Galbreath, C.B. John Brown. Bibliography. OAQ 30:180-289, July 1921.

Galbreath, C.B. Thomas Jefferson's views on slavery. OAQ 34:184-202, Apr. 1925.

GALLAGHER, BUELL G.

Lamott, W.C. Review of Buell Gallagher, Portrait of a pilgrim: A search for the Christian way in race relations. IRM 36:105-6, Jan. 1947.

Galpin, W.F. Fugitive slave law of 1850. The Jerry Rescue precipitated a clash between the government and local abolitionists. NYH 26:19-33, Jan. 1945.

Gardner, D.H. The emancipation of slaves in New Jersey. NJS 9:1-21, Jan. 1924.

Garretson, O.A. Travelling on the underground railroad in Iowa. IAJ 22:418-53, July 1924.

Garrison, C.W., ed. Letters of Atticus G. Haygood to Rutherford B. Hayes regarding the education of Negroes of the South. JSH 5:223-45, May 1939.

Garvie, B.S. Minstrel songs of other days. AME 7:945-55, Oct. 1912.

Garvie, C.F.C. South's problems. PUB 15:413-4, May 3, 1912.

Gaul, H.B. Negro spirituals. MUS 17:147-52, Apr. 1918.

Gee, C.S. John Brown's last letter, written to Lora Case. OAQ 40:185-9, Apr. 1931.

Gehrke, W.H. Negro slavery among the Germans in North Carolina. NCH 14:307-24, Oct. 1937.

Geiser, K.F. Anti-slavery movement, 1840-60, in the Western Reserve. MIV 5:73-98, 1912.

GEOGRAPHY

Emerson, F.V. Geographical influences in the distribution of slaves and slavery. AGS 43:13-26, June 1911 and following issues.

Hill, J.A. Effects of the northward migration of the Negro. ASS 17:34-46, 1923.

Mitchell, J.B. An analysis of population by race, nativity and residence. ARK 8:115-32, Summer 1949.

Taylor, Griffith. The distribution of future white settlement. GEO 12:375-402, July 1922.

Taylor, Griffith. Future white settlement: A rejoinder. GEO 13:130, Jan. 1923.

Valiah, P. Internal migration and racial composition of the Southern population. ASR 13:294-8, June 1948.

Willcox, W.F. On the future distribution of white settlement. GEO 12:646-7, Oct. 1922.

GEOPHAGY

Dickins, Dorothy, and R.N. Ford. Geophagy among Negro school children. ASR 7:59-65, Feb. 1942.

GEORGE, HENRY

Letters of S.P. Chase, Henry Clay, Henry George. INM 7: 123-32, Sept. 1911.

GEORGIA

Candler, M.A. Beginnings of slavery in Georgia. MAG 14: 342-51, July 1911.

Corry, J.P. Racial elements in colonial Georgia. GHQ 20: 30-40, Mar. 1936.

Coulter, E.M. History of a century on a Georgia plantation. MVH 16:334-46, Dec. 1929.

Flanders, R.B. The free Negro in ante-bellum Georgia. NCH 9:250-72, July 1932.

Flanders, R.B. Planters' problems in ante-bellum Georgia. GHQ 14:17-40, Mar. 1930.

Georgia and the African slave trade. GHQ 2:87-113, June 1918.

Georgia Presbyterian Church on secession and slavery. GHQ 1:263-5, Sept. 1917.

Grantham, D.W., Jr. Politics and the disfranchisement of the Negro. GHQ 32:1-21, Mar. 1948.

Henry, M.E., ed. Negro songs from Georgia. JAF 44:437-47, Oct.-Dec. 1931.

Holland, L.M. Republican primaries in Georgia. GHQ 30: 212-7, Sept. 1946.

Hollingsworth, R.R. Education and Reconstruction in Georgia. GHQ 19:112-33, June 1935 and following issue.

House, A.V., Jr. A Reconstruction share-cropper contract on a Georgia rice plantation. GHQ 26:156-65, June 1942.

GEORGIA (cont'd)

House, A.V., Jr., ed. Deterioration of a Georgia rice plantation during the Civil War. JSH 9:98-113, Feb. 1943.

Lawrence, J.B. Religious education of Negroes in the colony of Georgia. GHQ 14:41-57, Mar. 1930.

Letters pertaining to economic and social life of plantations in 1833-36. GHQ 14:150-73, June 1930.

Lombard, Mildred E., ed. Contemporary opinions of Georgia. A journal of life on a slave-holding plantation. GHQ 14:335-43, Dec. 1930.

Magoffin, Dorothy S. A Georgia planter and his plantation. NCH 15:354-77, Oct. 1938.

Montgomery, Horace. A Georgia precedent for the Freeport question. JSH 10:200-7, May 1944.

Potter, G.M., Jr. The rise of the plantation system in Georgia. GHQ 16:114-35, June 1932.

Rogers, W.M. Free Negro legislation in Georgia before 1865. GHQ 16:27-37, Mar. 1932.

Russ, W.A., Jr. Radical disfranchisement in Georgia, 1867-71. GHQ 19:175-209, Sept. 1935.

Stoddard, A.H. Origin, dialect, beliefs and characteristics of the Negroes of the South Carolina and Georgia coasts. GHQ 28:186-95, Sept. 1944.

Story of certain plantations. GHQ 24:342-73, Dec. 1940 and following issues.

Tebeau, C.W. Visitors' views of politics and life, 1865-80. GHQ 26:1-15, Mar. 1942.

Thompson, C. Mildred. The Freedmen's Bureau in Georgia in 1865-6. GHQ 5:40-9, Mar. 1921.

Ward, J.C., Jr. The Republican party in Bourbon Georgia, 1872-1890. JSH 9:196-209, May 1943.

GEORGIA, AVONDALE

Coulter, E.M. Avondale and Deerbrook, Ga., plantation documents. GHQ 17:150-9, June 1933 and following issues.

GEORGIA, BEAVER BEND

Jordan, W.T., ed. A system of operation of Beaver Bend plantation, Georgia, 1862. JSH 7:76-84, Feb. 1941.

GEORGIA, BRAMPTON

Story of Brampton plantation. GHQ 27:28-55, Mar. 1933.

GEORGIA, BREWTON HILL

Causton's Bluff, Deptford, Brewton Hill: Three allied plantations. GHQ 23:28-54, Mar. 1939 and following issue.

GEORGIA, CAUSTON'S BLUFF

Causton's Bluff, Deptford, Brewton Hill: Three allied plantations. GHQ 23:28-54, Mar. 1939 and following issue.

GEORGIA, DEERBROOK

Coulter, E.M. Avondale and Deerbrook, Ga., plantation documents. GHQ 17:150-9, June 1933 and following issues.

GEORGIA, DEPTFORD

Causton's Bluff, Deptford, Brewton Hill: Three allied plantations. GHQ 23:28-54, Mar. 1939 and following issue.

GEORGIA, DRAKIES

Story of the Drakies plantation. GHQ 24:207-35, Sept. 1940.

GEORGIA, HERMITAGE

Story of the Hermitage plantation. GHQ 27:56-87, Mar. 1943.

GEORGIA, MULBERRY GROVE

Mulberry Grove, Georgia, in colonial times. GHQ 23: 236-52, Sept. 1939.

GEORGIA, RAE'S HALL

Story of Rae's Hall plantation. GHQ 26:225-48, Sept.-Dec. 1942 and following issue.

GEORGIA, RICHMOND OAKGROVE

Story of Richmond Oakgrove plantation. GHQ 24:22-42, Mar. 1940 and following issue.

GEORGIA, ROYAL VALE

Plantation of the Royal Vale. GHQ 27:88-110, Mar. 1943.

GEORGIA, WHITEHALL

Story of Whitehall plantation. GHQ 25:340-63, Dec. 1941 and following issue.

GERMAN-AMERICANS

Gehrke, W.H. Negro slavery among the Germans in North Carolina. NCH 14:307-24, Oct. 1937.

Herriott, F.I. Parts played by German citizens of U.S. in abolition of slavery. IHL 35:101-91, 1928.

GERMANS

Voss. L.D. Sally Mueller, the German slave. LHQ 12: 447-60, July 1929.

Gerofsky, M. Background of Reconstruction. WVA 6:295-360, July 1945 and following issue.

GHETTOES

Baldwin, James. The Harlem ghetto: Jewish-Negro relations. COM 5:165-70, Feb. 1948.

Petry, Ann. Harlem. A medieval ghetto in the heart of the biggest, richest city in the world. HOL 5:110-6, Apr. 1949.

GHOSTS

Kirgan, Sadie E. Tales the darkies tell of ghosts that walk in Freestone County, Texas. TEX 5:385-91, May 1930.

Gibb, H.L. Slaves in old Detroit, from a census of 1782. MHM 18:143-6, Spring 1934.

GIBBON, LARDNER

Bell, W.J., Jr. Relation of Herndon and Gibbon's exploration of the Amazon to North American slavery, 1850-5. HAH 19:494-503, Nov. 1939.

Gibbons, V.E., ed. Letters on the war in Kansas in 1856. KHQ 10:369-79, Nov. 1941.

Gibson, B.D. Negro agricultural extension work in U.S. IRM 10:385-95, July 1921.

Gibson, B.D. Review of D. Young, The American Negro. IRM 19: 306-7, Apr. 1930.

Giddens, Lucia. Birmingham's Negro quarter. TRA 53:40-1, July 1941.

Giddings, F.H. Slavery and its abolition in the U.S. TIM 1: 479-82, Mar. 1907.

GIDDINGS RESOLUTION

Savage, W.S. The origin of the Giddings Resolution, 1841. OAQ 47:20-39, Jan. 1938.

Gilmer, A.H. Boston and emancipation, 1863. MAG 16:141-7, Apr. 1913.

Gilmore, H. See Wilson, L.

Gittings, Victoria. What William saw; experiences of William Aquilla with the supernatural. JAF 58:135-7, Apr.-June 1945.

GLANVILLE, JEROME

Malin, J.C. Identification of the stranger at the Pottawatomie massacre. KHQ 9:3-12, Feb. 1940.

Glazer, N. The social scientists dissect prejudice. COM 1: 79-85, May 1946.

Glick, C.E. Collective behavior in race relations. ASR 13: 287-94, June 1948.

GOBINEAU, JOSEPH ARTHUR DE

Lockspeiser, E. Gobineau's friendship with Richard Wagner and the new racial cult. WOR 57-9, Feb. 1941.

Rahilly, A. Gobineau's theory of the inequality of races. DUB 159:125-40, July 1916.

Goddard, A.E. Some lessons from Hampton and Tuskegee Institutes. NEW 18:86-102, Jan. 1911.

GOLDSBOROUGH, GOV. CHARLES

Views on slavery of Gov. Charles Goldsborough, 1834. MDH 39:332-4, Dec. 1944.

GOLDSTEIN, NAOMI F.

Basset, T. Review of Naomi F. Goldstein, The roots of prejudice against the Negro in the U.S. MVH 35:684, Mar. 1949.

Gollock, G.A. Review of W.D. Weatherford, The Negro: From Africa to America. IRM 14:140-1, Jan. 1925.

Gonzales, J.E. William Pitt Kellogg, Reconstruction governor of Louisiana, 1873-77. LHQ 29:394-495, Apr. 1946.

Goodall, Elizabeth J. Review of E.M. Coulter, The South during Reconstruction. WVA 9:300-1, Apr. 1948.

Goodwin, Mary F. Christianizing and educating the Negro in colonial Virginia. PEH 1:143-52, Sept. 1932.

Goodwin, Mary F. Liberia--America's only foreign colonial settlement. VAM 55:338+, Oct. 1947.

Gordon, Maxine W. Race patterns and prejudice in Puerto Rico. ASR 14:294-301, Apr. 1949.

Gosnell, H.F. Political meetings in Chicago's "black belt." APS 28:254-8, Apr. 1934.

Gosnell, H.F. Review of G. Myrdal, An American dilemma. APS 38:995-6, Oct. 1944.

Govan, T.P. Was plantation slavery profitable? JSH 8: 513-35, Nov. 1942.

GOVERNMENT

Eno, J.N. Race in relation to solidarity, government. AME 27, 179-85, Apr. 1933.

Norton, H.K. Self-determination in the West Indies. The governments of the Caribbean. WDT 47:147-53, Jan. 1926.

GOVERNMENT, CONSTITUTIONAL

Burns, F.P. White supremacy in the South. The battle for constitutional government, 1866. LHQ 18:581-616, July 1935.

Graham, A.A. Abolition colony in Ohio. OAQ 30-43, 1895.

Graham, H. Toussaint L'Ouverture, the Napoleon of San Domingo. DUB 153:86-110, July 1913.

Granberry, E. Primitive Negroes in Florida's turpentine forests. TRA 58:32-5, Apr. 1932.

GRAND ARMY OF THE REPUBLIC

Davies, W.E. The problem of race segregation in the Grand Army of the Republic. JSH 13:354-72, Aug. 1947.

GRANDFATHER CLAUSE

Mabry, W.A. Louisiana politics and the "grandfather clause." NCH 13:290-310, Oct. 1936.

Grant, M. The physical basis of race. NIS 3:184-97, 1917.

Grant, M. Racial aspects of restriction of immigration. NIS 7:44-54, 1921.

Grantham, D.W., Jr. Politics and the disfranchisement of the Negro. GHQ 32:1-21, Mar. 1948.

Graves, John T. The Southern Negro and the war crisis. VQR 18:500-17, Autumn 1942.

GREAT BASIN

Creer, L.H. Spanish-American slave trade in the Great Basin, 1800-1853. NMH 24:171-83, July 1949.

GREAT BRITAIN

Clarke, C.M. "Uncle Tom's Cabin"--how it reached the British public. CHA 7th s. 11:81-2, Jan. 8, 1921.

Hamer, Philip M. Great Britain, the United States, and the Negro seamen acts, 1822-48. JSH 1:3-28, Feb. 1935 and following issue, which covers 1850-60.

Senior, W. An episode in the slave trade. Great Britain. COR n.s. 54:561-6, May 1923.

Smither, Harriet. Effect of English abolitionism on annexation of Texas. SWH 32:193-205, Jan. 1929.

Stuart, W. Dutch and English importation to New Jersey and New York. AME 16:347-67, Oct. 1922.

GREELEY, JULIA

Owens, Sr. M. Lilliana. Story of Julia Greeley, the colored angel of mercy. COL 20:176-8, Sept. 1948.

Green, Ernest. Upper Canada's black defenders. OHS 27:365-91, 1931.

Green, F.M. Writings of Walter Lynwood Fleming. JSH 2:497-521, Nov. 1936.

GREEN, HENRY

Buried at master's feet. AME 6:814-5, Aug. 1911.

Greene, C.R. Florida folk songs: Negro tunes and words. FLQ 9:103-5, June 1945.

GREENE, L.J.

Crenshaw, O. Review of L.J. Greene, The Negro in colonial New England. VAM 52:157-8, Apr. 1944.

Gregory, J.P., Jr. The question of slavery in the Kentucky constitutional convention of 1849. HIS 23:89-110, Apr. 1949.

GREGORY, J.W.

Oldham, J.H. Review of J.W. Gregory, The menace of colour. IRM 14:454-6, July 1925.

Review of J.W. Gregory, The menace of colour. SGM 41:246-7, July 1925.

Grey, F.W. Race questions in Canada. UNI 7:212-30, Apr. 1908.

Gridley, J.N. A case under Illinois black law in 1862. IHJ 4:401-25, Jan. 1912.

Griffeth, Lucile, ed. Brookdale farm: A record book, 1856-57. JMH 7:23-31, Jan. 1945.

GRIFFING, CHARLES S.S.

Filler, L., ed. John Brown in Ohio: An interview with Charles S.S. Griffing. OAQ 58:213-8, Apr. 1949.

Griffis, W.E. Does the Bible throw light on the race question? HOM 70:94-9, Aug. 1915.

Grim, P.R. Rev. John Rankin: His ancestry and early career. OAQ 46:215-56, July 1937.

Grossman, M. Caste or democracy? An American dilemma. CJR 7: 475-86, Oct. 1944.

Grosz, Agnes S. P.B.S. Pinchback: His political career in Louisiana. LHQ 27:527-612, Apr. 1944.

Gue, B.F. Iowa men in John Brown's raid. AMH 1:143-69, Mar. 1906.

GUIANA

Kirke, D.B. Bush Negroes of Dutch Guiana. CHA 7th s. 15:549-52, Aug. 1, 1925.

Guiness, R.B. Daniel Howell Hise, abolitionist and reformer. SOS 36:297-300, Nov. 1945.

Guiness, R.B. Revised historical viewpoints on Reconstruction. SOS 34:19-20, Jan. 1943 and following issues.

Haar, C.M. White indentured servants in colonial New York. AME 34:370-92, July 1940.

Haardt, Sara. The resulting enslavement of masters and mistresses of slaves in the old South. WDT 15:465-74, Apr. 1930.

Haines, Marian G. Tuskegee Institute. GOV 2:96-115, Nov. 1907.

HAITI

Graham, H. Toussaint L'Ouverture, the Napoleon of San Domingo. DUB 153:86-110, July 1913.

Protocol between the U.S.A. and the Republic of Haiti for the establishment of a claims commission. Oct. 3, 1919. (Text.) AJI Supp. 15:169-73, Apr. 1921.

Sears, L.M. Frederick Douglass: His career as U.S. minister to Haiti, 1889-91. HAH 21:222-38, May 1941.

Simpson, George E. Analysis of Haiti's social structure. ASR 6:640-9, Oct. 1941.

Simpson, George E. Four specialized ceremonies of the vodun cult in Northern Haiti. JAF 59:154-67, Apr.-June 1946.

HAITI (cont'd)

Simpson, George E. Two vodun-related ceremonies from Haiti. JAF 61:49-52, Jan.-Mar. 1948.

Treaty with the U.S. regarding the finances, economic development and tranquility of Haiti. (Text.) AJI Supp. 10:234-8, Oct. 1916.

What U.S. is doing for Santo Domingo, Nicaragua and Haiti. NGE 30:143-77, Aug. 1916.

Hale, A.R. Why miscegenation flourishes in the North. PRS 23:543-51, Apr. 1910.

Halpert, H. Some Negro riddles collected in New Jersey. JAF 56:200-2, July-Sept. 1943.

Halsell, Willie D., ed. Republican factionalism in Mississippi, 1882-4. JSH 84-101, Feb. 1941.

Halsted, M. John Brown's execution. OAQ 30:290-9, July 1921.

HAMELTON MASSACRE

Moody, Joel. Marais des Cygnes massacre. KAN 14:208-23, 1915-8.

Tannar, A.H. Marais des Cygnes and rescue of Ben Rice. KAN 14:224-34, 1915-8.

Hamer, Marguerite B. South Carolina. A century before manumission. NCH 17:232-6, July 1940.

Hamer, Philip M. Great Britain, the United States, and the Negro seamen acts, 1822-48. JSH 1:3-28, Feb. 1935 and following issue, which covers 1850-60.

Hamilton, J.G. DeR. Andrew Johnson, his Southern policy. NCA 16:65-60, 1915.

Hamilton, J.G. DeR. Lincoln's election an immediate menace to slavery in the states. AHR 37:700-11, July 1932.

Hamilton, J.G. DeR. Review of E.M. Coulter, The South during Reconstruction. JSH 14:134-6, Feb. 1948.

Hamilton, James A. Life and work of John Brown. NYS 5:148-57, Apr. 1924.

Hamilton, Oscar B. George Washington, colored, and the work of Silas Hamilton. IHJ 3:45-58, Oct. 1910.

HAMILTON, SILAS

Hamilton, Oscar B. George Washington, colored, and the work of Silas Hamilton. IHJ 3:45-58, Oct. 1910.

Hamilton, W.B., and W.D. McCain, eds. Inventories of the estate of Charles Percy, planter, 1794 and 1804. JMH 10: 290-316, Oct. 1948.

Hammond, I.W. New Hampshire slaves. GSM 4:199-203, Nov. 1907.

HAMPTON INSTITUTE

Goddard, A.E. Some lessons from Hampton and Tuskegee Institutes. NEW 18:86-102, Jan. 1911.

Hampton Normal and Agricultural Institute, Hampton, Va. AAB 51:64+, Aug. 1914.

Hand, J.P. Negro slavery in Illinois. IHL 15:42-50, 1910.

Handlin, Oscar. Prejudice and capitalist exploitation: Does economics explain racism? COM 6:79-85, July 1948.

Handlin, Oscar. Review of H.P. Fairchild, Race and nationality as factors in American life. COM 5:476-7, May 1948.

HANDY, W.C.

Osgood, H.O. Review of W.C. Handy, The Blues. MOD 4: 25-8, Nov.-Dec. 1926.

HANSEN, NICHOLAS

Stevens, Wayne E. Shaw-Hansen election contest. IHJ 7: 389-401, Jan. 1915.

HANWAY, CASPAR

Caspar Hanway and the fugitive slave law. MAG 21:148-50, Oct. 1915.

Hargis, Modeste. See Barr, Ruth B.

HARLEM

Baldwin, James. The Harlem ghetto: Jewish-Negro relations. COM 5:165-70, Feb. 1948.

The Harlem rendezvous and his Negro jazz orchestra. Edward Kennedy "Duke" Ellington. FTE 8:47+, Aug. 1933.

HARLEM (cont'd)

Ottley, Roi. Black Jews of Harlem. TRA 79:18-21, July 1942.

Petry, Ann. Harlem. A medieval ghetto in the heart of the biggest, richest city in the world. HOL 5:110-6, Apr. 1949.

Harlow, R.V. Gerrit Smith and the John Brown raid. AHR 38: 32-60, Oct. 1932.

Harlow, R.V. Rise and fall of emigrant aid movement in Kansas. AHR 41:1-25, Oct. 1935.

Harmon, D. Review of J.W. DeForest, A Union officer in the Reconstruction. PAM 72:432-3, Oct. 1948.

Harmon, G.D. Buchanan's attitude toward the admission of Kansas on the slavery question. PAM 53:51-91, Jan. 1929.

Harmon, G.D. Stephen A. Douglas--his leadership in Compromise of 1850, regarding government and question of slavery in territory acquired from Mexico. IHJ 21:452-90, Jan. 1929.

Harn, Julia E. Life and customs on plantations and in small communities of the ante-bellum South. GHQ 16:47-55, Mar. 1932 and previous and following issues.

Harrington, F.H. Nathaniel Banks. A study in anti-slavery politics. NEQ 9:626-54, Dec. 1936.

Harris, F.B. Reconstruction period: The career of Henry Clay Warmoth, governor. LHQ 30:523-653, Apr. 1947.

HARRIS, JOEL CHANDLER

Wolfe, B. Uncle Remus and the malevolent rabbit: The Negro in popular American culture. COM 8:31-41, July 1949.

HARRIS, JULIAN

Link, A.S., ed. The Progressive party's lily-white policy in 1912: Correspondence between Theodore Roosevelt and Julian Harris. JSH 10:480-90, Nov. 1944.

Harris, N.D. Negro servitude in Illinois. IHL 11:49-56, 1906.

Harrison, L. Cassius M. Clay's anti-slavery newspaper, the "True American": Opposition in Kentucky to his struggle for emancipation of the Negro. HIS 22:30-49, Jan. 1948.

HARRISON, RICHARD "KING"

Ardery, Julia S. Will of Richard "King" Harrison of Calvert Co., Md., granting freedom to his serving woman Kate Booth. KYR 46:637-46, Oct. 1958.

Harshaw, D.A. Philosophy of the Negro spiritual. HOM 95: 184-6, Mar. 1928.

Hart, A.B. Realities of suffrage. APP 2:149-70, 1905.

Hartridge, W.C. Refugees in Maryland from the St. Domingo slave revolt of 1793. MDH 38:103-22, June 1943.

Hartshorne, R. Racial maps of U.S. population. GEO 28:276-88, Apr. 1938.

Hartwell, E.C. Economics of slavery. HTM 4:50, Feb. 1913.

Harvey, J.R. Pioneer Negroes in Colorado. COL 26:165-76, July 1949.

Haseltine, G.C. Biographical sketch of William Wilberforce. ENG 57:59-65, July 1933.

Hastings, A.C.G. Slave traffickers. A capture thirty years ago. NAR 112:352-62, Mar. 1939.

HAWAII

Lee, L.L. Role and status of the Negro in the Hawaiian community. ASR 13:419-37, Aug. 1948.

Hawes, Lilla M. Amelia M. Murray on slavery; an unpublished letter. GHQ 33:314-7, Dec. 1949.

HAWKINS NEGROES

Porter, K.W. The Creek Indian-Negro tradition. The Hawkins Negroes go to Mexico. OKC 24:55-8, Spring 1946.

Hawley, C.A. Historical background of the Jasper Colony attitude toward slavery and the Civil War. IAJ 34:172-97, Apr. 1936.

Hawley, C.A. Whittier and Iowa. IAJ 34:115-43, Apr. 1936.

Hay, T.R. The question of arming the slaves. MVH 6:34-73, June 1919.

HAYES, RUTHERFORD B.

Garrison, C.W, ed. Letters of Atticus G. Haygood to Rutherford B. Hayes regarding the education of Negroes of the South. JSH 5:223-45, May 1939.

HAYGOOD, ATTICUS G.

Garrison, C.W., ed. Letters of Atticus G. Haygood to Rutherford B. Hayes regarding the education of Negroes of the South. JSH 5:223-45, May 1939.

Haynes, G.H. Biography of Charles Sumner. MAG 14:24-30, Aug. 1911 and following issues.

Haynes, George E. Effect of war conditions on Negro labor. ACA s. 8:299-312, Feb. 1919.

Haynes, N.S. Disciples of Christ and their attitude toward slavery. IHL 19:52-9, 1913.

Hearon, C. Mississippi Compromise of 1850. MSS 14:7-230, 1914.

Hearon, C. Nullification in Mississippi. MSS 12:37-71, 1912.

Heckman, O.S. The role of the Presbyterian Church in Southern Reconstruction, 1860-1880. NCH 20:219-37, July 1943.

Henry, H.M. Tennessee slave laws. THM 2:175-203, Sept. 1916.

Henry, M.E., ed. Negro songs from Georgia. JAF 44:437-47, Oct.-Dec. 1931.

HENSON, REV. JOSIAH

Ward, Aileen. Rev. Josiah Henson, the original Tom of "Uncle Tom's Cabin"; his story. DAL 20:335-8, Oct. 1940.

Herndon, D.T. Nashville convention of 1850 to protest against exclusion of slave holders from territories. AHS 5: 203-37, 1904.

HERNDON, WILLIAM LEWIS

Bell, W.J., Jr. Relation of Herndon and Gibbon's exploration of the Amazon to North American slavery, 1850-5. HAH 19:494-503, Nov. 1939.

Herring, Harriet L. The Clement attachment: An episode in Reconstruction industrial history. JSH 4:185-98, May 1938.

Herring, R. Black pastures. LON 22:239-49, July 1930.

Herriott, F.I. Parts played by German citizens of U.S. in abolition of slavery. IHL 35:101-91, 1928.

Herron, Stella. The African apprentice bill, 1858. MIV 8: 135-45, 1914-5.

Herskovits, Frances. See HERSKOVITS, M.J.

Herskovits, M.J. Effect of social selection on the American Negro. ASS 20:77-82, 1926.

Herskovits, M.J. Future steps in the study of Negro folklore. JAF 56:1-7, Jan.-Mar. 1943.

Herskovits, M.J. Review of H. Crum, Gullah: Negro life in the Caroline Sea Islands. ASR 6:423-4, June 1941.

Herskovits, M.J. Review of A.H. Fauset, Black gods of the metropolis: The cult practices of five Negro religious groups in Philadelphia. ROR 9:186-9, Jan. 1945.

Herskovits, M.J. Review of E. Franklin Frazier, The Negro family in Bahia, Brazil. ASR 8:394-404, Aug. 1943.

HERSKOVITS, M.J.

Johnson, G.B. Review of M.J. Herskovits, The myth of the Negro past. ASR 7:289-90, Apr. 1942.

Webb, J.L. Review of M.J. Herskovits and Frances S. Herskovits, Trinidad village: A study of a Protestant Negro culture. IRM 36:405-7, July 1947.

Hesseltine, W.B. Review of J.H. Franklin, From slavery to freedom. AHR 54:155-6, Oct. 1948.

Hesseltine, W.B., and Hazel C. Wolf. The Emancipation Proclamation and the Altoona conference. PAM 71:195-205, July 1947.

Hicks, Granville. Dr. Channing and the Creole case. AHR 37: 516-25, Apr. 1932.

Hiden, Mrs. P.W. Inventory and appraisement of a Virginia well-to-do planter's estate, 1760. WMQ 2d s. 16:600-1, Oct. 1936.

Higginson, Thomas W. John Greenleaf Whittier as abolitionist. BKN 26:259-62, Dec. 1907.

Highsmith, W.E. Some aspects of Reconstruction. JSH 13:460-91, Nov. 1947.

Hill, J.A. Effects of the northward migration of the Negro. ASS 17:34-46, 1923.

Hill, L.F. The abolition of the African slave trade to Brazil. HAH 11:169-97, May 1931.

Hill, L.P. Negro ideals, their effect and embarrassments. JRD 6:91-103, July 1915.

Hillis, N.D. Harriet Beecher Stowe and the Beecher family. MUN 46:191-201, Nov. 1911.

Himelhoch, J. Is there a bigot personality? A report on some preliminary studies. COM 3:277-84, Mar. 1947.

HISE, DANIEL HOWELL

Atherton, C.E. Daniel Howell Hise, abolitionist and reformer. MVH 26:343-58, Dec. 1939.

Guiness, R.B. Daniel Howell Hise, abolitionist and reformer. SOS 36:297-300, Nov. 1945.

HISTORIOGRAPHY

Beale, H.K. On rewriting Reconstruction history. AHR 45:807-27, July 1940.

Guiness, R.B. Revised historical viewpoints on Reconstruction. SOS 34:19-20, Jan. 1943 and following issues.

Hubbart, H.C. Revisionist interpretations of Douglas and his doctrine of popular sovereignty. SOS 25:103-7, Mar. 1934.

Phillips, U.B. Central theme of Southern history. AHR 34:30-43, Oct. 1928.

Simkins, F.B. New viewpoints of Southern Reconstruction. JSH 5:49-61, Feb. 1939.

Hoare, F.R. This racialism. DUB 204:126-39, Jan. 1939.

Hodder, F.H. Authorship of the Compromise of 1850. MVH 22: 525-36, Mar. 1936.

Hodder, F.H. Genesis of Kansas-Nebraska act. WHP 60:69-86, 1913.

Hodder, F.H. The railroad background of the Kansas-Nebraska act. MVH 12:3-22, June 1925.

Hodder, F.H. Some phases of the Dred Scott case. MVH 16:3-22, June 1929.

Hoernle, R.F.A. Racial problems in the Empire. WOR 6:49-53, Feb. 1939.

Hogan, P.E. Review of J.H. Franklin, From slavery to freedom. CHR 34:343-4, Oct. 1948.

Hogden, L. Biology and modern race dogmas. CJR 4:3-12, Feb. 1941.

HOLDEN, W.W.

Ewing, C.A.M. Two Reconstruction impeachments. NCH 15: 204-30, July 1938.

Holland, L.M. Republican primaries in Georgia. GHQ 30:212-7, Sept. 1946.

HOLLAND

Stuart, W. Dutch and English importation to New Jersey and New York. AME 16:347-67, Oct. 1922.

Hollingsworth, R.R. Education and Reconstruction in Georgia. GHQ 19:112-33, June 1935 and following issue.

Hollis, D. In the track of slave ships. CHA 7th s. 17:721-3, Oct. 15, 1927.

Hollister, H.A. Booker T. Washington. An appreciation. SCH 35:144+, Jan. 1916.

HOLMES, ROBIN

The case of Robin Holmes vs. Nathaniel Ford. ORE 23:111-37, June 1922.

HOLT, R.

Johnson, C.S. Review of R. Holt, George Washington Carver: An American biography. AHR 49:326-7, Jan. 1944.

Holzknecht, K.J. Negro song variants from Louisville. JAF 41:558-78, Oct.-Dec. 1928.

HOMILETICS

Stidger, W.L. Negro spirituelles, a new idea in homiletics. HOM 90:26-9, July 1925.

Honeyman, A. Van D. A slave sale of 1827. NJS 53:250-1, Oct. 1935.

HOODOO. See also BLACK MAGIC, OBEAH, VODUN

Hurston, Zora N. Hoodoo beliefs and practices in America. JAF 44:317-417, Oct.-Dec. 1931.

Hoole, W.S., ed. A Southerner's viewpoint of the Kansas situation, 1856-7. KHQ 3:43-68, Feb. 1934 and following issue.

Hopkins, Geraldine. Editions of the "Liberty Minstrel," a rare abolitionist document. MVH 18:60-4, June 1931.

Hornseth, R.A. See McCormick, T.C.

HOSSACK, JOHN

Speech delivered by John Hossack upon his conviction for violating the fugitive slave act, 1860. IHJ 41:67-74, Mar. 1948.

HOTEL THERESA, NEW YORK CITY

Hotel Theresa, New York City. AAB 45:465-7, Nov. 1913.

House, A.V., Jr. A Reconstruction share-cropper contract on a Georgia rice plantation. GHQ 26:156-65, June 1942.

House, A.V., Jr., ed. Deterioration of a Georgia rice plantation during the Civil War. JSH 9:98-113, Feb. 1943.

HOUSE SERVANTS

Settle, E. Ophelia. Social attitudes during the slave regime: Household servants versus field hands. ASS 28: 95-8, May 1934.

HOUSING

Abrams, C. Homes for Aryans only: Restrictive covenant spreads legal racism in America. COM 3:421-7, May 1947.

Housing problems for Negroes in New York City. Paul Laurence Dunbar apartments. ARC 59:5-12, Jan. 1929.

Smelser, M. Housing in Creole St. Louis, 1764-1821: An example of cultural change. LHQ 21:337-48, Apr. 1938.

Howard, J.T. Review of G.P. Jackson, ed., White and Negro spirituals. NEQ 17:332-3, June 1944.

HOWARD, GEN. OLIVER OTIS

Portrait. PRI 31:188, May 1918.

Howard, W.L. A plain explanation of the greatest social evil. PRS 23:640-7, May 1910.

Howay, F.W. The Negro immigration into Vancouver Island in 1858. BCH 3:101-13, Apr. 1939.

Howay, F.W. Negro immigration into Vancouver Island in 1858. RSC 3d s. 29:145-56, sec. 2, May 1935.

Howe, I., and B.J. Widick. The U.A.W. fights race prejudice; case history on the industrial front. COM 8:261-8, Sept. 1949.

Howell, Isabel. Story of John Armfield, slave-trader. THQ 2:3-29, Mar. 1943.

Hoyt, W.D., Jr. White servitude in Northampton, Maryland, 1772-4. MDH 33:126-33, June 1938.

Hubbart, H.C. Pro-Southern influences in the free West, 1840-65. MVH 20:45-62, June 1932.

Hubbart, H.C. Revisionist interpretations of Douglas and his doctrine of popular sovereignty. SOS 25:103-7, Mar. 1934.

Hudson, A.P. Some curious Negro names and their derivation. SFQ 2:170-93, Dec. 1938.

Hughes, E.C. Queries concerning industry and society growing out of a study of ethnic relations in industry. ASR 14: 211-20, Apr. 1949.

HUGHES, LANGSTON

Portrait. BKL 81:17, Oct. 1931.

Huhner, L. Some Jewish associates of John Brown. AJH 23: 55-78, 1915.

HUMANIZATION

Taylor, R.H. Humanizing the slave code in North Carolina. NCH 2:323-31, July 1925.

HUMOR

Burma, J.H. Humor as a technique in race conflict. ASR 11:710-5, Dec. 1946.

Humphrey, G.D. Public education for whites. JMH 3:26-36, Jan. 1941.

HUMPHREY, REV. LUTHER

Stutler, B.B. The "originals" of John Brown's letter to the Rev. Luther Humphrey. WVA 9:1-25, Oct. 1947.

Humphrey, N.D. Race can work toward democracy. SOS 35:246-8, Oct. 1944.

Hunt, H.F. Slavery among the Indians of Northwestern America. WAS 9:277-83, Oct. 1918.

Huntington, E. Climate, a neglected factor in race development. JRD 6:167-84, Oct. 1915.

HUNTINGTON, E.

Chisholm, G.C. Review of E. Huntington, Character of races. SGM 41:299-302, Sept. 15, 1925.

Hurdyk, Margaret. See BONGER, W.A.

Hurston, Zora N. Hoodoo beliefs and practices in America. JAF 44:317-417, Oct.-Dec. 1931.

Hurston, Zora N. Review of R. Tallant, Voodoo in New Orleans. JAF 60:436-8, Sept.-Dec. 1947.

HYMNS

Work, John W. Changing patterns in Negro folk songs. JAF 62:136-44, Apr.-June 1949.

IDEALS

HIll, L.P. Negro ideals, their effect and embarrassments. JRD 6:91-103, July 1915.

ILLINOIS

Aldrich, O.W. Illinois slavery. IHL 22:89-99, 1916.

Aldrich, O.W. Slavery or involuntary servitude in Illinois prior to and after admission as a state. IHJ 9:119-32, July 1916.

Cooley, Verna. Illinois and the underground railroad to Canada. IHL 23:76-98, 1917.

Correspondence of Gov. Edward Coles with Rev. Thomas Lippincott. IHJ 3:59-63, Jan. 1911.

Edward Coles, the man who saved Illinois from slavery. JAH 16:153-7, Apr.-June 1922.

Gridley, J.N. A case under Illinois black law in 1862. IHJ 4:401-25, Jan. 1912.

Hand, J.P. Negro slavery in Illinois. IHL 15:42-50, 1910.

Harris, N.D. Negro servitude in Illinois. IHL 11:49-56, 1906.

Haynes, N.S. Disciples of Christ and their attitude toward slavery. IHL 19:52-9, 1913.

Lemen, Joseph B. The Jefferson-Lemen anti-slavery pact. IHL 13:74-84, 1908.

Lyons, John F. Attitude of Presbyterians in Ohio, Indiana and Illinois toward slavery. PBY 11:69-82, June 1921.

Mulcaster, J.G. A quadroon girl of Southern Illinois. IHJ 28:214-7, Oct. 1935.

Riddell, W.R. International complications between Illinois and Canada arising out of slavery. IHJ 25:123-6, Apr.-July 1932.

Ryan, J.H. Illinois anti-slavery struggle and its effect on the Methodist Church. IHL 19:67-76, 1913.

Ryan, J.H. Underground railroad incident in Illinois. IHJ 8:23-30, Apr. 1915.

Schmidt, O.L. Illinois underground railroad. IHJ 18: 703-17, Oct. 1925.

ILLINOIS (cont'd)

Stevens, Wayne E. Shaw-Hansen election contest. IHJ 7: 389-401, Jan. 1915.

Swann, T.W. Jim Crow laws threatened in Illinois. PUB 16:246, Mar. 14, 1913.

Washburne, E.B. Sketch of Edward Coles, second governor of Illinois and of the slavery struggle of 1823-4. IHC 15, 1920.

ILLINOIS, ALTON

Bowers, A.L. Anti-slavery convention in Alton, Ill., in 1837. IHJ 20:329-56, Oct. 1927.

ILLINOIS, CHICAGO

Gosnell, H.F. Political meetings in Chicago's "black belt." APS 28:254-8, Apr. 1934.

Longini, Muriel D. Folk-songs of Chicago Negroes. JAF 52:96-111, Jan.-Mar. 1939.

Powell, Dorothy M. The Negro worker in Chicago industry. JOB 20:21-32, Jan. 1947.

ILLINOIS, DOUGLAS CO.

Reat, J.L. Slavery in Douglas Co., Ill. IHJ 11:177-9, July 1918.

ILLINOIS, GALESBURG

Muelder, H.R. Galesburg, Ill.; hot-bed of abolitionism. IHJ 35:216-35, Sept. 1942.

ILLINOIS, MCDONOUGH CO.

Blazer, D.N. Underground railroad in McDonough County, Ill. IHJ 15:579-91, Oct. 1922-Jan. 1923.

ILLINOIS, POPE COUNTY

Allen, John W. Slavery and Negro servitude in Pope County, Illinois. IHJ 42:411-23, Dec. 1949.

ILLINOIS COLLEGE

Rammelkamp, C.H. Anti-slavery movement and Illinois College. IHL 13:192-203, 1909.

Rammelkamp, C.H. Reverberations of the slavery conflict in Illinois College. MVH 14:447-61, Mar. 1928.

ILLUSTRATION

Crite, Alan R. Why I illustrate spirituals. WLD 1:44-5+, May 1938.

IMMIGRATION

Grant, M. Racial aspects of restriction of immigration. NIS 7:44-54, 1921.

Howay, F.W. The Negro immigration into Vancouver Island in 1858. BCH 3:101-13, Apr. 1939.

Howay, F.W. Negro immigration into Vancouver Island in 1858. RSC 3d s. 29:145-56, sec. 2, May 1935.

Woody, R.H. The labor and immigration problems of South Carolina during the Reconstruction period. MVH 18:195-212, Sept. 1931.

IMPEACHMENT

Ewing, C.A.M. Two Reconstruction impeachments. NCH 15: 204-30, July 1938.

IMPERIALISM

Fuller, J.D.P. Effect of the slavery issue on the movement to annex Mexico, 1846-48. MVH 21:31-48, June 1934.

INCOME

Quarles, Benjamin. Sources of abolitionist income. MVH 32:63-76, June 1945.

INDENTURED SERVANTS. See also SERVITUDE

Haar, C.M. White indentured servants in colonial New York. AME 34:370-92, July 1940.

Herron, Stella. The African apprentice bill, 1858. MIV 8:135-45, 1914-5.

Jervey, T.D. White indentured servants in South Carolina. SOC 12:163-71, Oct. 1911.

Miller, William. Effects of the American Revolution on indentured servitude. PAH 7:131-41, July 1940.

Smith, A.E. The indentured servant and land speculation in 17th century Maryland. AHR 40:467-72, Apr. 1935.

INDENTURES

Folsom, J.F. A slave indenture of colonial days. NJS 3d s. 10:111-5, July-Oct. 1915.

INDENTURES (cont'd)

Indentures. Original documents. INM 7:133-5, Sept. 1911.

INDIANA

Conklin, Julia S. Underground railroad in Indiana. INM 6:63-74, June 1910.

Dunn, J.P. Indiana's part in "Uncle Tom's Cabin." INM 7: 112-8, Sept. 1911.

Leslie, W.R. The constitutional significance of Indiana's statute of 1824 on fugitives from labor. JSH 13:338-53, Aug. 1947.

Lyons, John F. Attitude of Presbyterians in Ohio, Indiana and Illinois toward slavery. PBY 11:69-82, June 1921.

McDonald, E.E. The Negro in Indiana before 1881. INM 27: 291-306, Dec. 1931.

Money, C.H. Fugitive slave law of 1850. Indiana cases. INM 17:159-98, June 1921 and following issue.

Owen, D. Slavery in Indiana. Circumvention of Article VI, Ordinance of 1782. INM 36:110-6, June 1940.

Sherwood, H.N. Indiana and Negro deportation, 1817. MVH 9:414-21, 1919.

Trueblood, Lillie D. The story of John Williams, colored. INM 30:149-52, June 1934.

INDIANA, HENDRICKS CO.

Leak, R.R. Underground railroad in Hendricks Co., Indiana. INM 36:17-22, Mar. 1940.

INDIANA, INDIANAPOLIS

Riley, H.M. History of Negro elementary education in Indianapolis. INM 26:280-305, Sept. 1930.

INDIANA, KNOX CO.

McDonald, E.E. Disposal of Negro slaves by will in Knox Co., Indiana. INM 26:143-6, June 1930.

INDIANA, MONROE CO.

Smith, H.L. Aiding run-away slaves in Monroe Co. INM 13: 288-97, Sept. 1917.

INDIANA, NEWPORT

Waldrip, W.D. Underground railroad station at Newport, Ind. INM 7:64-76, June 1911.

INDIANA, RICHMOND

Abolition and Henry Clay's visit to Richmond, Ind., 1842. INM 4:117-28, Sept. 1908.

INDUSTRIAL RELATIONS

Ross, M. They did it in St. Louis: One man against folklore. COM 4:9-15, July 1947.

INDUSTRIALIZATION

Jernegan, M.W. Slavery and the beginnings of industrialization in the colonies. AHR 25:220-40, Jan. 1920.

INDUSTRY

Forbes, R.H. The black man's industries. GEO 23:230-47, Apr. 1933.

Howe, I., and B.J. Widick. The U.A.W. fights race prejudice; case history on the industrial front. COM 8:261-8, Sept. 1949.

Hughes, E.C. Queries concerning industry and society growing out of a study of ethnic relations in industry. ASR 14:211-20, Apr. 1949.

Northrup, H.R. Negroes in a war industry; the case of shipbuilding. JOB 16:160-72, July 1943.

Powell, Dorothy M. The Negro worker in Chicago industry. JOB 20:21-32, Jan. 1947.

INJURIES

Suit for damages for personal injuries to a slave, 1764. LHQ 5:58-62, Jan. 1922.

INSTITUTES. See also HAMPTON INSTITUTE, TUSKEGEE INSTITUTE, WEST VIRGINIA COLORED INSTITUTE

Goddard, A.E. Some lessons from Hampton and Tuskegee Institutes. NEW 18:86-102, Jan. 1911.

Hampton Normal and Agricultural Institute, Hampton, Va. AAB 51:64+, Aug. 1914.

Wright, John C. Teaching English at Tuskegee Institute. EBM 3:26-30, Oct. 1908.

INSTITUTIONS, POLITICAL

Barnes, H.E. The struggle of races and social groups as a factor in development of political and social institutions. JRD 9:394-419, Apr. 1919.

INSTITUTIONS, SOCIAL

Barnes, H.E. The struggle of races and social groups as a factor in development of political and social institutions. JRD 9:394-419, Apr. 1919.

INSURRECTIONS

Meader, J.R. Some Negro insurrections. AME 6:744-52, Apr. 1911.

Negro insurrection in Cuba. PUB 15:514-5, May 31, 1912; PUB 15:566, June 14, 1912.

White, W.W. The Texas slave insurrection of 1860. SWH 52:259-85, Jan. 1949.

Wish, H. The slave insurrection panic of 1856. JSH 5: 206-22, May 1939.

INTELLECTUAL DEVELOPMENT

Woodruff, C.E. Laws of racial and intellectual development. JRD 3:156-75, Oct. 1912.

INTELLIGENCE

Condenhove, H. Certain facets of Negro mentality in Central Africa. COR n.s. 55:207-21, Aug. 1923.

INTERIOR DECORATION

Szecsi, L. Negro sculpture in interior decoration. LST 7:326-7, June 1933.

INTERNATIONAL CONFERENCE ON THE NEGRO

Park, R.M. Tuskegee international conference on the Negro. JRD 3:117-20, July 1912.

INTERNATIONAL ORGANIZATIONS

Mead, E.D. International organizations for inter-racial good will. JRD 2:210-4, Oct. 1911.

INTERNATIONAL PROBLEMS

Riddell, W.R. International complications between Illinois and Canada arising out of slavery. IHJ 25:123-6, Apr.-July 1932.

INTERRACIAL CONTACTS

Ford, R.N. Study of white-Negro contacts. Scaling experience by a multiple response technique. ASR 6:9-23, Feb. 1941.

Frazier, E. Franklin. Negro-white contacts from the standpoint of the social structure of the Negro world. ASR 14:1-11, Feb. 1949.

INTERRACIALISM

Mead, E.D. International organizations for inter-racial good will. JRD 2:210-4, Oct. 1911.

INTOLERANCE

Minsky, L. Intolerance; a problem for psychiatrists? CJR 5:261-8, June 1942.

INVENTORIES

Hamilton, W.B., and W.D. McCain, eds. Inventories of the estate of Charles Percy, planter, 1794 and 1804. JMH 10:290-316, Oct. 1948.

Hiden, Mrs. P.W. Inventory and appraisement of a Virginia well-to-do planter's estate, 1760. WMQ 2d s. 16:600-1, Oct. 1936.

INVOLUNTARY SERVITUDE. See SLAVERY

IOWA

Bergmann, Leola N. The Negro in Iowa: Before the Civil War to World War II. IAJ 46:3-90, Jan. 1948.

Black, P.W. Lynching in Iowa. IAJ 10:151-254, Apr. 1912.

Coffin, N.E. Case of Archie P. Webb. ANN 3rd s. 11:200-14, July-Oct. 1913.

Garretson, O.A. Travelling on the underground railroad in Iowa. IAJ 22:418-53, July 1924.

Gue, B.F. Iowa men in John Brown's raid. AMH 1:143-69, Mar. 1906.

Hawley, C.A. Whittier and Iowa. IAJ 34:115-43, Apr. 1936.

Pelzer, L. Slavery and the Negro in Iowa. IAJ 2:471-84, Oct. 1904.

Teakle, T. Rendition of Barclay Coppoc. IAJ 10:503-66, Oct. 1912.

IOWA (cont'd)

Wick, B.L. Delia Webster--her part in the underground railroad movement in Iowa. ANN 3d s. 18:228-31, Jan. 1932.

Williams, Ora. Story of underground railway signals. ANN 27:297-303, Apr. 1946.

IRON INDUSTRY

Bruce, Kathleen. Slave labor in Virginia iron industry. WMQ 2d s. 6:289-302, Oct. 1932 and following issues.

Isely, J.A. Review of E.M. Coulter, The South during Reconstruction. MDH 43:146, June 1948.

ISOLATION

Telford, C.W. A race study of St. Helena Island Negroes with particular reference to what effect their isolation has had upon them. NDQ 21:126-35, Winter 1931.

Israel, S. Teaching of Report of President's Committee on Civil Rights. SOS 39:102-4, Mar. 1948.

Jackson, Mrs. F.N. Anti-slavery relics. CON 77:9-17, Jan. 1927.

JACKSON, G.P.

Howard, J.T. Review of G.P. Jackson, ed., White and Negro spirituals. NEQ 17:332-3, June 1944.

JACKSON, L.P.

Dabney, V. Review of L.P. Jackson, Free Negro labor and property holding in Virginia, 1830-60. VAM 51:212-3, Apr. 1913.

Jackson, S.L. Review of Benjamin Quarles, Frederick Douglass. NYH 29:443-4, Oct. 1948.

JAMAICA

Needham, C.K. Comparison of race conditions in Jamaica with those in U.S. JRD 4:189-203, Oct. 1913.

Parsons, Elsie. Ashanti influence in Negro folktales and customs in Jamaica. JAF 47:391-5, Oct.-Dec. 1934.

JAMAICA, WORTHY PARK

Phillips, U.B. A slave plantation in 1792-6: The Worthy Park plantation, Jamaica. AHR 19:543-58, Apr. 1914.

JASPER COLONY

Hawley, C.A. Historical background of the Jasper Colony attitude toward slavery and the Civil War. IAJ 34:172-97, Apr. 1936.

JAYHAWKERS

Lyman, W.A. Jayhawkers--origin of name and activity. KAN 14:203-7, 1915-8.

Mechem, K. The mythical jayhawk. KHQ 13:3-15, Feb. 1944.

JAZZ

The Harlem rendezvous and his Negro jazz orchestra. Edward Kennedy "Duke" Ellington. FTE 8:47+, Aug. 1933.

"JAZZERY"

Coward, H. "Jazzery," why the white races should ban it. NAR 90:395-400, Nov. 1927.

JEFFERSON, THOMAS

Galbreath, C.B. Thomas Jefferson's views on slavery. OAQ 34:184-202, Apr. 1925.

Lemen, Joseph B. The Jefferson-Lemen anti-slavery pact. IHL 13:74-84, 1908.

Jenkins, Frances. Education adapted to meet racial needs. SCH 37:126-8, Feb. 1918.

JENKINS, JOHN CARMICHAEL

Seal, A.G. John Carmichael Jenkins and his scientific management of his plantations. JMH 1:14-28, Jan. 1939.

Jente, R. Review of S.G. Champion, Racial proverbs. JAF 53:279-80, Oct.-Dec. 1940.

Jernegan, M.W. Slavery and the beginnings of industrialization in the colonies. AHR 25:220-40, Jan. 1920.

Jerrold, W. Centenary notes on Harriet Beecher Stowe. BKL 40:241-50, Sept. 1911.

JERRY RESCUE

Galpin, W.F. Fugitive slave law of 1850. The Jerry Rescue precipitated a clash between the government and local abolitionists. NYH 26:19-33, Jan. 1945.

Jervey, T.D. White indentured servants in South Carolina. SOC 12:163-71, Oct. 1911.

JEWISH-NEGRO RELATIONS

Baldwin, James. The Harlem ghetto: Jewish-Negro relations. COM 5:165-70, Feb. 1948.

Clark, K.B. Negro-Jewish relations: A complex social problem. COM 1:8-14, Feb. 1946.

JEWS

Huhner, L. Some Jewish associates of John Brown. AJH 23: 55-78, 1915.

Ottley, Roi. Black Jews of Harlem. TRA 79:18-21, July 1942.

JIM CROW

Folmsbee, Stanley J. The origin of the first "Jim Crow" law. JSH 15:235-47, May 1949.

Swann, T.W. Jim Crow laws threatened in Illinois. PUB 16:246, Mar. 14, 1913.

Johnson, A.K. Review of R. Tallant, Voodoo in New Orleans. SFQ 11:99-100, Mar. 1947.

JOHNSON, ANDREW

Andrews, Rena M. Andrew Johnson, his plan of restoration of the South to the Union in relation to that of Lincoln. THM n.s. 1:165-81, Apr. 1931.

Hamilton, J.G. DeR. Andrew Johnson, his Southern policy. NCA 16:65-80, 1915.

Johnson, C.S. The problem of Negro child education. ASR 1: 264-72, Apr. 1936.

Johnson, C.S. Racial attitudes of college students. ASS 28: 24-31, May 1934.

Johnson, C.S. Review of J.H. Franklin, From slavery to freedom. NYH 29:215-8, Apr. 1948.

Johnson, C.S. Review of R. Holt, George Washington Carver: An American biography. AHR 49:326-7, Jan. 1944.

Johnson, C.S. Review of B.J. Mathews, Booker T. Washington, educator and interracial interpreter. MVH 36:157-8, June 1949.

Johnson, C.S. Review of R.A. Warner, New Haven Negroes: A social history. NEQ 14:748-50, Dec. 1941.

JOHNSON, C.S.

Bain, R. Review of C.S. Johnson, Growing up in the black belt: Negro youth in the rural South. ASR 6:424-6, June 1941.

Cason, C.E. Review of C.S. Johnson, et al., The Negro in American civilization. VQR 6:594-600, Oct. 1930.

Roucek, J.S. Review of C.S. Johnson, Growing up in the black belt: Negro youth in the rural South. SOS 32: 284, Oct. 1941.

Johnson, G.B. Review of O.C. Cox, Caste, class and race: A study in social dynamics. VQR 24:455-9, Summer 1948.

Johnson, G.B. Review of M.J. Herskovits, The myth of the Negro past. ASR 7:289-90, Apr. 1942.

Johnson, G.B. See also ODUM, H.W.

JOHNSON, J.E.

Dexter, R.C. Review of J.E. Johnson, comp., The Negro problem. JIR 12:587-9, Apr. 1922.

Johnson, J.W. Negro in war-time. PUB 21:1218-9, Sept. 21, 1918.

Johnson, S.A. The Emigrant Aid Company in Kansas. KHQ 1: 429-41, Nov. 1932.

Johnson, S.A. The Emigrant Aid Company in the Kansas conflict. KHQ 6:21-33, Feb. 1937.

Johnson, W.H. Lincoln University, the pioneer institution in the world for the education of the Negro. PBY 14:142-3, Sept. 1930.

JONES, EDMUND W.

Ewing, C.A.M. Two Reconstruction impeachments. NCH 15: 204-30, July 1938.

Jones, L. Negro consciousness and democracy. PUB 15:820-2, Aug. 30, 1912.

Jones, M.A. The Negro and the South. VQR 3:1-12, Jan. 1927.

Jordan, P.D. Rev. William Salter and the slavery controversy, 1837-64. IAJ 33:99-122, Apr. 1935.

Jordan, W.T., ed. A system of operation of Beaver Bend plantation, Georgia, 1862. JSH 7:76-84, Feb. 1941.

JORDAN, W.T.

Flanders, R.B. Review of W.T. Jordan, Hugh Davis and his Alabama plantation. JSH 15:112-3, Feb. 1949.

Weaver, H. Review of W.T. Jordan, Hugh Davis and his Alabama plantation. MVH 35:686, Mar. 1949.

JUDGMENTS

Seeman, M. Moral judgment: A study in racial frames of reference. ASR 12:404-11, Aug. 1947.

JUDICIARY

Zornow, William F. Judicial modifications of the Maryland black code in the District of Columbia. MDH 44:18-32, Mar. 1949.

JULIAN, GEORGE W.

Clarke, Grace J. Anti-slavery letter of Daniel Worth to George W. Julian, and other documents. INM 26:152-7, June 1930.

KANSAS

Barry, Louise. The Emigrant Aid Company parties of 1854-5. KHQ 12:115-55, May 1943 and following issue.

Brown, S. John Brown and sons in Kansas territory. INM 31:142-50, June 1935.

Connelley, W.E., and A. Morrall. Proslavery activity in Kansas. KAN 14:123-42, 1915-8.

Fleming, W.L. Kansas territory and the Buford expedition of 1856. AHS 4:167-92, 1904.

Gibbons, V.E., ed. Letters on the war in Kansas in 1856. KHQ 10:369-79, Nov. 1941.

Harlow, R.V. Rise and fall of emigrant aid movement in Kansas. AHR 41:1-25, Oct. 1935.

Harmon, G.D. Buchanan's attitude toward the admission of Kansas on the slavery question. PAM 53:51-91, Jan. 1929.

Hoole, W.S., ed. A Southerner's viewpoint of the Kansas situation, 1856-7. KHQ 3:43-68, Feb. 1934 and following issue.

Johnson, S.A. The Emigrant Aid Company in Kansas. KHQ 1:429-41, Nov. 1932.

Johnson, S.A. The Emigrant Aid Company in the Kansas conflict. KHQ 6:21-33, Feb. 1937.

The Kansas fight against slavery. KAN 10:120-48+, 1908.

Langsdorf, Edgar. Samuel Clarke Pomeroy and the New England Emigrant Aid Company, 1854-8. KHQ 7:227-45, Aug. 1938 and following issue.

Lyman, W.A. Jayhawkers--origin of name and activity. KAN 14:203-7, 1915-8.

Lynch, W.O. Colonization of Kansas, 1854-1860. MIV 9: 380-2, 1919.

Malin, J.C. The proslavery background of the Kansas struggle. MVH 10:285-305, Dec. 1923.

Moody, Joel. Marais des Cygnes massacre. KAN 14:208-23, 1915-8.

Pantle, Alberta, ed. Larry Lapsley, 1840-97. Story of a Kansas freedman. KHQ 11:341-69, Nov. 1942.

Tannar, A.H. Marais des Cygnes massacre and rescue of Ben Rice. KAN 14:224-34, 1915-8.

Waters, J.G. Kansas and the Wyandotte convention. KAN 11:47-52, 1910.

Yost, Genevieve. History of lynchings in Kansas. KHQ 2: 182-219, May 1933.

KANSAS, LAWRENCE

Eastin, L.J. Notes on a proslavery march against Lawrence, Kan. KHQ 11:45-64, Feb. 1942.

KANSAS, OSAWATMIE

Celebration of John Brown's day. AME 5:980, Sept.-Oct. 1910.

KANSAS, POTTAWATOMIE

Malin, J.C. Identification of the stranger at the Pottawatomie massacre. KHQ 9:3-12, Feb. 1940.

KANSAS-NEBRASKA BILL

Hodder, F.H. Genesis of Kansas-Nebraska act. WHP 60: 69-86, 1913.

Klem, Mary J. The Kansas-Nebraska slavery bill and Missouri's part in the conflict. MIV 9:393-413, 1919.

Osborne, D.F. The sectional struggle over rights of slavery in new territory added to U.S. GHQ 15:223-51, Sept. 1931.

Parks, J.H. The Tennessee Whigs and the Kansas-Nebraska bill, 1854. JSH 10:308-30, Aug. 1944.

Karlin, J.A. New Orleans lynchings of 1891 and the American press. LHQ 24:187-204, Jan. 1941.

Kaufmann, M. A little bit prejudiced. COM 6:372-3, Oct. 1948.

Keasbey, A.Q. Slavery in New Jersey. NJS 3d s. 4:90-6, Jan.-Apr. 1907 and following issues.

Keith, E. Jean. Joseph Rogers Underwood of Kentucky and the American Colonization Society for the free people of color. HIS 22:117-32, Apr. 1938.

KELLOGG, WILLIAM PITT

Gonzales, J.E. William Pitt Kellogg, Reconstruction governor of Louisiana, 1873-77. LHQ 29:394-495, Apr. 1946.

Kemmerer, D.L. The suffrage franchise in colonial New Jersey. NJS 52:166-73, July 1934.

Kendall, J.S. Negro minstrels of New Orleans. LHQ 30:128-48, Jan. 1947.

Kendall, J.S. Slavery in New Orleans. LHQ 23:864-86, July 1940.

Kendall, J.S. Treatment of slaves in Louisiana. LHQ 22:142-65, Jan. 1939.

Kendall, L.C. John McDonogh, his scheme for the liberation of his slaves and their exportation to Liberia. LHQ 15: 646-54, Oct. 1932 and following issue.

Kendel, Julia. Reconstruction in Lafayette County. MSS 13: 223-72, 1913.

KENNEDY, LOUISE V.

Cason, C.E. Review of Louise V. Kennedy, The Negro peasant turns cityward. VQR 6:594-600, Oct. 1930.

Kennedy, Stetson. Nanigo in Florida. SFQ 4:153-6, Sept. 1940.

KENTUCKY

Clark, T.D. Slave trade between Kentucky and the cotton kingdom. MVH 21:331-42, Dec. 1934.

Eaton, C., ed. Minutes and resolutions of a Kentucky emancipation meeting in 1849. JSH 14:511-5, Nov. 1948.

Gregory, J.P., Jr. The question of slavery in the Kentucky constitutional convention of 1849. HIS 23:89-110, Apr. 1949.

Harrison, L. Cassius M. Clay's anti-slavery newspaper, the "True American": Opposition in Kentucky to his struggle for emancipation of the Negro. HIS 22:30-49, Jan. 1948.

Keith, E. Jean. Joseph Rogers Underwood of Kentucky and the American Colonization Society for the free people of color. HIS 22:117-32, Apr. 1938.

Wick, B.L. Delia Webster--her part in the underground railroad movement in Iowa. ANN 3d s. 18:228-31, Jan. 1932.

KENTUCKY, LEXINGTON

Coleman, J.W., Jr. Lexington, Ky., slave dealers and their Southern trade. HIS 21:1-23, Jan. 1938.

KENTUCKY, LOUISVILLE

Holzknecht, K.J. Negro song variants from Louisville. JAF 41:558-78, Oct.-Dec. 1928.

Kephart, W.M. Is the American Negro becoming lighter? An analysis of the sociological and biological trends. ASR 13:437-43, Aug. 1948.
Comment by J.T. Blue, Jr., ASR 13:766-7, Dec. 1948.

KESSELMAN, L.C.

Truman, D.B. Review of L.C. Kesselman, The social politics of FEPC; a study in reform pressure movements. APS 43:377-8, Apr. 1949.

KETRING, RUTH A.

Lynch, Bertha T. Review of Ruth A. Ketring, Charles Osburn in the anti-slavery movement. INM 33:78-9, Mar. 1937.

King, Emma. Some aspects of the work of the Society of Friends for Negro education in North Carolina. NCH 1: 403-11, Oct. 1924.

King, Ethel. The New York Negro plot of 1741. USC 20:173-80, 1931.

King, J.F. Evolution of the free slave trade principle in Spanish colonial administration. HAH 22:34-56, Feb. 1942.

King, J.F. The Negro in continental Spanish America: A select bibliography. HAH 24:547-58, Aug. 1944.

King, J.F. The suppression of the slave trade in the Latin American republics. HAH 24:387-411, Aug. 1944.

KING, THOMAS STARR

How Thomas Starr King saved California to the Union during the slavery discussion. CAL 3:10-5, Oct.-Nov. 1929.

Kirgan, Sadie E. Tales the darkies tell of ghosts that walk in Freestone County, Texas. TEX 5:385-91, May 1930.

Kirke, D.B. Bush Negroes of Dutch Guiana. CHA 7th s. 15: 549-52, Aug. 1, 1925.

Klem, Mary J. The Kansas-Nebraska slavery bill and Missouri's part in the conflict. MIV 9:393-413, 1919.

Klement, F. Review of J.W. DeForest, A Union officer in the Reconstruction. WIM 32:225-6, Dec. 1948.

KLINEBERG, O.

Farnsworth, P.R. Review of O. Klineberg, Characteristics of the American Negro. ASR 9:589-90, Oct. 1944.

Klingberg, F.J. Missionary activity of the S.P.G. among the African immigrants of colonial Pennsylvania and Delaware. PEH 11:126-53, June 1942.

Klingberg, F.J. Review of Herbert Aptheker, Essays in the history of the American Negro. JSH 12:280-1, May 1946.

Klingberg, F.J. Review of E.M. Coleman, ed., Creole Voices: Poems in French by free men of color. PEH 12:396-8, Dec. 1943.

Klingberg, F.J. Review of E. Conrad, Harriet Tubman: Story of a Maryland slave. PEH 12:396-7, Dec. 1943.

Klingberg, F.J. The Society for the Propagation of the Gospel program for Negroes in colonial New York. PEH 8:306-71, Dec. 1939.

Klingberg, F.J. See also ABEL, ANNIE HELOISE

Klingberg, F.W. Operation Reconstruction: A report on Southern unionist planters. NCH 25:466-84, Oct. 1948.

Knabenshue, S.S. The underground railroad. OAQ 14:396-403, Oct. 1905.

Knight, E.W. Notes on career of John Chavis, Negro Presbyterian preacher and teacher, 1763(?)- , as a teacher of Southern white children and of his ministry. NCH 7: 326-45, July 1930.

Knopland, P. Review of Louis Adamic, A nation of nations. WIM 29:457-60, June 1946.

Knox, Winifred. American Negro poetry. BKL 81:16-7, Oct. 1931.

Koch, F.J. Marking the old "abolition holes" at Ripley. OAQ 22:308-18, Apr. 1913.

Koenig, S. Review of A.M. Rose and Carolyn Rose, America divided: Minority group relations in the U.S. ASR 14: 435-7, June 1949.

Koontz, L.K. Review of Carey McWilliams, Brothers under the skin. PHR 12:418-9, Dec. 1943.

Kraus, M. Slavery reform in the 18th century. PAM 60:53-66, Jan. 1936.

KU KLUX KLAN

Activities of the Ku Klux Klan in Saskatchewan. QUE 35: 592-609, Autumn 1928.

Alexander, T.B. Kukluxism in Tennessee, 1865-69: A technique for the overthrow of radical Reconstruction. THQ 8:195-219, Sept. 1949.

Bradley, P. Psycho-analyzing the Ku Klux Klan. AMR 2: 683-6, Nov.-Dec. 1924.

Duffus, R.L. Salesmen of hate. WWL 42:461-9, Oct. 1923 and following issue.

Ku Klux Klans of the Reconstruction period in Missouri. MOH 37:441-50, July 1943.

McNeilly, J.S. Enforcement act of 1871 and Ku Klux Klan in Mississippi. MSS 9:109-71, 1906.

Mecklin, J.M. Ku Klux Klan and the democratic tradition. AMR 2:241-51, May-June 1924.

Weir, Sally R. Reminiscences of the Ku Klux Klan. MET 26:97-106, Apr. 1907.

Kull, I.S. Slavery in New Jersey. AME 24:443-72, Oct. 1930.

KUNERS, JOHN

McMillan, D. Story of John Kuners. JAF 39:53-7, Jan.-Mar. 1926.

Kyle, J.W. Reconstruction in Panola Co. MSS 19:9-98, 1913.

Laack, J.A. Biographical sketch of Jonathan Walker. WIM 32:312-20, Mar. 1949.

LABOR

Carmichael, Maude. Federal experiments with Negro labor on abandoned plantations in Arkansas. ARK 1:101-16, June 1942.

Haynes, George E. Effect of war conditions on Negro labor. ACA s. 8:299-312, Feb. 1919.

Herron, Stella. The African apprentice bill, 1858. MIV 8:135-45, 1914-5.

Morris, R.B. White bondage and compulsory labor in ante-bellum South Carolina. SOC 49:191-207, Oct. 1948.

Phillips, U.B. Plantations with slave labor and free. AHR 30:738-53, July 1925.

Sitterson, J.C. Hired labor on sugar plantations of the ante-bellum South. JSH 14:192-205, May 1948.

Spraggins, T.L. Mobilization of Negro labor for the Department of Virginia and North Carolina, 1861-5. NCH 24:160-97, Apr. 1947.

Trexler, H.A. The opposition of planters to employment of slaves as laborers by the Confederacy. MVH 27:211-24, Sept. 1940.

Woody, R.H. The labor and immigration problems of South Carolina during the Reconstruction period. MVH 18: 195-212, Sept. 1931.

LAFFAN, SIR JOSEPH de COURCY

Cocke, R.H. Sir Joseph de Courcy Laffan's views on slavery. WMQ 2d s. 19:42-8, Jan. 1939.

Lamott, W.C. Review of Buell Gallagher, Portrait of a pilgrim: A search for the Christian way in race relations. IRM 36:105-6, Jan. 1947.

Land, Mary. John Brown's Ohio environment. OAQ 57:24-47, Jan. 1948.

LAND

Smith, A.E. The indentured servant and land speculation in 17th century Maryland. AHR 40:467-72, Apr. 1935.

LAND MONOPOLY

Danziger, S. Segregation and land monopoly. PUB 19: 891-2, Sept. 22, 1916.

LANDLORDS

Tenant farms and landlords. PRS 25:801-8, June 1911.

Landon, F. Anthony Burns in Canada. OHS 22:162-6, 1925.

Landon, F. Canada's part in freeing the slaves. OHS 17: 74-84, 1919.

Landon, F. The Canadian anti-slavery group before the Civil War. UNI 17:540-7, Dec. 1918.

Landon, F. The fugitive slave in Canada before the American Civil War. UNI 18:270-9, Apr. 1919.

Landon, F. Negro colonization schemes in Upper Canada before 1860. RSC 3d s. 23:73+, sec. 2, May 1929.

Landon, F. Refugee Negroes from the United States in Ontario. DAL 5:523-31, Jan. 1926.

Landon, F. Review of Annie Heloise Abel and F.J. Klingberg, eds., A side-light on Anglo-American relations, 1839-58. CAN 9:72-3, Mar. 1928.

Landon, F. Social conditions among the Negroes in Upper Canada before 1865. OHS 22:144-61, 1925.

Landon, F. The work of the American Missionary Association among the Negro refugees in Canada West, 1848-64. OHS 21:198-205, 1924.

LANDOWNERS

Riggs, J.B. Early Maryland landowners in the vicinity of Washington. CHS 48:249-63, 1949.

LANDOWNERSHIP

Coles, H.L., Jr. Slaveownership and landownership in Louisiana, 1850-1860. JSH 9:381-94, Aug. 1943.

Langsdorf, Edgar. Samuel Clarke Pomeroy and the New England Emigrant Aid Company, 1854-8. KHQ 7:227-45, Aug. 1938 and following issue.

LANGUAGE

Taylor, G. Evolution and distribution of race, culture and language. GEO 11:54-119, Jan. 1921.

LAPSLEY, LARRY

Pantle, Alberta, ed. Larry Lapsley, 1840-97. Story of a Kansas freedman. KHQ 11:341-69, Nov. 1942.

Lash, J.S. The American Negro and American literature: A check list of significant commentaries. BUB 19:33-6, Jan.-Apr. 1947 and previous issue.

LATIN AMERICA. See also SOUTH AMERICA, SPANISH AMERICA

King, J.F. The suppression of the slave trade in the Latin American republics. HAH 24:387-411, Aug. 1944.

Laughlin, C.J. Plantation architecture in Louisiana. MAR 41:210-3, Oct. 1948.

Lawrence, J.B. Religious education of Negroes in the colony of Georgia. GHQ 14:41-57, Mar. 1930.

LAWRENCE, JACOB

Jacob Lawrence, his pictures of the South-to-North migration of Negroes that began during the First World War. FOR 24:102-9, Nov. 1941.

McCausland, Elizabeth. Jacob Lawrence, the man and his work. MAR 38:251-4, Nov. 1945.

LAWS

Folmsbee, Stanley J. The origin of the first "Jim Crow" law. JSH 15:235-47, May 1949.

Henry, H.M. Tennessee slave laws. THM 2:175-203, Sept. 1916.

McLoughlin, James J. The black code. LHS 8:28-35, 1916; MIV 8:210-6, 1914-5.

Stephenson, G.T. Racial distinctions in Southern law. APS 1:44-61, Nov. 1906.

Swann, T.W. Jim Crow laws threatened in Illinois. PUB 16:246, Mar. 14, 1913.

Violette, E.M. Black code in Missouri. MIV 6:287-316, 1913.

Walter, D.O. Proposals for a federal anti-lynching law. APS 28:436-42, June 1934.

Zornow, William F. Judicial modifications of the Maryland black code in the District of Columbia. MDH 44:18-32, Mar. 1949.

Lawson, Holda J. The Negro in American drama: Bibliography. BUB 17:7-8, Jan.-Apr. 1940 and following issue.

LAWSUITS

Suit for damages for personal injuries to a slave, 1764. LHQ 5:58-62, Jan. 1922.

Leach, Marguerite. The aftermath of Reconstruction in Louisiana. LHQ 32:631-717, July 1949.

LEAGUE OF NATIONS

DuBois, W.E.B. Liberia, the League and the United States. FOR 11:682-95, July 1933.

Leak, R.R. Underground railroad in Hendricks Co., Indiana. INM 36:17-22, Mar. 1940.

Learned, H.B. Reaction of Philip Phillips to the repeal of the Missouri Compromise. MVH 8:303-17, Mar. 1922.

LEASES

Prichard, W., ed. Lease of a Louisiana plantation and slaves. LHQ 21:995-7, Oct. 1938.

Leckie, J.D. Slavery in Mohammedan countries. CHA 7th s. 15:276-7, Apr. 4, 1925.

Lee, A. McC. Review of G. Watson, Action for unity. COM 3: 497-8, May 1947.

Lee, L.L. Role and status of the Negro in the Hawaiian community. ASR 13:419-37, Aug. 1948.

Lee, T.Z. Chief Justice Taney and the Dred Scott decision. AIR 22:142-4, 1923.

Lees, G.F. Ras Tafari and his people. WDT 44:121-9, July 1924.

Leftwich, G.J. Reconstruction in Monroe Co. MSS 9:53-84, 1906.

LEGAL STATUS

Bates, Thelma. The legal status of the Negro in Florida. FHS 6:159-81, Jan. 1928.

Trieber, J. Legal status of Negroes in Arkansas before the Civil War. ARA 3:175-83, 1911.

LEGENDS

Taylor, Helen L., ed. Negro beliefs and place legends from New Castle, Del. JAF 51:92-4, Jan.-Mar. 1938.

LEGISLATION

Randall, J.G. Part played by Sen. John Sherman in financial legislation during Reconstruction. MVH 19: 382-93, Dec. 1932.

Rogers, W.M. Free Negro legislation in Georgia before 1865. GHQ 16:27-37, Mar. 1932.

LE JAU, REV. FRANCIS

Pennington, E.L. Work of Rev. Francis Le Jau in colonial South Carolina among Indians and Negro slaves. JSH 1: 442-58, Nov. 1935.

LEMEN, JAMES

Lemen, Joseph B. The Jefferson-Lemen anti-slavery pact. IHL 13:74-84, 1908.

Lemen, Joseph B. The Jefferson-Lemen anti-slavery pact. IHL 13:74-84, 1908.

Lepage, P.C. Arts and crafts of Negroes. INT 78:577-80, Mar. 1924.

Lerche, C.O., Jr. Congressional interpretation of the guarantee of a republican form of government during Reconstruction. JSH 15:192-211, May 1949.

Lescohier, D.D. Causes of race prejudice and possible solutions of the problem. AMR 4:495-506, Dec. 1926.

Leslie, W.R. The constitutional significance of Indiana's statute of 1824 on fugitives from labor. JSH 13:338-53, Aug. 1947.

Lestage, H.O., Jr. The White League in Louisiana and its participation in Reconstruction riots, 1866-74. LHQ 18:617-95, July 1935.

LETTERS

Coleman, C.H. Three Vallandigham letters, 1865. OAQ 43: 461-4, Oct. 1934.

Letter from John Brown on the wool trade, 1849. MAG 16: 36-8, Jan. 1913.

Letter from Secretary of State concerning John Brown. MAG 20:184, Mar.-Apr. 1915.

Letter regarding Negro criminal. PUB 14:843-4, Aug. 18, 1911.

Letters of John Brown. VAM 9:385-94, April 1902 and following issues.

Letters of S.P. Chase, Henry Clay, Henry George. INM 7: 123-32, Sept. 1911.

Letters pertaining to economic and social life of plantations in 1833-36. GHQ 14:150-73, June 1930.

Letters to Dr. William E. Channing on slavery and the annexation of Texas. NEQ 5:587-601, July 1932.

Marshall, Ruth. Duane Mowry, ed. Property in Negroes: A Southern slaveholding woman's plea to Sen. J.R. Doolittle. AME 8:530-2, June 1913.

Nebbit, L. Letter of a colored child of the Sacred Heart. AMC 24:179-81, June 1913.

Padgett, J.A., ed. Letters from North Carolina--Reconstruction period. NCH 20:259-82, July 1943, previous and following issues.

Padgett, J.A., ed. Letters to Thaddeus Stevens regarding Reconstruction. NCH 18:171-95, Apr. 1941 and following issues.

Rothert, O.A. Two letters by Cassius Clay, 1862 and 1869. HIS 12:162-9, July 1938.

Stone, Lucie P., ed. Letter written in 1844 regarding slavery by a member of the Society of Friends. JAH 6: 613-5, July-Sept. 1912.

Stutler, B.B. The "originals" of John Brown's letter to the Rev. Luther Humphrey. WVA 9:1-25, Oct. 1947.

Thurston, Mrs. C.B. Letter of 1859. News of the John Brown raid on Harper's Ferry. MDH 39:162-3, June 1944.

Whittington, G.P., ed. Facts concerning the loyalty of slaves in Northern Louisiana in 1863 as shown in the letters of J.H. Ransdell to Gov. T.O. Moore. LHQ 14: 487-502, Oct. 1931.

Levi, Kate E. The Wisconsin press and slavery. WIM 9:423-34, July 1926.

Lewinson, P. Review of John Dollard, Class and caste in a Southern town. AHR 43:428-9, Jan. 1938.

Lewis, A.N. Amistad slave case, 1840. CNT 11:125-8, Jan. 1907.

Lewonson, P. Review of W.E.B. DuBois, Black folk then and now. MVH 26:580-1, Mar. 1940.

Leys, N. Review of L. Stoddard, Rising tide of color against white supremacy. IRM 10:566-8, Oct. 1921.

LIBERIA

Buell, R.L. Conditions of slavery in Liberia. VQR 7: 161-71, Apr. 1931.

DuBois, W.E.B. Liberia, the League and the United States. FOR 11:682-95, July 1933.

Fisher, H.P. The Catholic Church in Liberia. AMC 40: 249-310, Sept. 1929.

Goodwin, Mary F. Liberia--America's only foreign colonial settlement. VAM 55:338+, Oct. 1947.

Kendall, L.C. John McDonogh, his scheme for the liberation of his slaves and their exportation to Liberia. LHQ 15:646-54, Oct. 1932 and following issue.

Parson, A.B. Beginnings of the Episcopal Church ministry in Liberia. PEH 7:154-77, June 1938.

Shunk, E.W. "Ohio in Africa," a plan for a colony of Ohio free-Negro emigrants in Liberia, c. 1850. OAQ 51: 70-87, Apr.-June 1942.

Simpson, Lucretia C. Henry Clay and Liberia. JAH 16: 237-45, July-Sept. 1922.

LIBERTY

Crane, V.W. Benjamin Franklin on slavery and American liberties. PAM 62:1-11, Jan. 1938.

"LIBERTY MINSTREL"

Hopkins, Geraldine. Editions of the "Liberty Minstrel," a rare abolitionist document. MVH 18:60-4, June 1931.

LIBERTY PARTY

Rayback, J.G. The Liberty party leaders of Ohio: Exponents of anti-slavery coalition. OAQ 57:165-78, Apr. 1948.

LIBRARIANS

Bogle, Sarah C.N. Training for Negro librarians. ALA 25:133, Apr. 1931.

Phillips, Edna. A plan for cooperation between evening school teachers and librarians in the educational development of racial groups. ALA 26:29-30, Jan. 1932.

LIBRARIES

The colored library, Knoxville, Tenn. PLY 24:5-8, Jan. 1919.

Mulhauser, R. Library services to Negroes. BUB 13:155-7, Jan.-Apr. 1929 and following issue.

Work with Negroes. ALA 17:274-9, July 1923.

LIEBER, FRANCIS

Freidel, F. Francis Lieber, Charles Sumner, and slavery. JSH 9:75-93, Feb. 1943.

LIFE SPAN

Sydnor, C.S. Life span of Mississippi slaves. AHR 35:566-74, Apr. 1930.

Lilly, E.P. Review of Madeleine H. Rice, American Catholic opinions in the slavery controversy. MVH 31:294-6, Sept. 1944.

Linaker, R.H. A silver slave brand. CON 69:161-4, July 1924.

LINCOLN, ABRAHAM

Andrews, Rena M. Andrew Johnson, his plan of restoration of the South to the Union in relation to that of Lincoln. THM n.s. 1:165-81, Apr. 1931.

Cole, A.C. Lincoln's election an immediate menace to slavery in the states? AHR 36:740-67, July 1931.

Hamilton, J.G. DeR. Lincoln's election an immediate menace to slavery in the states. AHR 37:700-11, July 1932.

Young, J.H. Anna Elizabeth Dickinson--her campaign during the Civil War period for and against Lincoln. MVH 31:59-80, June 1944.

LINCOLN UNIVERSITY

Johnson, W.H. Lincoln University, the pioneer institution in the world for the education of the Negro. PBY 14: 142-3, Sept. 1930.

Lindsay, P. Review of L. Erlich, God's angry man. BKL 85: 240-1, Dec. 1933.

Link, A.S., ed. The Progressive party's lily-white policy in 1912: Correspondence between Theodore Roosevelt and Julian Harris. JSH 10:480-90, Nov. 1944.

Linwood, F. Review of Robert E. Speer, Race and race relations. IRM 14:285-7, Apr. 1925.

LIPPINCOTT, REV. THOMAS

Correspondence of Gov. Edward Coles with Rev. Thomas Lippincott. IHJ 3:59-63, Jan. 1911.

Lissfelt, Mildred B. Review of E.M. Coulter, The South during Reconstruction. SOS 39:133-4, Mar. 1948.

Lissfelt, Mildred B. Review of J.H. Franklin, From slavery to freedom. SOS 39:134, Mar. 1948.

LITERATURE

Herring, R. Black pastures. LON 22:239-49, July 1930.

Knox, Winifred. American Negro poetry. BKL 81:16-7, Oct. 1931.

Lash, J.S. The American Negro and American literature: A check list of significant commentaries. BUB 19:33-6, Jan.-Apr. 1947 and previous issue.

Park, R.E. Negro race consciousness as reflected in race literature. AMR 1:505-17, Sept.-Oct. 1923.

Simms, H.H. Abolition literature, 1830-40, a critical analysis. JSH 6:368-82, Aug. 1940.

Webb, J.W. Irwin Russell and Negro folk literature. SFQ 12:137-49, June 1948.

LLOYD, A.Y.

Sydnor, C.S. Review of A.Y. Lloyd, The slavery controversy, 1831-60. NCH 17:278-80, July 1940.

Locke, Alain. The American Negro as artist. AMA 23:210-30, Sept. 1931.

Locke, Alain. Exhibition of African art at Museum of Modern Art. AMA 28:270-8, May 1935.

Lockley, Frederick. Oregon slavery documentary records. ORE 17:107-15, June 1916.

Lockspeiser, E. Gobineau's friendship with Richard Wagner and the new racial cult. WOR 57-9, Feb. 1941.

Logan, R.W. Review of F. Tannenbaum, Slave and citizen: The Negro in the Americas. HAH 27:665-6, Nov. 1947.

Lombard, Mildred E., ed. Contemporary opinions of Georgia. A journal of life on a slave-holding plantation. GHQ 14: 335-43, Dec. 1930.

Longini, Muriel D. Folk-songs of Chicago Negroes. JAF 52: 96-111, Jan.-Mar. 1939.

Lonn, Ella. Review of Benjamin Quarles, Frederick Douglass. AHR 54:156-7, Oct. 1948.

Lorain, C.T. Review of W.E.B. DuBois, Black folk then and now. AHR 46:95-6, Oct. 1940.

LOUISIANA

Coles, H.L., Jr. Slaveownership and landownership in Louisiana, 1850-1860. JSH 9:381-94, Aug. 1943.

Engelsman, J.C. Work of the Freedman's Bureau in Louisiana. LHQ 32:145-224, Jan. 1949.

Fauset, A.H. Folk-tales from Alabama, Mississippi, and Louisiana. JAF 40:214-303, June-Sept. 1927.

Gonzales, J.E. William Pitt Kellogg, Reconstruction governor of Louisiana, 1873-77. LHQ 29:394-495, Apr. 1946.

Grosz, Agnes S. P.B.S. Pinchback: His political career in Louisiana. LHQ 27:527-612, Apr. 1944.

Harris, F.B. Reconstruction period: The Career of Henry Clay Warmoth, governor. LHQ 30:523-653, Apr. 1947.

Herron, Stella. The African apprentice bill, 1858. MIV 8:135-45, 1914-5.

Highsmith, W.E. Some aspects of Reconstruction. JSH 13: 460-91, Nov. 1947.

Kendall, J.S. Treatment of slaves in Louisiana. LHQ 22: 142-65, Jan. 1939.

Laughlin, C.J. Plantation architecture in Louisiana. MAR 41:210-3, Oct. 1948.

Leach, Marguerite. The aftermath of Reconstruction in Louisiana. LHQ 32:631-717, July 1949.

Lestage, H.O., Jr. The White League in Louisiana and its participation in Reconstruction riots, 1866-74. LHQ 18:617-95, July 1935.

McDaniel, Hilda M. Francis T. Nicholls and the end of Reconstruction. LHQ 32:357-513, Apr. 1949.

McLoughlin, James J. The black code. LHS 8:28-35, 1916; MIV 8:210-6, 1914-5.

Mabry, W.A. Louisiana politics and the "grandfather clause." NCH 13:290-310, Oct. 1936.

Moody, V.A. Slavery on Louisiana sugar plantations. LHQ 7:191-303, Apr. 1924.

Porter, Betty. The history of Negro education in Louisiana. LHQ 25:728-831, July 1942.

Prichard, W. A Louisiana sugar plantation under the slavery regime. MVH 14:168-78, Sept. 1927.

Prichard, W., ed. Lease of a Louisiana plantation and slaves. LHQ 21:995-7, Oct. 1938.

Rice, Eliza G. Louisiana planters' plea for self-government of slaves, 1849. JAH 3:621-6, Oct.-Dec. 1909.

Russ, W.A., Jr. Disfranchisement in Louisiana, 1862-70. LHQ 18:557-80, July 1935.

Sanders, A.G., tr. H.P. Dart, ed. Documents covering the beginning of the African slave trade in Louisiana, 1718. LHQ 14:103-77, Apr. 1931.

Schuler, Kathryn R. Women in public affairs during Reconstruction. LHQ 19:668-750, July 1936.

LOUISIANA (cont'd)

Seale, Lee, and Marianna Seale. A Louisiana Negro ceremony: Easter Rock. JAF 55:212-8, Oct.-Dec. 1942.

Shugg, R.W. A Louisiana co-operationist protest against secession. LHQ 19:199-203, Jan. 1936.

Sitterson, J.C. The William J. Minor plantations: A study in ante-bellum absentee ownership. JSH 9:59-74, Feb. 1943.

White, Alice P. The plantation experience of Joseph and Lavinia Erwin, 1807-36: Records and papers. LHQ 27: 343-478, Apr. 1944.

White, M.J. Louisiana and the secession movement of the early fifties. MIV 8:278-88, 1916.

Whittington, G.P., ed. Facts concerning the loyalty of slaves in Northern Louisiana in 1863 as shown in the letters of J.H. Ransdell to Gov. T.O. Moore. LHQ 14: 487-502, Oct. 1931.

Williams, T.H. Unification movement: Its influence on Louisiana's Reconstruction history. JSH 11:349-69, Aug. 1945.

LOUISIANA, DONALDSONVILLE

Durel, L.C. Donaldsonville, La., Creole civilization, 1850, according to the newspaper "Le Vigilant." LHQ 31:981-94, Oct. 1948.

LOUISIANA, NEW ORLEANS

Copeland, F. The New Orleans press and the Reconstruction. LHQ 30:149-337, Jan. 1947.

Karlin, J.A. New Orleans lynchings of 1891 and the American press. LHQ 24:187-204, Jan. 1941.

Kendall, J.S. Negro minstrels of New Orleans. LHQ 30: 128-48, Jan. 1947.

Kendall, J.S. Slavery in New Orleans. LHQ 23:864-86, July 1940.

Negro businessmen of New Orleans. FTE 40:112+, Nov. 1949.

Perkins, A.E., comp. Riddles from Negro school children in New Orleans, La. JAF 35:105-15, Apr.-June 1922.

Simms, Marion. Black magic in New Orleans yesterday and today. TRA 81:18-9, July 1943.

Slave auction, New Orleans. HTM 3:188, Oct. 1912.

L'OUVERTURE, TOUSSAINT

Graham, H. Toussaint L'Ouverture, the Napoleon of San Domingo. DUB 153:86-110, July 1913.

LOVEJOY, REV. ELIJAH P.

Brown, J.N. Lovejoy's influence on John Brown. MAG 23: 97-102, Sept.-Oct. 1916.

Official report of the killing of Rev. Elijah P. Lovejoy. IHJ 4:499-503, Jan. 1912.

LOYALTY

Whittington, G.P., ed. Facts concerning the loyalty of slaves in Northern Louisiana in 1863 as shown in the letters of J.H. Ransdell to Gov. T.O. Moore. LHQ 14: 487-502, Oct. 1931.

Lyman, W.A. Jayhawkers--origin of name and activity. KAN 14: 203-7, 1915-8.

Lynch, Bertha T. Review of Ruth A. Ketring, Charles Osburn in the anti-slavery movement. INM 33:78-9, Mar. 1937.

Lynch, W.O. Antislavery tendencies of the Democratic party in the Northwest, 1848-50. MVH 11:319-31, Dec. 1924.

Lynch, W.O. Colonization of Kansas, 1854-1860. MIV 9:380-2, 1919.

LYNCHING

Black, P.W. Lynching in Iowa. IAJ 10:151-254, Apr. 1912.

Bloom, L.B., ed. Lt. John Bourke's description of a lynching in Tucson, N.M., in 1873. NMH 19:233-42, July 1944 and following issue.

Cooley, S. Civic backsliding. PUB 18:753-4, Aug. 6, 1915.

Karlin, J.A. New Orleans lynchings of 1891 and the American press. LHQ 24:187-204, Jan. 1941.

Lynching without "error of law." PUB 20:956, Oct. 5, 1917.

Milton, G.F. The impeachment of lynching. VQR 8:247-56, Apr. 1932.

LYNCHING (cont'd)

Walter, D.O. Proposals for a federal anti-lynching law. APS 28:436-42, June 1934.

Yost, Genevieve. History of lynchings in Kansas. KHQ 2: 182-219, May 1933.

LYON, REV. JAMES A.

Bettersworth, J.K., ed. Mississippi unionism: The case of Mr. Lyon. JMH 1:37-52, Jan. 1939.

Lyons, John F. Attitude of Presbyterians in Ohio, Indiana and Illinois toward slavery. PBY 11:69-82, June 1921.

McCain, W.D. See Hamilton, W.B.

McCain, William D. The emancipation of Indiana Osborne. JMH 8:97-8, Apr. 1946.

McCarron, Anna T. Prudence Crandall's trial. CNT 12:225-32, Apr.-June 1908.

McCausland, Elizabeth. Jacob Lawrence, the man and his work. MAR 38:251-4, Nov. 1945.

McClendon, R. Earl. Status of the ex-Confederate states as seen in the readmission of U.S. Senators. AHR 41:702-9, July 1936.

McCormac, E.I., and R.R. Stenberg. The Dred Scott case, 1857. MVH 19:565-77, Mar. 1933.

McCormick, T.C., and R.A. Hornseth. The Negro in Madison, Wisconsin. ASR 12:519-25, Oct. 1947.

McDaniel, Hilda M. Francis T. Nicholls and the end of Reconstruction. LHQ 32:357-513, Apr. 1949.

McDonald, Capt. "Bill." See Paine, A.B.

McDonald, E.E. Disposal of Negro slaves by will in Knox Co., Indiana. INM 26:143-6, June 1930.

McDonald, E.E. The Negro in Indiana before 1881. INM 27: 291-306, Dec. 1931.

MCDONOGH, JOHN

Kendall, L.C. John McDonogh, his scheme for the liberation of his slaves and their exportation to Liberia. LHQ 15:646-54, Oct. 1932 and following issue.

McDowell, Tremaine. Webster's words on abolitionists. NEQ 7:315, June 1934.

McElfresh, Mona H. President's Committee on Civil Rights. ALA 42:74-5, Feb. 1948.

McGroarty, W.B. Settlement by colonies of emancipated Negroes in Brown Co., Ohio, 1818-46. WMQ 2d s. 21: 208-26, July 1941.

McGue, D.B. John Taylor, a slave-born pioneer. COL 18:161-8, Sept. 1941.

MACIVER, R.M.

Swisher, C.B. Review of R.M. MacIver, The more perfect Union: A program for the control of inter-group discrimination in the U.S. APS 42:998-9, Oct. 1948.

McKenzie, Ruth I. An evaluation of racial prejudice towards Negroes in various countries. DAL 20:197-205, July 1940.

MCKINNEY, R.I.

Faulkner, W.J. Review of R.I. McKinney, Religion in higher education among Negroes. IRM 36:408-9, July 1947.

McLean, Mrs. C.F. History of slaves and slavery. AMH 4:237-50, May 1909 and following issues; and AME 4:531-41, Aug. 1909 and following issues.

MacLean, M.S. Review of B.J. Mathews, Booker T. Washington, educator and interracial interpreter. AHR 54:630-1, Apr. 1949.

McLoughlin, James J. The black code. LHS 8:28-35, 1916; MIV 8:210-6, 1914-5.

McMillan, D. Story of John Kuners. JAF 39:53-7, Jan.-Mar. 1926.

McNeilly, J.S. Enforcement act of 1871 and Ku Klux Klan in Mississippi. MSS 9:109-71, 1906.

McNeilly, J.S. Reconstruction in Mississippi, 1874-96. MSS 12:283-474, 1912.

McNeilly, J.S. Reconstruction in Mississippi, 1863-90. MSS Cent. s. 2:165-535, 1918.

MCWILLIAMS, CAREY

Koontz, L.K. Review of Carey McWilliams, Brothers under the skin. PHR 12:418-9, Dec. 1943.

Mabry, W.A. Louisiana politics and the "grandfather clause." NCH 13:290-310, Oct. 1936.

Mabry, W.A. Negro suffrage and fusion rule in North Carolina. NCH 12:79-102, Apr. 1935.

Mabry, W.A. Review of E.M. Coulter, The South during Reconstruction. NCH 25:522-4, Oct. 1948.

Mabry, W.A. The white supremacy campaign in suffrage amendment, 1900. NCH 13:1-24, Jan. 1936.

Macer-Wright, P. "Uncle Tom's Cabin" and the "crusader in crinoline" who wrote it. WOR 59-62, July 1942.

Magee, Hattie. Reconstruction in Lawrence and Jefferson Davis Counties. MSS 11:163-204, 1910.

MAGIC

Simms, Marion. Black magic in New Orleans yesterday and today. TRA 81:18-9, July 1943.

Magoffin, Dorothy S. A Georgia planter and his plantation. NCH 15:354-77, Oct. 1938.

MAINE, BRUNSWICK

"Uncle Tom's Cabin" written in Brunswick, Me. SJM 5:160, Aug.-Oct. 1917.

Malin, J.C. Identification of the stranger at the Pottawatomie massacre. KHQ 9:3-12, Feb. 1940.

Malin, J.C. John Brown and the Manes incident. KHQ 7:376-8, Nov. 1938.

Malin, J.C. The John Brown legend in pictures. KHQ 8:339-41, Nov. 1939; 9:339-42, Nov. 1940.

Malin, J.C. The proslavery background of the Kansas struggle. MVH 10:285-305, Dec. 1923.

MANAGEMENT

Seal, A.G. John Carmichael Jenkins and his scientific management of his plantations. JMH 1:14-28, Jan. 1939.

MANES, POINDEXTER

Malin, J.C. John Brown and the Manes incident. KHQ 7: 376-8, Nov. 1938.

Mangus, A.R. A study of prejudice against the Negro. NDQ 21:5-14, Dec. 1930.

MANUMISSION. See also EMANCIPATION

Ardery, Julia S. Will of Richard "King" Harrison of Calvert Co., Md., granting freedom to his serving woman Kate Booth. KYR 46:637-46, Oct. 1958.

Clemence, Stella R. Deed and notes covering emancipation of a Negro slave woman in 1585. HAH 10:51-7, Feb. 1930.

First manumission society, 1815. INM 7:184-7, Dec. 1911.

Kendall, L.C. John McDonogh, his scheme for the liberation of his slaves and their exportation to Liberia. LHQ 15:646-54, Oct. 1932 and following issue.

Sherwood, H.N. Colonization of manumitted slaves in Ohio. John Randolph's bequest. MVH 5:39-59, 1912.

Trabue, C.C. Voluntary emancipation of slaves in Tennessee. THM 4:50-68, Mar. 1918.

MAPS

Hartshorne, R. Racial maps of U.S. population. GEO 28: 276-88, Apr. 1938.

MARAIS DES CYGNES MASSACRE

Moody, Joel. Marais des Cygnes massacre. KAN 14:208-23, 1915-8.

Tannar, A.H. Marais des Cygnes massacre and rescue of Ben Rice. KAN 14:224-34, 1915-8.

MARITAL STATUS

Cox, O.C. Sex ratio and marital status among Negroes. ASR 5:937-47, Dec. 1940.

MARKETING

Sitterson, J.C. Financing and marketing the sugar crop of the old South. JSH 10:188-99, May 1944.

Marsh, W.L. The need for men. ENG 42:51-5, Jan. 1926.

Marshall, Ruth. Duane Mowry, ed. Property in Negroes: A Southern slaveholding woman's plea to Sen. J.R. Doolittle. AME 8:530-2, June 1913.

Martin, A.E. Anti-slavery activities in the Methodist Church. THM 2:98-109, June 1916.

Martin, A.E. Anti-slavery press. MVH 2:509-28, Mar. 1916.

Martin, A.E. Tennessee anti-slavery societies. THM 1:261-81, Dec. 1915.

Martin, P.A. Slavery and abolition in Brazil. HAH 13:151-96, May 1933.

MARYLAND

Hartridge, W.C. Refugees in Maryland from the St. Domingo slave revolt of 1793. MDH 38:103-22, June 1943.

Protection Society of Maryland. MDH 1:358-62, June 1907.

Riggs, J.B. Early Maryland landowners in the vicinity of Washington. CHS 48:249-63, 1949.

Russ, W.A., Jr. Disfranchisement in Maryland, 1861-7. MDH 28:309-28, Dec. 1933.

Smith, A.E. The indentured servant and land speculation in 17th century Maryland. AHR 40:467-72, Apr. 1935.

Views on slavery of Gov. Charles Goldsborough, 1834. MDH 39:332-4, Dec. 1944.

Zornow, William F. Judicial modifications of the Maryland black code in the District of Columbia. MDH 44:18-32, Mar. 1949.

MARYLAND, CALVERT CO.

Ardery, Julia S. Will of Richard "King" Harrison of Calvert Co., Md., granting freedom to his serving woman Kate Booth. KYR 46:637-46, Oct. 1958.

MARYLAND, NORTHAMPTON

Hoyt, W.D., Jr. White servitude in Northampton, Maryland, 1772-4. MDH 33:126-33, June 1938.

Mason, Frances. Review of J.S. Tilley, The coming of the glory. VAM 57:436-9, Oct. 1949.

MASSACHUSETTS

Siebert, W.H. The underground railroad in Massachusetts. NEQ 9:447-67, Sept. 1936.

MASSACHUSETTS, BOSTON

Gilmer, A.H. Boston and emancipation, 1863. MAG 16:141-7, Apr. 1913.

Sherwin, O. Boston: The case of Anthony Burns, Negro. NEQ 19:212-23, June 1946.

MASSACHUSETTS, HINGHAM

Studley, Marian H. An August First anti-slavery picnic. NEQ 16:567-77, Dec. 1943.

MASSACHUSETTS, MILFORD

O'Donnell, W.G. Race relations in a New England town. NEQ 14:235-42, June 1941.

MASSACRES

Moody, Joel. Marais des Cygnes massacre. KAN 14:208-23, 1915-8.

Tannar, A.H. Marais des Cygnes massacre and rescue of Ben Rice. KAN 14:224-34, 1915-8.

MATHEMATICIANS

Phillips, F.L. The life of Benjamin Banneker. CHS 20:114-20, 1917.

MATHEWS, B.J.

Johnson, C.S. Review of B.J. Mathews, Booker T. Washington, educator and interracial interpreter. MVH 36:157-8, June 1949.

MacLean, M.S. Review of B.J. Mathews, Booker T. Washington, educator and interracial interpreter. AHR 54:630-1, Apr. 1949.

MATHEWS, B.J. (cont'd)

Wharton, V.L. Review of B.J. Mathews, Booker T. Washington, educator and interracial interpreter. JSH 15: 267-8, May 1949.

Mead, E.D. International organizations for inter-racial good will. JRD 2:210-4, Oct. 1911.

Meader, J.R. Harper's Ferry raid. AME 7:29-36, Jan. 1912.

Meader, J.R. Some Negro insurrections. AME 6:744-52, Apr. 1911.

Means, P.A. Race appreciation and democracy. JRD 9:180-8, Oct. 1918.

MEASUREMENT

Odum, H.W. Standards of measurement in race development. JRD 5:364-83, Apr. 1915.

Mechem, K. The mythical jayhawk. KHQ 13:3-15, Feb. 1944.

Mecklin, J.M. Ku Klux Klan and the democratic tradition. AMR 2:241-51, May-June 1924.

MEDIUMS

Gittings, Victoria. What William saw; experiences of William Aquilla with the supernatural. JAF 58:135-7, Apr.-June 1945.

Meehan, T.F. Mission work among colored Catholics. USC 8: 116-28, June 1915.

Merkel, B.G. The underground railroad and the Missouri borders, 1840-60. MOH 37:271-85, Apr. 1943.

Merton, R.K. Fact and factitiousness in ethnic opinionnaires. ASR 5:13-28, Feb. 1940.

METHODIST CHURCH

Martin, A.E. Anti-slavery activities in the Methodist Church. THM 2:98-109, June 1916.

Posey, W.B. Influence of slavery upon the Methodist Church in the early South and Southwest. MVH 17:530-42, Mar. 1931.

Ryan, J.H. Illinois anti-slavery struggle and its effect on the Methodist Church. IHL 19:67-76, 1913.

Simkins, F.S. White Methodism in South Carolina during Reconstruction. NCH 5:35-64, Jan. 1928.

Sweet, W.W. The Methodist Church and Reconstruction. IHL 20:83-94, 1914.

Sweet, W.W. Methodist Episcopal Church and Reconstruction. IHJ 7:147-65, Oct. 1914.

Winter, H. Early Methodism and slavery in Missouri, 1819-44; the division of Methodism in 1845. MOH 37:1-18, Oct. 1942.

MEXICAN WAR

Fuller, J.D.P. Slavery propaganda during the Mexican War. SWH 38:235-45, Apr. 1935.

MEXICO

Beltran, G.A. The slave trade in Mexico. HAH 24:412-31, Aug. 1944.

Clemence, Stella R. Deed and notes covering emancipation of a Negro slave woman in 1585. HAH 10:51-7, Feb. 1930.

Fuller, J.D.P. Effect of the slavery issue on the movement to annex Mexico, 1846-48. MVH 21:31-48, June 1934.

Harmon, G.D. Stephen A. Douglas--his leadership in Compromise of 1850, regarding government and question of slavery in territory acquired from Mexico. IHJ 21:452-90, Jan. 1929.

Porter, K.W. The Creek Indian-Negro tradition. The Hawkins Negroes go to Mexico. OKC 24:55-8, Spring 1946.

Roncal, J. The Negro race in Mexico: A statistical study. HAH 24:530-40, Aug. 1944.

Stenberg, R.R. The motivation of the Wilmot Proviso to a bill for the purchase of Mexican territory, prohibiting slavery therein. MVH 18:535-40, Mar. 1932.

MIAMI UNIVERSITY

Rodabaugh, J.H. Miami University, Calvinism and the anti-slavery movement. OAQ 48:66-73, Jan. 1939.

MICHIGAN

Aiken, Martha D. The underground railroad. MHM 6:597-610, no. 4, 1922.

MICHIGAN (cont'd)

Dancy, J.C. The Negro people in Michigan. MHM 24:221-40, Spring 1940.

MICHIGAN, BATTLECREEK

Barnes, Charles E. Battlecreek as a station on the underground railway. MPC 38:279-85, 1912.

MICHIGAN, DETROIT

Gibb, H.L. Slaves in old Detroit, from a census of 1782. MHM 18:143-6, Spring 1934.

Riddell, W.R. A Negro slave in Canadian Detroit, 1795. MHM 18:48-52, Winter 1934.

Middleton, A.P. The strange story of Job Ben Solomon, the African, 1750. WMQ 3d s. 5:342-50, July 1948.

MIGRATION

Florant, L.C. Negro internal migration. ASR 7:782-91, Dec. 1942.

Hill, J.A. Effects of the northward migration of the Negro. ASS 17:34-46, 1923.

Jacob Lawrence, his pictures of the South-to-North migration of Negroes that began during the First World War. FOR 24:102-9, Nov. 1941.

Valian, P. Internal migration and racial composition of the Southern population. ASR 13:294-8, June 1948.

Milburn, P. Emancipation of slaves in the District of Columbia. CHS 16:96-119, 1913.

Miller, E.C. John Brown's ten years in Northwestern Pennsylvania. PAH 15:24-33, Jan. 1948.

Miller, H.A. Changing concepts of race. ASR 21:106-12, 1927.

Miller, K. The Negro in New England. HGM 34:538-48, June 1926.

Miller, K.D. Some racial factors in American life. HOM 85:312-9, Apr. 1923.

Miller, P. Review of J.W. DeForest, A Union officer in the Reconstruction. NEQ 21:392-4, Sept. 1948.

Miller, William. Effects of the American Revolution on indentured servitude. PAH 7:131-41, July 1940.

MILLIN, SARAH G.

Callaway, A. Review of Sarah G. Millin, God's step-children. IRM 18:612-5, Oct. 1929.

Milling, C.J. "Delia Holmes," a neglected Negro ballad. SFQ 1:3-8, Dec. 1937.

Milton, G.F. The impeachment of lynching. VQR 8:247-56, Apr. 1932.

MINER, MYRTILLA

Wells, L.G. Story of Myrtilla Miner. NYH 24:358-75, July 1943.

MINISTRY

Knight, E.W. Notes on career of John Chavis, Negro Presbyterian preacher and teacher, 1763(?)- , as a teacher of Southern white children and of his ministry. NCH 7:326-45, July 1930.

Minor, R.C. The career of James Preston Poindexter, Negro statesman, in Columbus, Ohio. OAQ 56:266-86, July 1947.

MINOR, WILLIAM J.

Sitterson, J.C. The William J. Minor plantations: A study in ante-bellum absentee ownership. JSH 9:59-74, Feb. 1943.

MINORITY GROUPS

Saenger, G. Effect of the war on our minority groups. ASR 8:15-22, Feb. 1943.

Minsky, L. Intolerance; a problem for psychiatrists? CJR 5:261-8, June 1942.

MINSTRELS

Garvie, B.S. Minstrel songs of other days. AME 7:945-55, Oct. 1912.

MINSTRELS (cont'd)

Kendall, J.S. Negro minstrels of New Orleans. LHQ 30: 128-48, Jan. 1947.

MISCEGENATION

de Rivera, B. How women can halt "the great black plague." PRS 23:417-20, Mar. 1910.

Hale, A.R. Why miscegenation flourishes in the North. PRS 23:543-51, Apr. 1910.

Howard, W.L. A plain explanation of the greatest social evil. PRS 23:640-7, May 1910.

MISSIONS

Dickinson, C.H. Samuel Armstrong's contribution to Christian missions. IRM 10:509-24, Oct. 1921.

Fisher, H.P. The Catholic Church in Liberia. AMC 40: 249-310, Sept. 1929.

Goodwin, Mary F. Christianizing and educating the Negro in colonial Virginia. PEH 1:143-52, Sept. 1932.

Klingberg, F.J. Missionary activity of the S.P.G. among the African immigrants of colonial Pennsylvania and Delaware. PEH 11:126-53, June 1942.

Klingberg, F.J. The Society for the Propagation of the Gospel program for Negroes in colonial New York. PEH 8:306-71, Dec. 1939.

Meehan, T.F. Mission work among colored Catholics. USC 8:116-28, June 1915.

Murphy, Miriam T. Catholic missionary work among the colored people of the United States, 1776-1866. AMC 35:101-36, June 1924.

Parson, A.B. Beginnings of the Episcopal Church ministry in Liberia. PEH 7:154-77, June 1938.

Theobald, Stephen L. Catholic missionary work among the colored people of the United States (1776-1866). AMC 35:325-44, Dec. 1924.

MISSISSIPPI

Barnhart, John D., ed. Letters on Reconstruction on the lower Mississippi, 1864-78. MVH 21:387-96, Dec. 1934.

Bettersworth, J.K., ed. Mississippi unionism: The case of Mr. Lyon. JMH 1:37-52, Jan. 1939.

Donald, D.H. The role of the scalawag in Mississippi Reconstruction. JSH 10:447-60, Nov. 1944.

Fauset, A.H. Folk-tales from Alabama, Mississippi and Louisiana. JAF 40:214-303, June-Sept. 1927.

Halsell, Willie D., ed. Republican factionalism in Mississippi, 1882-4. JSH 7:84-101, Feb. 1941.

Hearon, C. Mississippi Compromise of 1850. MSS 14:7-230, 1914.

Hearon, C. Nullification in Mississippi. MSS 12:37-71, 1912.

Humphrey, G.D. Public education for whites. JMH 3:26-36, Jan. 1941.

McCain, William D. The emancipation of Indiana Osborne. JMH 8:97-8, Apr. 1946.

McNeilly, J.S. Enforcement act of 1871 and Ku Klux Klan in Mississippi. MSS 9:109-71, 1906.

McNeilly, J.S. Reconstruction in Mississippi, 1874-96. MSS 12:283-474, 1912.

McNeilly, J.S. Reconstruction in Mississippi, 1863-90. MSS Cent. s. 2:165-535, 1918.

A Mississippian's view of civil rights, states rights and the Reconstruction background. JMH 10:181-239, July 1948.

Osborn, G.C. Life of a Southern plantation owner during Reconstruction as revealed in the Clay Sharkey papers. JMH 6:103-12, Apr. 1944.

Osborn, G.C. Plantation life in central Mississippi as revealed in the Clay Sharkey papers. JMH 3:277-88, Oct. 1941.

Reconstruction in various counties. MSS 10:115-61, 1909.

Seal, A.G., ed. A Mississippian's defense of slavery. JMH 2:212-31, Oct. 1940.

Stone, A.H. The basis of white political control in Mississippi. JMH 6:225-36, Oct. 1944.

Sydnor, C.S. The free Negro in Mississippi before the Civil War. AHR 32:769-88, July 1927.

Sydnor, C.S. Life span of Mississippi slaves. AHR 35:566-74, Apr. 1930.

Timberlake, Elsie. Did the Reconstruction give Mississippi new schools? MSS 12:72-93, 1912.

MISSISSIPPI (cont'd)

Washington, Booker T. Progress of the Negro race in Mississippi. WWL 13:409-13, Mar. 1909.

MISSISSIPPI, BRIERFIELD

Murphee, D. Hurricane and Brierfield: The Jefferson Davis plantations on Palmyra Island, Miss. JMH 9:98-107, Apr. 1947.

MISSISSIPPI, BROOKDALE

Griffeth, Lucile, ed. Brookdale farm: A record book, 1856-57. JMH 7:23-31, Jan. 1945.

MISSISSIPPI, HINDS CO.

Wells, W.C. Reconstruction and its destruction in Hinds Co., Miss. MHS 9:85-108, 1906.

MISSISSIPPI, HURRICANE

Murphee, D. Hurricane and Brierfield: The Jefferson Davis plantations on Palmyra Island, Miss. JMH 9:98-107, Apr. 1947.

MISSISSIPPI, JEFFERSON DAVIS CO.

Magee, Hattie. Reconstruction in Lawrence and Jefferson Davis Counties. MSS 11:163-204, 1910.

MISSISSIPPI, LAFAYETTE CO.

Kendel, Julia. Reconstruction in Lafayette County. MSS 13:223-72, 1913.

MISSISSIPPI, LAWRENCE CO.

Magee, Hattie. Reconstruction in Lawrence and Jefferson Davis Counties. MSS 11:163-204, 1910.

MISSISSIPPI, MONROE CO.

Leftwich, G.J. Reconstruction in Monroe Co. MSS 9:53-84, 1906.

MISSISSIPPI, NATCHEZ

Hamilton, W.B., and W.D. McCain, eds. Inventories of the estate of Charles Percy, planter, 1794 and 1804. JMH 10:290-316, Oct. 1948.

Seal, A.G. John Carmichael Jenkins and his scientific management of his plantations. JMH 1:14-28, Jan. 1939.

MISSISSIPPI, PALMYRA ISLAND

Murphee, D. Hurricane and Brierfield: The Jefferson Davis plantations on Palmyra Island, Miss. JMH 9:98-107, Apr. 1947.

MISSISSIPPI, PANOLA CO.

Kyle, J.W. Reconstruction in Panola Co. MSS 19:9-98, 1913.

MISSISSIPPI, PLEASANT HILL

Stephenson, W.H. A quarter-century at Pleasant Hill. MVH 23:355-74, Dec. 1936.

MISSISSIPPI, PONTOTOC CO.

Reconstruction in Pontotoc Co. MSS 11:229-69, 1910.

MISSISSIPPI, SCOTT CO.

Cooper, F. Reconstruction in Scott Co., Miss. MSS 13:99-222, 1913.

MISSOURI

Klem, Mary J. The Kansas-Nebraska slavery bill and Missouri's part in the conflict. MIV 9:393-413, 1919.

Ku Klux Klans of the Reconstruction period in Missouri. MOH 37:441-50, July 1943.

Merkel, B.G. The underground railroad and the Missouri borders, 1840-60. MOH 37:271-85, Apr. 1943.

Nelson, E.J. Missouri slavery, 1861-5. MOH 28:260-74, July 1934.

Ryle, W.H. Slavery and party realignment in the Missouri state election of 1856. MOH 39:320-32, Apr. 1945.

Sampson, F.A., and W.C. Breckenridge. Bibliography of slavery in Missouri. MOH 2:233-44, Apr. 1908.

Trexler, H.A. Slavery in Missouri territory. MOH 3:179-97, Apr. 1909.

Trexler, H.A. The value and sale of the Missouri slave. MOH 8:69-85, Jan. 1914.

Violette, E.M. Black code in Missouri. MIV 6:287-316, 1913.

MISSOURI (cont'd)

Winter, H. Early Methodism and slavery in Missouri, 1819-44; the division of Methodism in 1845. MOH 37: 1-18, Oct. 1942.

MISSOURI, ST. LOUIS

Ross, M. They did it in St. Louis: One man against folklore. COM 4:9-15, July 1947.

Smelser, M. Housing in Creole St. Louis, 1764-1821: An example of cultural change. LHQ 21:337-48, Apr. 1938.

MISSOURI COMPROMISE

Learned, H.B. Reaction of Philip Phillips to the repeal of the Missouri Compromise. MVH 8:303-17, Mar. 1922.

Osborne, D.F. The sectional struggle over rights of slavery in new territory added to U.S. GHQ 15:223-51, Sept. 1931.

Mitchell, J.B. An analysis of population by race, nativity and residence. ARK 8:115-32, Summer 1949.

MOB LAW

Mob law and the Negro. PUB 20:810-1, Aug. 24, 1917.

MOHAMMEDAN COUNTRIES

Leckie, J.D. Slavery in Mohammedan countries. CHA 7th s. 15:276-7, Apr. 4, 1925.

Mokitimi, S. Review of H.V. Richardson, Dark glory: A picture of the church among the Negroes of the rural South. IRM 37:462-4, Oct. 1948.

Money, C.H. Fugitive slave law of 1850. Indiana cases. INM 17:159-98, June 1921 and following issue.

Montague, Ashley. See Ashley-Montague, M.F.

Montgomery, Horace. A Georgia precedent for the Freeport question. JSH 10:200-7, May 1944.

Moody, Joel. Marais des Cygnes massacre. KAN 14:208-23, 1915-8.

Moody, V.A. Slavery on Louisiana sugar plantations. LHQ 7: 191-303, Apr. 1924.

MOON, H.L.

Strong, D.S. Review of H.L. Moon, Balance of power, the Negro vote. APS 42:1220-1, Dec. 1948.

Mooney, C.C. Institutional and statistical aspects of slavery in Tennessee. THQ 1:195-228, Sept. 1942.

Mooney, C.C. Review of E.M. Coulter, The South during Reconstruction. INM 44:110-2, Mar. 1948.

Mooney, C.C. Review of E. Franklin Frazier, The Negro in the U.S. JSH 15:543-5, Nov. 1949.

Moore, A.B. One hundred years of Reconstruction of the South. JSH 9:153-80, May 1943.

Moore, R.H. Review of V.L. Wharton, The Negro in Mississippi. JMH 9:268-9, Oct. 1947.

MOORE, GOV. T.O.

Whittington, G.P., ed. Facts concerning the loyalty of slaves in Northern Louisiana in 1863 as shown in the letters of J.H. Ransdell to Gov. T.O. Moore. LHQ 14: 487-502, Oct. 1931.

MORAL JUDGMENTS

Seeman, M. Moral judgment: A study in racial frames of reference. ASR 12:404-11, Aug. 1947.

MORALITY

Wallis, W.D. Moral and racial prejudice. JRD 5:212-29, Oct. 1914.

Moroney, T.B. Review of Carter G. Woodson, A century of Negro migration. CHR 6:527-9, Jan. 1921.

Morrall, A. See Connelley, W.E.

Morris, R.B. White bondage and compulsory labor in ante-bellum South Carolina. SOC 49:191-207, Oct. 1948.

Morris, R.L. Review of B.A. Botkin, ed., Lay my burden down: A folk history of slavery. ARK 5:411-2, Winter 1946.

MORRIS, THOMAS

Swing, J.B. Thomas Morris, Ohio pioneer. OAQ 10:352-60, Jan. 1902.

Morse, J.T., Jr. Moorfield Storey, 1845-1929. HGM 38:291-302, Mar. 1930.

Morton, R.L. Review of J.C. Robert, The road from Monticello, a study of the Virginia slavery debate of 1832. WMQ 2d s. 22:70-5, Jan. 1942.

Moseley, J.A.R. The citizens white primary in Marion Co., Texas, of 1898. SWH 49:524-31, Apr. 1946.

Moses, E.R. Differentials in crime rates between Negroes and whites, based on comparisons of four socio-economically equated areas. ASR 12:411-20, Aug. 1947.

MOVIES

Noble, P. Influence of screen portrayal of the Negro upon the colour bar in America. WOR 53-6, June 1944.

Mowry, D. Negro colonization. AME 5:975-6, Sept.-Oct. 1910.

Mowry, Duane. New York Democratic convention's "corner stone" resolution, 1847. IHJ 3:88-90, Oct. 1910.

MOWRY, DUANE, ED.

Marshall, Ruth. Duane Mowry, ed. Property in Negroes: A Southern slaveholding woman's plea to Sen. J.R. Doolittle. AME 8:530-2, June 1913.

Marshall, Ruth. Mowry, Duane, ed. Property in Negroes: A Southern slaveholding woman's plea to Sen. J.R. Doolittle. AME 8:530-2, June 1913.

Muelder, H.R. Galesburg, Ill.; hot-bed of abolitionism. IHJ 35:216-35, Sept. 1942.

MUELLER, SALLY

Voss, L.D. Sally Mueller, the German slave. LHQ 12:447-60, July 1929.

Muir, A.F. The free Negro in Harris Co., Texas. SWH 46:214-38, Jan. 1943.

Mulcaster, J.G. A quadroon girl of Southern Illinois. IHJ 28:214-7, Oct. 1935.

Mulhauser, R. Library services to Negroes. BUB 13:155-7, Jan.-Apr. 1929 and following issue.

Murdock, R.K. Review of V.L. Wharton, The Negro in Mississippi. MDH 43:72, Mar. 1948.

Murphee, D. Hurricane and Brierfield: The Jefferson Davis plantations on Palmyra Island, Miss. JMH 9:98-107, Apr. 1947.

Murphy, Miriam T. Catholic missionary work among the colored people of the United States, 1776-1866. AMC 35:101-36, June 1924.

MURRAY, AMELIA M.

Hawes, Lilla M. Amelia M. Murray on slavery; an unpublished letter. GHQ 33:314-7, Dec. 1949.

MUSEUM OF MODERN ART

Locke, Alain. Exhibition of African art at Museum of Modern Art. AMA 28:270-8, May 1935.

MUSIC. See also FOLK SONGS, SONGS, SPIRITUALS

Damon, S.F. The Negro in early American songsters. BSA 28:132-63, 1934.

Harshaw, D.A. Philosophy of the Negro spiritual. HOM 95:184-6, Mar. 1928.

Milling, C.J. "Delia Holmes," a neglected Negro ballad. SFQ 1:3-8, Dec. 1937.

MUTINY

Hicks, Granville. Dr. Channing and the Creole case. AHR 37:516-25, Apr. 1932.

"MY OLD KENTUCKY HOME"

Clark, T.D. The slavery background of Foster's "My Old Kentucky Home." HIS 10:1-17, Jan. 1936.

MYRDAL, GUNNAR

Gosnell, H.F. Review of G. Myrdal, An American dilemma. APS 38:995-6, Oct. 1944.

Reedman, J.N. Review of G. Myrdal, An American dilemma. IRM 34:211-4, Apr. 1945.

Young, K. Review of G. Myrdal, An American dilemma. ASR 9:326-30, June 1944.
Comment: G. Nettler, ASR 9:686-8, Dec. 1944.

N., V.E.P. The chief problem of the South. TIM 1:399-406, Mar. 1907.

NAMES

Hudson, A.P. Some curious Negro names and their derivation. SFQ 2:170-93, Dec. 1938.

NANIGO

Kennedy, Stetson. Nanigo in Florida. SFQ 4:153-6, Sept. 1940.

Naruse, J. War and the concordia of race. JRD 5:268-75, Jan. 1915.

NASHOBA

Emerson, O.B. Frances Wright and her Nashoba experiment. THQ 6:291-314, Dec. 1947.

NASHVILLE CONVENTION

Herndon, D.T. Nashville convention of 1850 to protest against exclusion of slave holders from territories. AHS 5:203-37, 1904.

Sioussat, St. G.L. The Compromise of 1850 and the Nashville convention. THM 4:215-47, Dec. 1918.

NATIONALISM

Bernanos, Georges. Nation against race. DUB 209:1-6, July 1941.

NATIONALITY

Newbegin, Marion I. Race and nationality. GEJ 50:313-35, Nov. 1917.

Robison, Sophia M. Effects of the factors of race and nationality on the registration of behavior as delinquent in New York City in 1930. ASS 28:37-44, May 1934.

NATIVITY

Mitchell, J.B. An analysis of population by race, nativity and residence. ARK 8:115-32, Summer 1949.

Nebbit, L. Letter of a colored child of the Sacred Heart. AMC 24:179-81, June 1913.

NEBRASKA, NEBRASKA CITY

Overturf, W. John Brown's cabin at Nebraska City. NHS 21:92-100, Apr.-June 1940.

Needham, C.K. Comparison of race conditions in Jamaica with those in U.S. JRD 4:189-203, Oct. 1913.

NEGRO HISTORY WEEK

Crawford, Myrtle B. Instructions for producing pageant for Negro History Week. SOS 32:27-31, Jan. 1941.

NEGRO PLOT OF 1741

Clarke, T.W. The Negro plot in New York City of 1741. NYH 25:167-81, Apr. 1944.

NEGRO SEAMEN ACTS

Hamer, Philip M. Great Britain, the United States, and the Negro seamen acts, 1822-48. JSH 1:3-28, Feb. 1935 and following issue, which covers 1850-60.

NEGRO-JEWISH RELATIONS

Baldwin, James. The Harlem ghetto: Jewish-Negro relations. COM 5:165-70, Feb. 1948.

Clark, K.B. Negro-Jewish relations: A complex social problem. COM 1:8-14, Feb. 1946.

Nelson, B.H. Aspects of Negro life in North Carolina during the Civil War. NCH 25:143-66, Apr. 1948.

Nelson, B.H. Legislative control of the Southern free Negro, 1861-65. CHR 32:28-46, Apr. 1946.

Nelson, E.J. Missouri slavery, 1861-5. MOH 28:260-74, July 1934.

Nettler, G. See Young, K.

NEW ENGLAND

Adams, J.T. Disfranchisement of Negroes in New England. AHR 30:543-7, Apr. 1925.

Dounan, Elizabeth. The New England slave trade after the Revolution. NEQ 3:251-78, Apr. 1930.

Miller, K. The Negro in New England. HGM 34:538-48, June 1926.

NEW ENGLAND (cont'd)

O'Donnell, W.G. Race relations in a New England town. NEQ 14:235-42, June 1941.

NEW ENGLAND EMIGRANT AID COMPANY. See EMIGRANT AID COMPANY

NEW HAMPSHIRE

Hammond, I.W. New Hampshire slaves. GSM 4:199-203, Nov. 1907.

Perry, C.E. The voice of New Hampshire in the slave controversy. NWH 61:63-6, Feb.-Mar. 1929.

NEW JERSEY

Connolly, J.C. Slavery and the causes operating against its extension in colonial New Jersey. NJS n.s. 14: 181-202, Apr. 1929.

Folsom, J.F. A slave indenture of colonial days. NJS 3d s. 10:111-5, July-Oct. 1915.

Gardner, D.H. The emancipation of slaves in New Jersey. NJS 9:1-21, Jan. 1924.

Halpert, H. Some Negro riddles collected in New Jersey. JAF 56:200-2, July-Sept. 1943.

Honeyman, A. Van D. A slave sale of 1827. NJS 53:250-1, Oct. 1935.

Keasbey, A.Q. Slavery in New Jersey. NJS 3d s. 4:90-6, Jan.-Apr. 1907 and following issues.

Kemmerer, D.L. The suffrage franchise in colonial New Jersey. NJS 52:166-73, July 1934.

Kull, I.S. Slavery in New Jersey. AME 24:443-72, Oct. 1930.

Stuart, W. Dutch and English importation to New Jersey and New York. AME 16:347-67, Oct. 1922.

Stuart, W. White servitude in New York and New Jersey. AME 15:19-37, Jan. 1921.

NEW JERSEY, HUNTERDON CO.

Schmidt, H. Slavery and attitudes toward slavery in Hunterdon Co., N.J. NJS 58:151-69, July 1940 and following issue.

NEW MEXICO, TUCSON

Bloom, L.B., ed. Lt. John Bourke's description of a lynching in Tucson, N.M., in 1873. NMH 19:233-42, July 1944 and following issue.

NEW YORK

Beyer, R.L. Slavery in colonial New York. JAH 23:102-8, 1929.

Bishop, Shelton H. A history of St. Philip's Church: The first colored parish in the Diocese of New York. PEH 15:298-317, Dec. 1917.

Haar, C.M. White indentured servants in colonial New York. AME 34:370-92, July 1940.

King, Ethel. The New York Negro plot of 1741. USC 20: 173-80, 1931.

Klingberg, F.J. The Society for the Propagation of the Gospel program for Negroes in colonial New York. PEH 8:306-71, Dec. 1939.

Northrup, H.R. Proving ground for fair employment: Some lessons from New York State's experience. COM 4:552-6, Dec. 1947.

Stuart, W. Dutch and English importation to New Jersey and New York. AME 16:347-67, Oct. 1922.

Stuart, W. White servitude in New York and New Jersey. AME 15:19-37, Jan. 1921.

NEW YORK, CHAUTAUQUA CO.

Bailey, William S. The underground railroad in southern Chautauqua County, N.Y. NYH 16:53-63, Jan. 1935.

NEW YORK, LAKE PLACID

Rex, Millicent B. John Brown's life and burial at Lake Placid. AME 25:141-9, Apr. 1931.

NEW YORK, NEW YORK

Clarke, T.W. The Negro plot in New York City of 1741. NYH 25:167-81, Apr. 1944.

Housing problems for Negroes in New York City. Paul Laurence Dunbar apartments. ARC 59:5-12, Jan. 1929.

Petry, Ann. Harlem. A medieval ghetto in the heart of the biggest, richest city in the world. HOL 5:110-6, Apr. 1949.

NEW YORK, NEW YORK (cont'd)

Robison, Sophia M. Effects of the factors of race and nationality on the registration of behavior as delinquent in New York City in 1930. ASS 28:37-44, May 1934.

NEW YORK, SYRACUSE

Galpin, W.F. Fugitive slave law of 1850. The Jerry Rescue precipitated a clash between the government and local abolitionists. NYH 26:19-33, Jan. 1945.

Newbegin, Marion I. Race and nationality. GEJ 50:313-35, Nov. 1917.

NEWSPAPERS

Allen, C.E. The slavery question in Catholic newspapers, 1850-65. USC 26:99-169, 1936.

Copeland, F. The New Orleans press and the Reconstruction. LHQ 30:149-337, Jan. 1947.

Durel, L.C. Donaldsville, La., Creole civilization, 1850, according to the newspaper "Le Vigilant." LHQ 31:981-94, Oct. 1948.

Fortune press analysis: Negroes. FTE 13:233+, May 1945.

Harrison, L. Cassius M. Clay's anti-slavery newspaper, the "True American": Opposition in Kentucky to his struggle for emancipation of the Negro. HIS 22:30-49, Jan. 1948.

Karlin, J.A. New Orleans lynchings of 1891 and the American press. LHQ 24:187-204, Jan. 1941.

Levi, Kate E. The Wisconsin press and slavery. WIM 9: 423-34, July 1926.

Martin, A.E. Anti-slavery press. MVH 2:509-28, Mar. 1916.

Perkins, H.C. The defense of slavery in the Northern press on the eve of the Civil War. JSH 9:501-31, Nov. 1943.

Walsh, Anetta C. Three anti-slavery newspapers published in Ohio prior to 1823. OAQ 31:171-212, Apr. 1922.

NICARAGUA

What U.S. is doing for Santo Domingo, Nicaragua and Haiti. NGE 30:143-77, Aug. 1916.

NICHOLLS, FRANCIS T.

McDaniel, Hilda M. Francis T. Nicholls and the end of Reconstruction. LHQ 32:357-513, Apr. 1949.

NIGERIA

Catching slave-traders in Nigeria. WWL 19:331-6, Feb. 1912.

Turner, L.D. Contrasts of Brazilian ex-slaves with Nigeria. VQR 27:55-67, Jan. 1942.

Nixon, H.C. Review of E.M. Coulter, The South during Reconstruction. VQR 24:454-5, Summer 1948.

Noble, P. Influence of screen portrayal of the Negro upon the colour bar in America. WOR 53-6, June 1944.

NOLAN, NICHOLAS

Carroll, H.B. Nolan's "lost nigger" expedition of 1877. SWH 44:55-75, July 1940.

NORTH

Carsel, W. The slaveholders' indictment of Northern wage slavery. JSH 6:504-20, Nov. 1940.

Hale, A.R. Why miscegenation flourishes in the North. PRS 23:543-51, Apr. 1910.

Negro in the North. PUB 20:571-2, June 15, 1917.

Perkins, H.C. The defense of slavery in the Northern press on the eve of the Civil War. JSH 9:501-31, Nov. 1943.

NORTH CAROLINA

Autobiography of Omar ibn Said, slave in North Carolina, 1831. AHR 30:787-95, July 1925.

Ewing, C.A.M. Two Reconstruction impeachments. NCH 15: 204-30, July 1938.

Franklin, J.H. The free Negro in the economic life of ante-bellum North Carolina. NCH 19:239-59, July 1942 and following issue.

Franklin, J.H. Negro members of the Protestant Episcopal Church in ante-bellum North Carolina. PEH 13:216-34, Sept. 1944.

NORTH CAROLINA (cont'd)

Gehrke, W.H. Negro slavery among the Germans in North Carolina. NCH 14:307-24, Oct. 1937.

King, Emma. Some aspects of the work of the Society of Friends for Negro education in North Carolina. NCH 1: 403-11, Oct. 1924.

Mabry, W.A. Negro suffrage and fusion rule in North Carolina. NCH 12:79-102, Apr. 1935.

Mabry, W.A. The white supremacy campaign in suffrage amendment, 1900. NCH 13:1-24, Jan. 1936.

Nelson, B.H. Aspects of Negro life in North Carolina during the Civil War. NCH 25:143-66, Apr. 1948.

Padgett, J.A., ed. Letters from North Carolina--Reconstruction period. NCH 20:259-82, July 1943, previous and following issues.

Riddell, Justice. The story of Governor Sothel, one-time slave. DAL 9:475-80, Jan. 1930.

Riddell, W.R. A half-told story of real white slavery in the 17th century. NCH 9:299-303, July 1932.

Russ, W.A., Jr. Radical disfranchisement in North Carolina, 1867-8. NCH 11:271-83, Oct. 1934.

St. Clair, K.E. Debtor relief in North Carolina during Reconstruction, 1865. NCH 18:215-35, July 1941.

Taylor, R.H. Humanizing the slave code in North Carolina. NCH 2:323-31, July 1925.

Taylor, R.H. Slave conspiracies in North Carolina. NCH 5:20-34, June 1928.

Todd, Willie G. North Carolina Baptists and slavery. NCH 24:135-59, Apr. 1947.

Winston, S. Negro bootleggers in Eastern North Carolina. ASR 8:692-7, Dec. 1943.

NORTH CAROLINA, GUILFORD CO.

Farrison, W.E. Negro population of Guilford Co., N.C., before the Civil War. NCH 21:319-29, Oct. 1944.

Northrup, H.R. Negroes in a war industry; the case of shipbuilding. JOB 16:160-72, July 1943.

Northrup, H.R. Proving ground for fair employment: Some lessons from New York State's experience. COM 4:552-6, Dec. 1947.

Northrup, H.R. Race discrimination in trade unions. COM 2: 124-31, Aug. 1946.

NORTHRUP, HENRY

Curtis, Agnes B. A strange story of a Negro and his white deliverer. JAH 18:349-55, Oct.-Dec. 1924.

NORTHRUP, SOLOMON

Curtis, Agnes B. A strange story of a Negro and his white deliverer. JAH 18:349-55, Oct.-Dec. 1924.

NORTHWEST

Hunt, H.F. Slavery among the Indians of Northwestern America. WAS 9:277-83, Oct. 1918.

Lynch, W.O. Antislavery tendencies of the Democratic party in the Northwest, 1848-50. MVH 11:319-31, Dec. 1924.

Potts, Alma G. Slavery in the old Northwest. SOS 33: 70+, Feb. 1942.

Norton, F.C. Negro slaves in Connecticut. CNT 5:320-8, June 1899.

Norton, H.K. Self-determination in the West Indies. The governments of the Caribbean. WDT 47:147-53, Jan. 1926.

NOVA SCOTIA

Oliver, W.P. Cultural progress of the Negro in Nova Scotia. DAL 29:203-300, Oct. 1949.

NULLIFICATION

Hearon, C. Nullification in Mississippi. MSS 12:37-71, 1912.

Nye, R.B. Albion W. Tourgee--his ideas concerning Reconstruction problems in the South. OAQ 50:101-14, Apr.-June 1941.

Nye, R.B. Marius Racine Robinson, his activities in the Ohio anti-slavery movement. OAQ 55:138-54, Apr.-June 1946.

NYE, R.B.

Filler, L. Review of R.B. Nye, Fettered freedom: Civil liberties and the slavery controversy. AHR 55:162-4, Oct. 1949.

O'Dell, R.F. Review of R.B. Nye, Fettered freedom: Civil liberties and the slavery controversy. MHM 33:379, Dec. 1949.

OBEAH. See also BLACK MAGIC, HOODOO, VODUN

Thirsk, R. Obeah in the West Indies. CHA 7th s. 7:247-50, Mar. 17, 1917.

Udal, J.S. Obeah in the West Indies. FLL 26:255-95, Sept. 1915.

O'CONNELL, DANIEL

Wayland, Francis F. Slavebreeding in America: The Stevenson-O'Connell imbroglio of 1838. VAM 50:47-54, Jan. 1942.

O'Dell, R.F. Review of R.B. Nye, Fettered freedom: Civil liberties and the slavery controversy. MHM 33:379, Dec. 1949.

O'Donnell, W.G. Race relations in a New England town. NEQ 14:235-42, June 1941.

Odum, Anna K. Folk-songs from Tennessee. JAF 27:255-65, July-Sept. 1914.

Odum, H.W. Problems of the Southern states. JRD 6:185-91, Oct. 1915.

Odum, H.W. Standards of measurement in race development. JRD 5:364-83, Apr. 1915.

ODUM, H.W.

Bain, R. Review of H.W. Odum and G.B. Johnson, The Negro and his songs. AMR 4:104-7, Jan.-Feb. 1926.

OHIO

Alilunas, Leo. Fugitive slave cases in Ohio prior to 1850. OAQ 49:160-84, Apr.-June 1940.

Coleman, C.H. Three Vallandigham letters, 1865. OAQ 43:461-4, Oct. 1934.

Ellsworth, C.S. Ohio legislative attack upon abolition schools. MVH 21:379-86, Dec. 1934.

Filler, L., ed. John Brown in Ohio: An interview with Charles S.S. Griffing. OAQ 58:213-8, Apr. 1949.

Fugitive or rescue case of 1857 in Ohio. OAQ 16:292-309, July 1907.

Galbreath, C.B. Anti-slavery movement in Ohio. OAQ 30: 355-95, Oct. 1921.

Galbreath, C.B. The fugitive slave law, 1839. OAQ 34: 216-40, Apr. 1925.

Graham, A.A. Abolition colony in Ohio. OAQ 30-43, 1895.

Land, Mary. John Brown's Ohio environment. OAQ 57:24-47, Jan. 1948.

Lyons, John F. Attitude of Presbyterians in Ohio, Indiana and Illinois toward slavery. PBY 11:69-82, June 1921.

Nye, R.B. Marius Racine Robinson, his activities in the Ohio anti-slavery movement. OAQ 55:138-54, Apr.-June 1946.

Ohio fugitive slave law of 1839. ONW 13:69-72, Apr.-Oct. 1910.

Price, R. The Ohio Anti-Slavery Society's convention of 1836. OAQ 45:173-88, Apr. 1936.

Rayback, J.G. The Liberty party leaders of Ohio: Exponents of anti-slavery coalition. OAQ 57:165-78, Apr. 1948.

Rodabaugh, J.H. Miami University, Calvinism and the anti-slavery movement. OAQ 48:66-73, Jan. 1939.

Sherwood, H.N. Colonization of manumitted slaves in Ohio. John Randolph's bequest. MVH 5:39-59, 1912.

Shunk, E.W. "Ohio in Africa," a plan for a colony of Ohio free-Negro emigrants in Liberia, c. 1850. OAQ 51:70-87, Apr.-June 1942.

Siebert, W.H. Beginnings of the underground railroad in Ohio. OAQ 56:70-93, Jan. 1947.

OHIO (cont'd)

Siebert, W.H. A Quaker section of the underground railroad in Northern Ohio. OAQ 39:429-502, July 1930.

Siebert, W.H. The underground railroad in Ohio. OAQ 4: 44-63, 1895.

Swing, J.B. Thomas Morris, Ohio pioneer. OAQ 10:352-60, Jan. 1902.

Van Fossan, W.H. Biography of Clement L. Vallandigham. OAQ 23:256-67, July 1914.

Walsh, Anetta C. Three anti-slavery newspapers published in Ohio prior to 1823. OAQ 31:171-212, Apr. 1922.

Wilson, C.J. People's attitude toward the Negro in early Ohio. OAQ 39:717-68, Oct. 1930.

OHIO, BROWN CO.

McGroarty, W.B. Settlement by colonies of emancipated Negroes in Brown Co., Ohio, 1818-46. WMQ 2d s. 21:208-26, July 1941.

OHIO, COLUMBUS

Minor, R.C. The career of James Preston Poindexter, Negro statesman, in Columbus, Ohio. OAQ 56:266-86, July 1947.

OHIO, GRANVILLE

Price, R. Anti-abolition disturbances of 1836 in Granville, Ohio. OAQ 45:365-8, Oct. 1936.

OHIO, MECHANICSBURG

Watts, R.M. The underground railroad in Mechanicsburg, Ohio. OAQ 43:209-54, July 1934.

OHIO, OBERLIN

Burroughs, W.G. Oberlin's part in the slavery conflict. OAQ 20:269-334, Apr.-July 1911.

OHIO, PUTNAM

Sheppard, T.J. Putnam, Ohio, as an abolition centre. OAQ 19:266-9, July 1910.

OHIO, RIPLEY

Koch, F.J. Marking the old "abolition holes" at Ripley. OAQ 22:308-18, Apr. 1913.

"OHIO IN AFRICA"

Shunk, E.W. "Ohio in Africa," a plan for a colony of Ohio free-Negro emigrants in Liberia, c. 1850. OAQ 51: 70-87, Apr.-June 1942.

OKLAHOMA

Forbes, G. Part played by Indian slavery in removal of tribes to Oklahoma. OKC 16:163-70, June 1938.

Porter, K.W. The Creek Indian-Negro tradition. The Hawkins Negroes go to Mexico. OKC 24:55-8, Spring 1946.

Oldham, J.H. Review of J.W. Gregory, The menace of colour. IRM 14:454-6, July 1925.

Oliver, W.P. Cultural progress of the Negro in Nova Scotia. DAL 29:203-300, Oct. 1949.

OPINIONNAIRES

Merton, R.K. Fact and factitiousness in ethnic opinionnaires. ASR 5:13-28, Feb. 1940.

ORCHESTRAS

The Harlem rendezvous and his Negro jazz orchestra. Edward Kennedy "Duke" Ellington. FTE 8:47+, Aug. 1933.

ORDINANCE OF 1782

Owen, D. Slavery in Indiana. Circumvention of Article VI, Ordinance of 1782. INM 36:110-6, June 1940.

OREGON

The case of Robin Holmes vs. Nathaniel Ford. ORE 23: 111-37, June 1922.

Davenport, T.W. Slavery in Oregon. ORE 9:309-73, Dec. 1908.

Davenport, T.W., and G.H. Williams. Oregon agitation up to 1801. ORE 8:189-273, Sept. 1908.

Lockley, Frederick. Oregon slavery documentary records. ORE 17:107-15, June 1916.

Slavery agitation in Oregon up to 1861. ORE 8:189-273, Sept. 1908.

ORIGINS

Stoddard, A.H. Origin, dialect, beliefs and characteristics of the Negroes of the South Carolina and Georgia coasts. GHQ 28:186-95, Sept. 1944.

Osborn, G.C. Life of a Southern plantation owner during Reconstruction, as revealed in the Clay Sharkey papers. JMH 6:103-12, Apr. 1944.

Osborn, G.C. Plantation life in central Mississippi as revealed in the Clay Sharkey papers. JMH 3:277-88, Oct. 1941.

Osborn, H.F. Race progress and its relation to social progress. NIS 9:8-18, 1924.

Osborne, D.F. The sectional struggle over rights of slavery in new territory added to U.S. GHQ 15:223-51, Sept. 1931.

OSBORNE, INDIANA

McCain, William D. The emancipation of Indiana Osborne. JMH 8:97-8, Apr. 1946.

Osgood, H.O. Review of W.C. Handy, The Blues. MOD 4:25-8, Nov.-Dec. 1926.

"OSSAWATTOMIE BROWN"

Swayze, L.E. "Ossawattomie Brown," an old play on John Brown. KHQ 6:34-59, Feb. 1937.

Ottley, Roi. Black Jews of Harlem. TRA 79:18-21, July 1942.

OTTLEY, ROI

Redding, J.S. Review of R. Ottley, Black odyssey: The story of the Negro in America. MVH 36:117, June 1949.

Ousley, F.L. Review of E.M. Coulter, The South during Reconstruction. SWH 52:248-50, Oct. 1948.

OVERSEERS

Sydnor, C.S. The relation between a slave owner and his overseers. NCH 14:31-8, Jan. 1937.

Overturf, W. John Brown's cabin at Nebraska City. NHS 21:92-100, Apr.-June 1940.

Ovington, Mary W. Certain books on the Negro. EXL 2:263-4, June 1925.

OVINGTON, MARY W.

Chamberlain, A.F. Review of Mary W. Ovington, Half a man. JRD 2:345-6, Jan. 1912.

Owen, D. Slavery in Indiana. Circumvention of Article VI, Ordinance of 1782. INM 36:110-6, June 1940.

Owens, Sr. M. Lilliana. Story of Julia Greeley, the colored angel of mercy. COL 20:176-8, Sept. 1948.

OWNERS

Slave owners, Spotsylvania Co., Va., 1783. VAM 4:292-8, Jan. 1897.

OWNERSHIP

Sitterson, J.C. The William J. Minor plantations: A study in ante-bellum absentee ownership. JSH 9:59-74, Feb. 1943.

Owsley, F.L. Review of D. Dumond, Antislavery origins of the Civil War in the U.S. NCH 17:186-8, Apr. 1940.

Padgett, J.A., ed. Letters from North Carolina--Reconstruction period. NCH 20:259-82, July 1943, previous and following issues.

Padgett, J.A., ed. Letters to Thaddeus Stevens regarding Reconstruction. NCH 18:171-95, Apr. 1941 and following issues.

PAGEANTS

Crawford, Myrtle B. Instructions for producing pageant for Negro History Week. SOS 32:27-31, Jan. 1941.

Paine, A.B. Truth about the Brownsville, Texas, affair, by Capt. "Bill" McDonald. PRS 20:221-35, Sept. 1908.

Pantle, Alberta, ed. Larry Lapsley, 1840-97. Story of a Kansas freedman. KHQ 11:341-69, Nov. 1942.

PAPERS

Chamberlain, A.F. Universal Races Congress: Papers and proceedings. JRD 2:494-7, Apr. 1912.

PAPERS (cont'd)

Wilkins, Mary, ed. The American Cotton Planters' Ass'n: Papers, 1865-6. THQ 7:335-61, Dec. 1948 and following issue.

Paquet, L.A. Slaves and slavery in Canada. RSC 3d s. 7: 139-49, sec. 1, 1913.

Park, R.E. Assimilation in secondary groups with particular reference to the Negro. ASS 8:66-83, 1913.

Park, R.E. Negro race consciousness as reflected in race literature. AMR 1:505-17, Sept.-Oct. 1923.

Park, R.M. Tuskegee international conference on the Negro. JRD 3:117-20, July 1912.

Parks, E.T. Review of W.H. Callcott, The Caribbean policy of the U.S. JSH 9:430-2, Aug. 1943.

Parks, E.W. Frances Wright--founder of the emancipating labor society, Nashoba, Tenn. THM 2d s. 2:74-86, Jan. 1932.

Parks, J.H. John Bell and the Compromise of 1850. JSH 9: 328-56, Aug. 1943.

Parks, J.H. The Tennessee Whigs and the Kansas-Nebraska bill, 1854. JSH 10:308-30, Aug. 1944.

Parson, A.B. Beginnings of the Episcopal Church ministry in Liberia. PEH 7:154-77, June 1938.

Parsons, Elsie. Ashanti influence in Negro folktales and customs in Jamaica. JAF 47:391-5, Oct.-Dec. 1934.

Parsons, Elsie. Folk-tales of Negroes. FLL 28:408-14, Dec. 1917.

Patricia, Sr. Margaret. White servitude in the American colonies. AMC 42:12-53, Mar. 1931.

Patton, J.W. Review of H. Crum, Gullah: Negro life in the Caroline Sea Islands. MVH 28:300, Sept. 1941.

PAUL LAURENCE DUNBAR APARTMENTS

Housing problems for Negroes in New York City. Paul Laurence Dunbar apartments. ARC 59:5-12, Jan. 1929.

Pearce, H.J., Jr. Review of E.M. Coulter, The South during Reconstruction. GHQ 32:71-2, Mar. 1948.

Pelzer, L. Slavery and the Negro in Iowa. IAJ 2:471-84, Oct. 1904.

Pendergraft, D. The political career of Thomas Corwin and the conservative Republican reaction, 1858-61. OAQ 57:1-23, Jan. 1948.

Pendleton, Helen B. Negro in war-time. PUB 21:1290, Oct. 12, 1918.

Pennington, E.L. Philanthropic activities of the Bray Associates among the Negroes. PAM 58:1-25, Jan. 1934.

Pennington, E.L. Work of Rev. Francis Le Jau in colonial South Carolina among Indians and Negro slaves. JSH 1:442-58, Nov. 1935.

PENNSYLVANIA

Historic account of slavery in Pennsylvania. AME 17:399-426, Oct. 1923.

Klingberg, F.J. Missionary activity of the S.P.G. among the African immigrants of colonial Pennsylvania and Delaware. PEH 11:126-53, June 1942.

Miller, E.C. John Brown's ten years in Northwestern Pennsylvania. PAH 15:24-33, Jan. 1948.

Riddell, W.R. Slave trade in pre-Revolutionary Pennsylvania. PAM 52:1-28, Jan. 1928.

Turner, E.R. Abolition of slavery in Pennsylvania. PAM 36:129-42, Apr. 1912.

Turner, E.R. Slavery in colonial Pennsylvania. PAM 35:141-51, Apr. 1911.

Turner, E.R. Underground railroad. PAM 36:309-18, July 1912.

PENNSYLVANIA, ALTOONA

Hesseltine, W.B., and Hazel C. Wolf. The Emancipation Proclamation and the Altoona conference. PAM 71:195-205, July 1947.

PENNSYLVANIA, GERMANTOWN

Binder-Johnson, Hildegard. Germantown (Pa.) protest of 1688 against Negro slavery. PAM 65:145-56, Apr. 1941.

PENNSYLVANIA, PHILADELPHIA

Wilkinson, N.B. The Philadelphia free produce attack on slavery. PAM 66:294-313, July 1942.

PEONAGE

Peonage in Southern states. PUB 14:555, June 16, 1911.

PERCY, CHARLES

Hamilton, W.B., and W.D. McCain, eds. Inventories of the estate of Charles Percy, planter, 1794 and 1804. JMH 10:290-316, Oct. 1948.

Perkins, A.E. Negro spirituals from the far South. JAF 35: 223-49, July-Sept. 1922.

Perkins, A.E., comp. Riddles from Negro school children in New Orleans, La. JAF 35:105-15, Apr.-June 1922.

Perkins, D. Review of R.P. Warren, John Brown, the making of a martyr. VQR 6:614-8, Oct. 1930.

Perkins, H.C. The defense of slavery in the Northern press on the eve of the Civil War. JSH 9:501-31, Nov. 1943.

Perlman, Philip B. See CLARK, TOM C.

Perrow, E.C. Songs and rhymes of the South. JAF 26:123-73, Apr.-June 1913.

Perry, C.E. The voice of New Hampshire in the slave controversy. NWH 61:63-6, Feb.-Mar. 1929.

PERSONALITY

Himelhoch, J. Is there a bigot personality? A report on some preliminary studies. COM 3:277-84, Mar. 1947.

Reuter, E.B. The personality of mixed bloods. ASS 22:52-9, 1928.

PESSIMISM

Weatherly, U.S. Racial pessimism. ASS 18:1-17, 1923.

Petry, Ann. Harlem. A medieval ghetto in the heart of the biggest, richest city in the world. HOL 5:110-6, Apr. 1949.

Phayre, I. The slave trade today. ENG 60:55-65, Jan. 1935.

Phelan, R.V. Slavery in central United States. WHP 252-64, 1905.

PHILANTHROPY

Garrison, C.W., ed. Beginnings of Slater Fund for carrying education to the Negroes of the South. JSH 5:223-45, May 1939.

Pennington, E.L. Philanthropic activities of the Bray Associates among the Negroes. PAM 58:1-25, Jan. 1934.

Phileo, Mrs. Calvin. See CRANDALL, PRUDENCE

Phillips, D.E. Slaves who fought in the Revolution. JAH 5:143-6, Jan.-Mar. 1911.

Phillips, Edna. A plan for cooperation between evening school teachers and librarians in the educational development of racial groups. ALA 26:29-30, Jan. 1932.

Phillips, F.L. The life of Benjamin Banneker. CHS 20:114-20, 1917.

PHILLIPS, PHILIP

Learned, H.B. Reaction of Philip Phillips to the repeal of the Missouri Compromise. MVH 8:303-17, Mar. 1922.

Phillips, U.B. Central theme of Southern history. AHR 34:30-43, Oct. 1928.

Phillips, U.B. Plantations with slave labor and free. AHR 30:738-53, July 1925.

Phillips, U.B. A slave plantation in 1792-6: The Worthy Park Plantation, Jamaica. AHR 19:543-58, Apr. 1914.

PHILOSOPHY

Harshaw, D.A. Philosophy of the Negro spiritual. HOM 95:184-6, Mar. 1928.

PHYSIOGRAPHY

Taylor, Griffith. The distribution of future white settlement. GEO 12:375-402, July 1922.

Willcox, W.F. On the future distribution of white settlement. GEO 12:646-7, Oct. 1922.

PHYSIOLOGY

Grant, M. The physical basis of race. NIS 3:184-97, 1917.

PICNICS

Studley, Marian H. An August First anti-slavery picnic. NEQ 16:567-77, Dec. 1943.

PICTURES

Jacob Lawrence, his pictures of the South-to-North migration of Negroes that began during the First World War. FOR 24:102-9, Nov. 1941.

Malin, J.C. The John Brown legend in pictures. KHQ 8: 339-41, Nov. 1939; 9:339-42, Nov. 1940.

Pierson, D. The Negro in Bahia, Brazil. ASR 4:524-33, Aug. 1939.

Pillsbury, A.E. Sketch of Parker Pillsbury. GRA 54:73-6, Mar. 1922.

PILLSBURY, PARKER

Filler, L., ed. Parker Pillsbury: Biographical sketch. NEQ 19:315-37, Sept. 1946.

Pillsbury, A.E. Sketch of Parker Pillsbury. GRA 54: 73-6, Mar. 1922.

PINCHBACK, P.B.S.

Grosz, Agnes S. P.B.S. Pinchback: His political career in Louisiana. LHQ 27:527-612, Apr. 1944.

PIONEERS

Harvey, J.R. Pioneer Negroes in Colorado. COL 26:165-76, July 1949.

McGue, D.B. John Taylor, a slave-born pioneer. COL 18: 161-8, Sept. 1941.

PLANTATION SYSTEM

Brewer, W.M. Effects of the plantation system on the ante-bellum South. GHQ 11:250-73, Sept. 1927.

Govan, T.P. Was plantation slavery profitable? JSH 8: 513-35, Nov. 1942.

PLANTATIONS

Abbey, Kathryn T. History of El Destino and Chemonie (Fla.) plantations and documents pertaining thereto (1828-68). FHS 7:179-213, Jan. 1929 and following issues.

Adams, Fannie L.G. A childhood spent at Hayfield plantation near Fredericksburg, Va., during the Civil War. WMQ 2d s. 23:292-7, July 1948.

Bruce, W.C. A plantation retrospect of the Reconstruction period after the Civil War. VQR 7:546-61, Oct. 1931.

Carmichael, Maude. Federal experiments with Negro labor on abandoned plantations in Arkansas. ARK 1:101-16, June 1942.

Causton's Bluff, Deptford, Brewton Hill: Three allied plantations. GHQ 23:28-54, Mar. 1939 and following issue.

Coulter, E.M. Avondale and Deerbrook, Ga., plantation documents. GHQ 17:150-9, June 1933 and following issues.

Coulter, E.M. History of a century on a Georgia plantation. MVH 16:334-46, Dec. 1929.

Coulter, E.M. Planters' wants in the days of the Confederacy. GHQ 12:38-52, Mar. 1928.

Dimmick, J. Sir William Berkley's plantation at Green Spring, Va. WMQ 2d s. 9:129-30, Apr. 1929.

Fleming, W.L. Plantation life in the South. JAH 3: 233-46, Apr.-June 1909.

Griffeth, Lucile, ed. Brookdale farm: A record book, 1856-57. JMH 7:23-31, Jan. 1945.

Hamilton, W.B., and W.D. McCain, eds. Inventories of the estate of Charles Percy, planter, 1794 and 1804. JMH 10:290-316, Oct. 1948.

Harn, Julia E. Life and customs on plantations and in small communities of the ante-bellum South. GHQ 16:47-55, Mar. 1932 and previous and following issues.

Hiden, Mrs. P.W. Inventory and appraisement of a Virginia well-to-do planter's estate, 1760. WMQ 2d s. 16:600-1, Oct. 1936.

House, A.V., Jr. A Reconstruction share-cropper contract on a Georgia rice plantation. GHQ 2:156-65, June 1942.

PLANTATIONS (cont'd)

House, A.V. Jr., ed. Deterioration of a Georgia rice plantation during the Civil War. JSH 9:98-113, Feb. 1943.

Jordan, W.T., ed. A system of operation of Beaver Bend plantation, Georgia, 1862. JSH 7:76-84, Feb. 1941.

Laughlin, C.J. Plantation architecture in Louisiana. MAR 41:210-3, Oct. 1948.

Letters pertaining to economic and social life of plantations in 1833-36. GHQ 14:150-73, June 1930.

Lombard, Mildred E., ed. Contemporary opinions of Georgia. A journal of life on a slave-holding plantation. GHQ 14:335-43, Dec. 1930.

Magoffin, Dorothy S. A Georgia planter and his plantation. NCH 15:354-77, Oct. 1938.

Management of Negroes on Southern estates. THM 5:97-100, July 1919.

Moody, V.A. Slavery on Louisiana sugar plantations. LHQ 7:191-303, Apr. 1924.

Mulberry Grove, Georgia, in colonial times. GHQ 23:236-52, Sept. 1939.

Murphee, D. Hurricane and Brierfield, the Jefferson Davis plantations on Palmyra Island, Miss. JMH 9:98-107, Apr. 1947.

Osborn, G.C. Plantation life in central Mississippi as revealed in the Clay Sharkey papers. JMH 3:277-88, Oct. 1941.

Phillips, U.B. Plantations with slave labor and free. AHR 30:738-53, July 1925.

Phillips, U.B. A slave plantation in 1792-6: The Worthy Park plantation, Jamaica. AHR 19:543-58, Apr. 1914.

Plantation of the Royal Vale. GHQ 27:88-110, Mar. 1943.

Potter, G.M., Jr. The rise of the plantation system in Georgia. GHQ 16:114-35, June 1932.

Prichard, W. A Louisiana sugar plantation under the slavery regime. MVH 14:168-78, Sept. 1927.

Prichard, W., ed. Lease of a Louisiana plantation and slaves. LHQ 21:995-7, Oct. 1938.

Seal, A.G. John Carmichael Jenkins and his scientific management of his plantations. JMH 1:14-28, Jan. 1939.

Sitterson, J.C. Hired labor on sugar plantations of the ante-bellum South. JSH 14:192-205, May 1948.

Sitterson, J.C. The William J. Minor plantations: A study in ante-bellum absentee ownership. JSH 9:59-74, Feb. 1943.

Stephenson, W.H. A quarter-century at Pleasant Hill. MVH 23:355-74, Dec. 1936.

Story of Brampton plantation. GHQ 27:28-55, Mar. 1933.

Story of certain plantations. GHQ 24:342-73, Dec. 1940 and following issues.

Story of Rae's Hall plantation. GHQ 26:225-48, Sept.-Dec. 1942 and following issue.

Story of Richmond Oakgrove plantation. GHQ 24:22-42, Mar. 1940 and following issue.

Story of the Drakies plantation. GHQ 24:207-35, Sept. 1940.

Story of the Hermitage plantation. GHQ 27:56-87, Mar. 1943.

Story of Whitehall plantation. GHQ 25:340-63, Dec. 1941 and following issue.

White, Alice P. The plantation experience of Joseph and Lavinia Erwin, 1807-36: Records and papers. LHQ 27: 343-478, Apr. 1944.

White, W.W. History of a slave plantation. SWH 26:79-127, Oct. 1922.

Whitehall plantation. GHQ 25:340-63, Dec. 1941.

PLANTERS

Flanders, R.B. Planters' problems in ante-bellum Georgia. GHQ 14:17-40, Mar. 1930.

Klingberg, F.W. Operation Reconstruction: A report on Southern unionist planters. NCH 25:466-84, Oct. 1948.

Magoffin, Dorothy S. A Georgia planter and his plantation. NCH 15:354-77, Oct. 1938.

Osborn, G.C. Life of a Southern plantation owner during Reconstruction, as revealed in the Clay Sharkey papers. JMH 6:103-12, Apr. 1944.

PLANTERS (cont'd)

Rice, Eliza G. Louisiana planters' plea for self-government of slaves, 1849. JAH 3:621-6, Oct.-Dec. 1909.

Trexler, H.A. The opposition of planters to employment of slaves as laborers by the Confederacy. MVH 27:211-24, Sept. 1940.

White, Alice P. The plantation experience of Joseph and Lavinia Erwin, 1807-36: Records and papers. LHQ 27: 343-478, Apr. 1944.

Wilkins, Mary, ed. The American Cotton Planters' Ass'n: Papers, 1865-6. THQ 7:335-61, Dec. 1948 and following issue.

PLOTS

King, Ethel. The New York Negro plot of 1741. USC 20: 173-80, 1931.

POETRY

Knox, Winifred. American Negro poetry. BKL 81:16-7, Oct. 1931.

POINDEXTER, JAMES PRESTON

Minor, R.C. The career of James Preston Poindexter, Negro statesman, in Columbus, Ohio. OAQ 56:266-86, July 1947.

POLITICAL CONVENTIONS

Mowry, Duane. New York Democratic convention's "corner stone" resolution, 1847. IHJ 3:88-90, Oct. 1910.

POLITICAL PARTIES

Ryle, W.H. Slavery and party realignment in the Missouri state election of 1856. MOH 39:320-32, Apr. 1945.

POLITICAL REPRESENTATION

Simpson, A.F. The political significance of slave representation, 1787-1821. JSH 7:315-42, Aug. 1941.

POLITICS

Dickson, Harris. The Negro in politics. HAM 23:225-36, Aug. 1909.

Driggs, O.T., Jr. Arkansas politics: The essence of the Powell Clayton regime, 1868-1871. ARK 8:1-75, Spring 1949.

Gosnell, H.F. Political meetings in Chicago's "black belt." APS 28:254-8, Apr. 1934.

Grantham, D.W., Jr. Politics and the disfranchisement of the Negro. GHQ 32:1-21, Mar. 1948.

Harrington, F.H. Nathaniel Banks. A study in anti-slavery politics. NEQ 9:626-54, Dec. 1936.

Mabry, W.A. Louisiana politics and the "grandfather clause." NCH 13:290-310, Oct. 1936.

Moseley, J.A.R. The citizens white primary in Marion Co., Texas, of 1898. SWH 49:524-31, Apr. 1946.

Pendergraft, D. The political career of Thomas Corwin and the conservative Republican reaction, 1858-61. OAQ 57:1-23, Jan. 1948.

Reilley, E.C. Politico-economic considerations in Western Reserve's early slavery controversy. OAQ 52: 141-57, Apr.-June 1943.

Stone, A.H. The basis of white political control in Mississippi. JMH 6:225-36, Oct. 1944.

Strong, D.S. The rise of Negro voting in Texas. APS 42:510-22, June 1948.

Tebeau, C.W. Visitors' views of politics and life, 1865-80. GHQ 26:1-15, Mar. 1942.

Woodward, C.V. Tom Watson and the Negro in agrarian politics. JSH 4:14-33, Feb. 1938.

Young, J.H. Anna Elizabeth Dickinson--her campaign during the Civil War period for and against Lincoln. MVH 31:59-80, June 1944.

POLL TAX

Strong, D.S. The poll tax: The case of Texas. APS 38: 693-709, Aug. 1944.

POMEROY, SAMUEL CLARKE

Langsdorf, Edgar. Samuel Clarke Pomeroy and the New England Emigrant Aid Company, 1854-8. KHQ 7:227-45, Aug. 1938 and following issue.

POPULAR CULTURE

Wolfe, B. Uncle Remus and the malevolent rabbit: The Negro in popular American culture. COM 8:31-41, July 1949.

POPULAR SOVEREIGNTY

Hubbart, H.C. Revisionist interpretations of Douglas and his doctrine of popular sovereignty. SOS 25:103-7, Mar. 1934.

POPULATION

Farrison, W.E. Negro population of Guilford Co., N.C., before the Civil War. NCH 21:319-29, Oct. 1944.

Hartshorne, R. Racial maps of U.S. population. GEO 28: 276-88, Apr. 1938.

Mitchell, J.B. An analysis of population by race, nativity and residence. ARK 8:115-32, Summer 1949.

Valian, P. Internal migration and racial composition of the Southern population. ASR 13:294-8, June 1948.

POPULISM

Woodward, C.V. Tom Watson and the Negro in agrarian politics. JSH 4:14-33, Feb. 1938.

Porter, Betty. The history of Negro education in Louisiana. LHQ 25:728-831, July 1942.

Porter, Dorothy B. Early American Negro writings: A bibliographical study with a preliminary check list of the published writings of American Negroes, 1760-1835. BSA 39:192-268, Third Quarter, 1945.

Porter, James A. Versatile interests of the early Negro artist: A neglected chapter of American art history. AIA 24:16-27, Jan. 1936.

PORTER, JAMES A.

Franklin, John H. Review of James A. Porter, Modern Negro art. NCH 21:172-3, Apr. 1944.

Review of J.A. Porter, Negro art. AMA 27:33-8, Jan. 1934.

Porter, K.W. The Creek Indian-Negro tradition. The Hawkins Negroes go to Mexico. OKC 24:55-8, Spring 1946.

Porter, K.W. The Negro Abraham; his life among the Seminole Indians. FHS 25:1-43, July 1946.

Porter, K.W. Negroes and Indians on the Texas frontier, 1834-74. SWH 53:151-63, Oct. 1949.

Porter, K.W. Notes on Seminole Negroes in the Bahamas. FHS 24:56-60, July 1945.

Porter, K.W. Varied parts played by Negroes in the American fur trade. MNN 15:421-33, Dec. 1934.

Posey, W.B. Influence of slavery upon the Methodist Church in the early South and Southwest. MVH 17:530-42, Mar. 1931.

Posey, W.B. The slavery question in the Presbyterian Church in the old Southwest. JSH 15:311-24, Aug. 1949.

Potter, G.M., Jr. The rise of the plantation system in Georgia. GHQ 16:114-35, June 1932.

Potts, Alma G. Slavery in the old Northwest. SOS 33:70+, Feb. 1942.

Powdermaker, Hortense. Discussion of recent books on the race problem. CJR 6:203-4, Apr. 1943.

Powell, Dorothy M. The Negro worker in Chicago industry. JOB 20:21-32, Jan. 1947.

Pratt, L.R. Development of Negroes in the U.S. AME 6: 529-34, June 1911.

PREACHERS

Knight, E.W. Notes on career of John Chavis, Negro Presbyterian preacher and teacher, 1763(?)- , as a teacher of Southern white children and of his ministry. NCH 7:326-45, July 1930.

PRESBYTERIAN CHURCH

Georgia Presbyterian Church on secession and slavery. GHQ 1:263-5, Sept. 1917.

Heckman, O.S. The role of the Presbyterian Church in Southern Reconstruction, 1860-1880. NCH 20:219-37, July 1943.

PRESBYTERIAN CHURCH (cont'd)

Knight, E.W. Notes on career of John Chavis, Negro Presbyterian preacher and teacher, 1763(?)- , as a teacher of Southern white children and of his ministry. NCH 7:326-45, July 1930.

Lyons, John F. Attitude of Presbyterians in Ohio, Indiana and Illinois toward slavery. PBY 11:69-82, June 1921.

Posey, W.B. The slavery question in the Presbyterian Church in the old Southwest. JSH 15:311-24, Aug. 1949.

Staiger, C.B. Abolitionism and the Presbyterian schism of 1837-8. MVH 36:391-414, Dec. 1949.

PREJUDICE

Ellis, G.W. Psychology of American race prejudice. JRD 5:297-315, Jan. 1915.

Glazer, N. The social scientists dissect prejudice. COM 1:79-85, May 1946.

Handlin, Oscar. Prejudice and capitalist exploitation: Does economics explain racism? COM 6:79-85, July 1948.

Howe, I., and B.J. Widick. The U.A.W. fights race prejudice; case history on the industrial front. COM 8:261-8, Sept. 1949.

Kaufmann, M. A little bit prejudiced. COM 6:372-3, Oct. 1948.

Lescohier, D.D. Causes of race prejudice and possible solutions of the problem. AMR 4:495-506, Dec. 1926.

McKenzie, Ruth I. An evaluation of racial prejudice towards Negroes in various countries. DAL 20:197-205, July 1940.

Mangus, A.R. A study of prejudice against the Negro. NDQ 21:5-14, Dec. 1930.

Minsky, L. Intolerance; a problem for psychiatrists? CJR 5:261-8, June 1942.

Thompson, J.V. Pathways to prejudice. CJR 4:464-75, Oct. 1941.

Wallis, W.D. Moral and racial prejudice. JRD 5:212-29, Oct. 1914.

Woodard, J.W. Some implications from our present knowledge concerning prejudice. ASR 11:344-56, June 1946.

PRESIDENT'S COMMITTEE ON CIVIL RIGHTS

Israel, S. Teaching of Report of President's Committee on Civil Rights. SOS 39:102-4, Mar. 1948.

McElfresh, Mona H. President's Committee on Civil Rights. ALA 42:74-5, Feb. 1948.

Wechsler, James A., and Nancy F. Wechsler. Report of President's Committee on Civil Rights: One year later. COM 6:297-304, Oct. 1948.

Price, R. Anti-abolition disturbances of 1836 in Granville, Ohio. OAQ 45:365-8, Oct. 1936.

Price, R. The Ohio Anti-Slavery Society's convention of 1836. OAQ 45:173-88, Apr. 1936.

Prichard, W. A Louisiana sugar plantation under the slavery regime. MVH 14:168-78, Sept. 1927.

Prichard, W., ed. Lease of a Louisiana plantation and slaves. LHQ 21:995-7, Oct. 1938.

PRIMARY ELECTIONS

Holland, L.M. Republican primaries in Georgia. GHQ 30: 212-7, Sept. 1946.

Moseley, J.A.R. The citizens white primary in Marion Co., Texas, of 1898. SWH 49:524-31, Apr. 1946.

Weeks, O.D. The white primary: 1944-48. APS 42:500-10, June 1948.

PRIMITIVE PEOPLE

Granberry, E. Primitive Negroes in Florida's turpentine forests. TRA 58:32-5, Apr. 1932.

Pritchard, W. Review of E.M. Coulter, The South during Reconstruction. LHQ 31:150-4, Jan. 1948.

Pritchard, W., ed. Origin and activities of the "White League." LHQ 23:525-43, Apr. 1940.

PROCEEDINGS

Chamberlain, A.F. Universal Races Congress: Papers and proceedings. JRD 2:494-7, Apr. 1912.

PROGRESS

Cooley, S. Progress of Negroes. PUB 18:875, Sept. 10, 1915.

Oliver, W.P. Cultural progress of the Negro in Nova Scotia. DAL 29:203-300, Oct. 1949.

Osborn, H.F. Race progress and its relation to social progress. NIS 9:8-18, 1924.

Washington, Booker T. Progress of the Negro race in Mississippi. WWL 13:409-13, Mar. 1909.

PROGRESSIVE PARTY

Link, A.S., ed. The Progressive party's lily-white policy in 1912: Correspondence between Theodore Roosevelt and Julian Harris. JSH 10:480-90, Nov. 1944.

PROPAGANDA

Fuller, J.D.P. Slavery propaganda during the Mexican War. SWH 38:235-45, Apr. 1935.

PROPERTY

Marshall, Ruth. Duane Mowry, ed. Property in Negroes: A Southern slaveholding woman's plea to Sen. J.R. Doolittle. AME 8:530-2, June 1913.

PRO-SLAVERY MOVEMENT. See also ANTI-ABOLITIONIST MOVEMENT

Connelley, W.E., and A. Morrall. Proslavery activity in Kansas. KAN 14:123-42, 1915-8.

Eastin, L.J. Notes on a proslavery march against Lawrence, Kan. KHQ 11:45-64, Feb. 1942.

Hubbart, H.C. Pro-Southern influence in the free West, 1840-65. MVH 20:45-62, June 1932.

Malin, J.C. The proslavery background of the Kansas struggle. MVH 10:285-305, Dec. 1923.

Moody, Joel. Marais des Cygnes massacre. KAN 14:208-23, 1915-8.

Perkins, H.C. The defense of slavery in the Northern press on the eve of the Civil War. JSH 9:501-31, Nov. 1943.

Stampp, K.M. The Southern refutation of the proslavery argument. NCH 21:35-45, Jan. 1944.

Tannar, A.H. Marais des Cygnes and rescue of Ben Rice. KAN 14:224-34, 1915-8.

PROTECTION SOCIETY OF MARYLAND

Protection Society of Maryland. MDH 1:358-63, June 1907.

PROTESTANT EPISCOPAL CHURCH

Bishop, Shelton H. A history of St. Philip's Church: The first colored parish in the Diocese of New York. PEH 15:298-317, Dec. 1917.

Bragg, George F., Jr. The Negro race and the Episcopal Church. PEH 4:47-52, Mar. 1935.

Franklin, J.H. Negro members of the Protestant Episcopal Church in ante-bellum North Carolina. PEH 13:216-34, Sept. 1944.

Parson, A.B. Beginnings of the Episcopal Church ministry in Liberia. PEH 7:154-77, June 1938.

PSYCHIATRISTS

Minsky, L. Intolerance; a problem for psychiatrists? CJR 5:261-8, June 1942.

PSYCHOANALYSIS

Bradley, P. Psycho-analyzing the Ku Klux Klan. AMR 2: 683-6, Nov.-Dec. 1924.

PSYCHOLOGY

Ellis, G.W. Psychology of American race prejudice. JRD 5:297-315, Jan. 1915.

Reuter, E.B. The personality of mixed bloods. ASS 22: 52-9, 1928.

PUBLIC AFFAIRS

Schuler, Kathryn R. Women in public affairs during Reconstruction. LHQ 19:668-750, July 1936.

PUBLIC CONVEYANCES

Stephenson, G.T. Separation of the races in public conveyances. APS 3:180-204, May 1909.

Puckett, N.N. Negro character as revealed in folk lore. ASS 28:12-23, May 1934.

PUERTO RICO

Gordon, Maxine W. Race patterns and prejudice in Puerto Rico. ASR 14:294-301, Apr. 1949.

PURITY

Woolley, R.W. Fight for race purity. PRS 23:3-11, Jan. 1910 and following issues.

QUADROONS

Mulcaster, J.G. A quadroon girl of Southern Illinois. IHJ 28:214-7, Oct. 1935.

QUAKERS. See SOCIETY OF FRIENDS

Quarles, Benjamin. Sources of abolitionist income. MVH 32:63-76, June 1945.

QUARLES, BENJAMIN

Broderick, F.L. Review of Benjamin Quarles, Frederick Douglass. NEQ 21:551-2, Dec. 1948.

Franklin, John H. Review of Benjamin Quarles, Frederick Douglass. MVH 35:515-6, Dec. 1948.

Jackson, S.L. Review of Benjamin Quarles, Frederick Douglass. NYH 29:443-4, Oct. 1948.

Lonn, Ella. Review of Benjamin Quarles, Frederick Douglass. AHR 54:156-7, Oct. 1948.

RACE

Dickson, Harris. Deterioration of the race. HAM 23:497-505, Oct. 1909.

Grant, M. The physical basis of race. NIS 3:184-97, 1917.

Grant, M. Racial aspects of restriction of immigration. NIS 7:44-54, 1921.

Grey, F.W. Race questions in Canada. UNI 7:212-30, Apr. 1908.

Griffis, W.E. Does the Bible throw light on the race question? HOM 70:94-9, Aug. 1915.

Humphrey, N.D. Race can work toward democracy. SOS 35:246-8, Oct. 1944.

Jenkins, Frances. Education adapted to meet racial needs. SCH 37:126-8, Feb. 1918.

Kephart, W.M. Is the American Negro becoming lighter? An analysis of the sociological and biological trends. ASR 13:437-43, Aug. 1948.
Comment by J.T. Blue, Jr., ASR 13:766-7, Dec. 1948.

Miller, H.A. Changing concepts of race. ASR 21:106-12, 1927.

Miller, K.D. Some racial factors in American life. HOM 85:312-9, Apr. 1923.

Mitchell, J.B. An analysis of population by race, nativity and residence. ARK 8:115-32, Summer 1949.

Newbegin, Marion I. Race and nationality. GEJ 50:313-35, Nov. 1917.

Osborn, H.F. Race progress and its relation to social progress. NIS 9:8-18, 1924.

Powdermaker, Hortense. Discussion of recent books on the race problem. CJR 6:203-4, Apr. 1943.

Race conflicts. PUB 20:666-7, July 13, 1917.

Rahilly, A. Gobineau's theory of the inequality of races. DUB 159:125-40, July 1916.

Ridgeway, William. Professor Ridgeway and racial origins. SCI 5:126-46, July 1910.

Robison, Sophia M. Effects of the factors of race and nationality on the registration of behavior as delinquent in New York City in 1930. ASS 28:37-44, May 1934.

Smith, R.M. Racial strains in Florida. FHS 11:16-32, July 1932.

Stephenson, G.T. Racial distinctions in Southern law. APS 1:44-61, Nov. 1906.

Stephenson, G.T. Separation of the races in public conveyances. APS 3:180-204, May 1909.

Stoutemyer, J.H. Certain experiments with backward races. JRD 5:438-66, Apr. 1916.

Strong, J. Race question from the Scriptural side. HOM 58:123-9, Aug. 1909.

Taylor, A.W. The church and the color line. HOM 92:479-81, Dec. 1926.

RACE (cont'd)

Taylor, E.G.R. Ideas current between 1580 and 1650 on influence of climate on racial characteristics. SGM 51:1-6, Jan. 1935.

Taylor, G. Evolution and distribution of race, culture and language. GEO 11:54-119, Jan. 1921.

Taylor, G. Future white settlement: A rejoinder. GEO 13:130, Jan. 1923.

Telford, C.W. A race study of St. Helena Island Negroes with particular reference to what effect their isolation has had upon them. NDQ 21:126-35, Winter 1931.

Thompson, E.W. White and black in the West Indies. IRM 19:183-94, Apr. 1930.

Tors, M. The value of racial mingling. WDT 47:532-5, May 1926.

Tumin, M.J. The idea of race dies hard: Current report on an old controversy. COM 8:80-5, July 1949.

Valian, P. Internal migration and racial composition of the Southern population. ASR 13:294-8, June 1948.

Wallis, W.D. Moral and racial prejudice. JRD 5:212-29, Oct. 1914.

Warner, C.D. Race and climate. OUT 44:38-9, Feb. 1917.

Weale, B.L.P. How color divides the world. WWL 14:598-604, Nov. 1909.

Weale, B.L.P. The position of the black man in the world today. WWL 15:237-43, Feb. 1910.

Weatherly, U.S. Racial elements in social assimilation. ASS 5:57-76, 1910.

Weatherly, U.S. Racial pessimism. ASS 18:1-17, 1923.

White is the finest race? STR 43:148-55, Feb. 1912.

Williams, Mildred, and W.L. Van Loan. Education for racial equality. SOS 34:308-11, Nov. 1943.

Wilson, C.J. People's attitude toward the Negro in early Ohio. OAQ 39:717-68, Oct. 1930.

Woodard, J.W. Some implications from our present knowledge concerning prejudice. ASR 11:344-56, June 1946.

Woodruff, C.E. Laws of racial and intellectual development. JRD 3:156-75, Oct. 1912.

Woolley, R.W. Fight for race purity. PRS 23:3-11, Jan. 1910 and following issues.

Work, M.N. Aspects and tendencies of the race problem. ASS 19:191-6, 1925.

Wright, R.C. The Southern white man and the Negro. VQR 9:175-94, Apr. 1933.

RACE APPRECIATION

Means, P.A. Race appreciation and democracy. JRD 9: 180-8, Oct. 1918.

RACE CONDITIONS

Needham, C.K. Comparison of race conditions in Jamaica with those in U.S. JRD 4:189-203, Oct. 1913.

RACE CONFLICT

Burma, J.H. Humor as a technique in race conflict. ASR 11:710-5, Dec. 1946.

RACE CONSCIOUSNESS

Park, R.E. Negro race consciousness as reflected in race literature. AMR 1:505-17, Sept.-Oct. 1923.

RACE DEVELOPMENT

Huntington, E. Climate, a neglected factor in race development. JRD 6:167-84, Oct. 1915.

Odum, H.W. Standards of measurement in race development. JRD 5:364-83, Apr. 1915.

RACE LITERATURE

Park, R.E. Negro race consciousness as reflected in race literature. AMR 1:505-17, Sept.-Oct. 1923.

RACE PATTERNS

Gordon, Maxine W. Race patterns and prejudice in Puerto Rico. ASR 14:294-301, Apr. 1949.

RACE PREJUDICE

Gordon, Maxine W. Race patterns and prejudice in Puerto Rico. ASR 14:294-301, Apr. 1949.

RACE PROBLEMS

Stone, A.H. Race problems in the South. SHA 11:20-37, Jan. 1907.

RACE RELATIONS

Frazier, E. Franklin. Sociological theory and race relations. ASR 12:261-71, June 1947.

Glick, C.E. Collective behavior in race relations. ASR 13:287-94, June 1948.

Marsh, W.L. The need for men. ENG 42:51-5, Jan. 1926.

O'Donnell, W.G. Race relations in a New England town. NEQ 14:235-42, June 1941.

Ross, M. They did it in St. Louis: One man against folklore. COM 4:9-15, July 1947.

Stone, A.H. Is race friction growing? ASS 2:69-110, 1907.

Stone, A.H. Race problem in the South. SHA 11:20-37, Jan. 1907.

Walker, H.J. Changes in the structure of race relations in the South. ASR 14:377-83, June 1949.

RACES, DISTRIBUTION OF

Corry, J.P. Racial elements in colonial Georgia. GHQ 20:30-40, Mar. 1936.

RACIAL ACCOMPLISHMENTS

DuBois, W.E.B. The Negro as a national asset. HOM 86:52-8, July 1923.

RACIAL ATTITUDES

Johnson, C.S. Racial attitudes of college students. ASS 28:24-31, May 1934.

RACIAL COOPERATION

Naruse, J. War and the concordia of race. JRD 5:268-75, Jan. 1915.

RACIAL DISTRIBUTION

Hartshorne, R. Racial maps of U.S. population. GEO 28:276-88, Apr. 1938.

RACIAL FRAMES OF REFERENCE

Seeman, M. Moral judgment: A study in racial frames of reference. ASR 12:404-11, Aug. 1947.

RACIAL MINGLING

Tors, M. The value of racial mingling. WDT 47:532-5, May 1926.

RACIAL MINORITIES

Burma, J.H. Racial minorities in wartime. SOS 35:157-8, Apr. 1944.

RACIAL MIXTURE

Reuter, E.B. The personality of mixed bloods. ASS 22: 52-9, 1928.

RACIAL ORIGINS

Ridgeway, William. Professor Ridgeway and racial origins. SCI 5:126-46, July 1910.

RACIAL PREJUDICE

Bernstein, David, and Adele Bernstein. Washington (D.C.): Tarnished symbol. Our capitol's treason against America. COM 6:397-403, Nov. 1948.

RACIAL PROBLEMS

Hoernle, R.F.A. Racial problems in the Empire. WOR 6: 49-53, Feb. 1939.

RACIAL RIVALRY

Bond, W.G. Race rivalry. ENG 43:74-9, July 1926.

RACIAL STRAINS

Smith, R.M. Racial strains in Florida. FHS 11:16-32, July 1932.

RACIAL THEORIES

Hogden, L. Biology and modern race dogmas. CJR 4:3-12, Feb. 1941.

RACIAL THEORY

Barnett, S.A. Light on theories of race. WOR 33-9, July 1945.

RACIALISM

Hoare, F.R. This racialism. DUB 204:126-39, Jan. 1939.

RACISM

Abrams, C. Homes for Aryans only: Restrictive covenant spreads legal racism in America. COM 3:421-7, May 1947.

Addams, Jane. Race problems of a democracy. ASS 14:206-15, 1919.

Baker, Emily V. Responsibility of the elementary teacher to overcome racial intolerance in future citizens. HIO 24:86-9, Feb. 1933.

Bernanos, Georges. Nation against race. DUB 209:1-6, July 1941.

Black, Stephen. Black men and white women. ENG 29:352-7, Oct. 1919.

Dickson, Harris. The unknowable Negro. HAM 23:728-42, June 1909 and following issues.

Handlin, Oscar. Prejudice and capitalist exploitation: Does economics explain racism? COM 6:79-85, July 1948.

Lockspeiser, E. Gobineau's friendship with Richard Wagner and the new racial cult. WOR 57-9, Feb. 1941.

Rahilly, A. Gobineau's theory of the inequality of races. DUB 159:125-40, July 1916.

RADICAL REPUBLICANS

Williams, H. General Banks and the radical Republicans in the Civil War. NEQ 12:268-80, June 1939.

Rahilly, A. Gobineau's theory of the inequality of races. DUB 159:125-40, July 1916.

RAILROADS

Hodder, F.H. The railroad background of the Kansas-Nebraska act. MVH 12:3-22, June 1925.

Rammelkamp, C.H. Anti-slavery movement and Illinois College. IHL 13:192-203, 1909.

Rammelkamp, C.H. Reverberations of the slavery conflict in Illinois College. MVH 14:447-61, Mar. 1928.

Rammelkamp, J. The Negro community in Providence, R.I., 1820-42. RIH 7:20-33, Jan. 1948.

Ramsdell, C.W. The natural limits of the expansion of slavery. MVH 16:151-71, Sept. 1929; also SWH 33:91-111, Oct. 1929.

Ramsdell, C.W. Review of H.P. Wilson, John Brown. SWH 17: 318-20, Jan. 1914.

Ramsdell, C.W. Review of J.A. Woodburn, The life of Thaddeus Stevens. SWH 17:93-5, July 1913.

Ranck, J.B. The attitude of James Buchanan towards slavery. PAM 51:126-42, Apr. 1927.

Randall, J.G. Part played by Sen. John Sherman in financial legislation during Reconstruction. MVH 19:382-93, Dec. 1932.

Randall, J.G. Review of J.H. Franklin, From slavery to freedom. MVH 35:288-9, Sept. 1948.

RANDOLPH, JOHN

Sherwood, H.N. Colonization of manumitted slaves in Ohio. John Randolph's bequest. MVH 5:39-59, 1912.

RANKIN, REV. JOHN

Grim, P.R. Rev. John Rankin: His ancestry and early career. OAQ 46:215-56, July 1937.

RANSDELL, J.H.

Whittington, G.P., ed. Facts concerning the loyalty of slaves in Northern Louisiana in 1863 as shown in the letters of J.H. Ransdell to Gov. T.O. Moore. LHQ 14: 487-502, Oct. 1931.

RANSOM, LOUIS LISCOLM

Fletcher, R.S. Ransom's painting of John Brown on his way to execution. KHQ 9:343-6, Nov. 1946.

RAS TAFARI

Lees, G.F. Ras Tafari and his people. WDT 44:121-9, July 1924.

Rayback, J.G. The Liberty party leaders of Ohio: Exponents of anti-slavery coalition. OAQ 57:165-78, Apr. 1948.

Reat, J.L. Slavery in Douglas Co., Ill. IHJ 11:177-9, July 1918.

RECONSTRUCTION

Alexander, T.B. Kukluxism in Tennessee, 1865-69: A technique for the overthrow of radical Reconstruction. THQ 8:195-219, Sept. 1949.

Andrews, Rena M. Andrew Johnson, his plan of restoration of the South to the Union in relation to that of Lincoln. THM n.s. 1:165-81, Apr. 1931.

Barnhart, John D., ed. Letters on Reconstruction on the lower Mississippi, 1864-78. MVH 21:387-96, Dec. 1934.

Beale, H.K. On rewriting Reconstruction history. AHR 45:807-27, July 1940.

Bentley, G.R. Political activity of the Freedmen's Bureau in Florida, 1865-70. FHS 28:28-37, July 1949.

Brown, I.V. American Freedmen's Union Commission--activities in Reconstruction under the direction of Lyman Abbott. JSH 15:22-38, Feb. 1949.

Bruce, W.C. A plantation retrospect of the Reconstruction period after the Civil War. VQR 7:546-61, Oct. 1931.

Buried at master's feet. AME 6:814-5, Aug. 1911.

Burns, F.P. White supremacy in the South. The battle for constitutional government, 1866. LHQ 18:581-616, July 1935.

Cooper, F. Reconstruction in Scott Co., Miss. MSS 13: 99-222, 1913.

Copeland, F. The New Orleans press and the Reconstruction. LHQ 30:149-337, Jan. 1947.

Donald, D.H. The role of the scalawag in Mississippi Reconstruction. JSH 10:447-60, Nov. 1944.

Dorris, J.T. Pardon and amnesty during the Civil War and Reconstruction: Excerpt from a forthcoming book. NCH 23:360-401, July 1946.

Ewing, C.A.M. Two Reconstruction impeachments. NCH 15: 204-30, July 1938.

Gerofsky, M. Background of Reconstruction. WVA 6:295-360, July 1945 and following issue.

Gonzales, J.E. William Pitt Kellogg, Reconstruction governor of Louisiana, 1873-77. LHQ 29:394-495, Apr. 1946.

Green, F.M. Writings of Walter Lynwood Fleming. JSH 2: 497-521, Nov. 1936.

Guiness, R.B. Revised historical viewpoints on Reconstruction. SOS 34:19-20, Jan. 1943 and following issues.

Halsell, Willie D., ed. Republican factionalism in Mississippi, 1882-4. JSH 7:84-101, Feb. 1941.

Hamilton, J.G. DeR. Andrew Johnson, his Southern policy. NCA 16:65-80, 1915.

Harris, F.B. Reconstruction period: The career of Henry Clay Warmoth, governor. LHQ 30:523-653, Apr. 1947.

Heckman, O.S. The role of the Presbyterian Church in Southern Reconstruction, 1860-1880. NCH 20:219-37, July 1943.

Herring, Harriet L. The Clement attachment: An episode in Reconstruction industrial history. JSH 4:185-98, May 1938.

Highsmith, W.E. Some aspects of Reconstruction. JSH 13:460-91, Nov. 1947.

Hollingsworth, R.R. Education and Reconstruction in Georgia. GHQ 19:112-33, June 1935 and following issue.

House, A.V., Jr. A Reconstruction share-cropper contract on a Georgia rice plantation. GHQ 26:156-65, June 1942.

Kendel, Julia. Reconstruction in Lafayette County. MSS 13:223-72, 1913.

Klingberg, F.W. Operation Reconstruction: A report on Southern unionist planters. NCH 25:466-84, Oct. 1948.

Ku Klux Klans of the Reconstruction period in Missouri. MOH 37:441-50, July 1943.

Kyle, J.W. Reconstruction in Panola Co. MSS 19:9-98, 1913.

Leach, Marguerite. The aftermath of Reconstruction in Louisiana. LHQ 32:631-717, July 1949.

Leftwich, G.J. Reconstruction in Monroe Co. MSS 9:53-84, 1906.

Lerche, C.O., Jr. Congressional interpretation of the guarantee of a republican form of government during Reconstruction. JSH 15:192-211, May 1949.

Lestage, H.O., Jr. The White League in Louisiana and its participation in Reconstruction riots, 1866-74. LHQ 18:617-95, July 1935.

McClendon, R. Earl. Status of the ex-Confederate states as seen in the readmission of U.S. senators. AHR 41:702-9, July 1936.

RECONSTRUCTION (cont'd)

McDaniel, Hilda M. Francis T. Nicholls and the end of Reconstruction. LHQ 32:357-513, Apr. 1949.

McNeilly, J.S. Reconstruction in Mississippi, 1874-96. MSS 12:283-474, 1912.

McNeilly, J.S. Reconstruction in Mississippi, 1863-90. MSS Cent. s. 2:165-535, 1918.

Magee, Hattie. Reconstruction in Lawrence and Jefferson Davis Counties. MSS 11:163-204, 1910.

Marshall, Ruth, Duane Mowry, ed. Property in Negroes: A Southern slaveholding woman's plea to Sen. J.R. Doolittle. AME 8:530-2, June 1913.

Moore, A.B. One hundred years of Reconstruction of the South. JSH 9:153-80, May 1943.

Nye, R.B. Albion W. Tourgee--his ideas concerning Reconstruction problems in the South. OAQ 50:101-14, Apr.-June 1941.

Osborn, G.C. Life of a Southern plantation owner during Reconstruction, as revealed in the Clay Sharkey papers. JMH 6:103-12, Apr. 1944.

Padgett, J.A., ed. Letters from North Carolina--Reconstruction period. NCH 20:259-82, July 1943, previous and following issues.

Padgett, J.A., ed. Letters to Thaddeus Stevens regarding Reconstruction. NCH 18:171-95, Apr. 1941 and following issues.

Randall, J.G. Part played by Sen. John Sherman in financial legislation during Reconstruction. MVH 19:382-93, Dec. 1932.

Reconstruction in Pontotoc Co. MSS 11:229-69, 1910.

Reconstruction in various counties. MSS 10:115-61, 1909.

Reynolds, John H. Presidential Reconstruction in Arkansas. ARA 1:352-61, 1906.

Russ, W.A., Jr. Anti-Catholic agitation. AMC 45:312-21, Dec. 1934.

Russ, W.A., Jr. Radical disfranchisement in Texas, 1867-70. SWH 38:40-52, July 1934.

Russ, W.A., Jr. Registration and disfranchisement under radical Reconstruction. MVH 21:163-80, Sept. 1931.

Russ, W.A., Jr. Was there danger of a second civil war during Reconstruction? MVH 25:39-58, June 1938.

St. Clair, K.E. Debtor relief in North Carolina during Reconstruction, 1865. NCH 18:215-35, July 1941.

Schuler, Kathryn R. Women in public affairs during Reconstruction. LHQ 19:668-750, July 1936.

Simkins, F.B. New viewpoints of Southern Reconstruction. JSH 5:49-61, Feb. 1939.

Simkins, F.S. White Methodism in South Carolina during Reconstruction. NCH 5:35-64, Jan. 1928.

Slavery and Reconstruction. J.R. Doolittle correspondence, 1848-65. SHA 11:94-105, Mar. 1907.

Smith, G.W. Carpetbag imperialism in Florida, 1862-8. FHS 27:99-130, Oct. 1948 and following issue.

Smith, W.H. Schuyler Colfax: His role in the development of Reconstruction policy. INM 39:323-44, Dec. 1943.

Stone, A.H. A Mississippian's view of civil rights, states rights, and the Reconstruction background. JMH 10:181-239, July 1948.

Stone, A.H. Post bellum Reconstruction--an American experience. JMH 3:227-45, July 1945.

Sweet, W.W. The Methodist Church and Reconstruction. IHL 20:83-94, 1914.

Sweet, W.W. Methodist Episcopal Church and Reconstruction. IHJ 7:147-65, Oct. 1914.

Tebeau, C.W. Visitors' views of politics and life, 1865-80. GHQ 26:1-15, Mar. 1942.

Thompson, C. Mildred. The Freedmen's Bureau in Georgia in 1865-6. GHQ 5:40-9, Mar. 1921.

Timberlake, Elsie. Did the Reconstruction give Mississippi new schools? MSS 12:72-93, 1912.

Tindall, George B. The campaign for the disfranchisement of Negroes in South Carolina. JSH 15:212-34, May 1949.

Ward, J.C., Jr. The Republican party in Bourbon Georgia, 1872-1890. JSH 9:196-209, May 1943.

Wells, W.C. Reconstruction and its destruction in Hinds Co., Miss. MHS 9:85-108, 1906.

Wilkins, Mary, ed. The American Cotton Planters' Ass'n: Papers, 1865-6. THQ 7:335-61, Dec. 1948 and following issue.

RECONSTRUCTION (cont'd)

Williams, Helen, and H. Williams. Wisconsin Republicans and Reconstruction, 1865-70. WIM 23:17-39, Sept. 1939.

Williams, T.H. Reconstruction. An analysis of some attitudes. JSH 12:469-86, Nov. 1946.

Williams, T.H. Unification movement: Its influence on Louisiana's Reconstruction history. JSH 11:349-69, Aug. 1945.

Woody, R.H. The labor and immigration problems of South Carolina during the Reconstruction period. MVH 18:195-212, Sept. 1931.

Young, J.H. Anna Elizabeth Dickinson--a woman abolitionist views the South in 1875. GHQ 32:241-51, Dec. 1948.

RECORDS

Lockley, Frederick. Oregon slavery documentary records. ORE 17:107-15, June 1916.

White, Alice P. The plantation experience of Joseph and Lavinia Erwin, 1807-36: Records and papers. LHQ 27: 343-478, Apr. 1944.

Redding, J.S. Review of R. Ottley, Black odyssey: The story of the Negro in America. MVH 36:117, June 1949.

Reed, C.D. Tribute to George Washington Carver. ANN 3d s. 24:248-53, Jan. 1943.

Reedman, J.N. Review of G. Myrdal, An American dilemma. IRM 34:211-4, Apr. 1945.

REFORM

Kraus, M. Slavery reform in the 18th century. PAM 60: 53-66, Jan. 1936.

REFORMERS

Guiness, R.B. Daniel Howell Hise, abolitionist and reformer. SOS 36:297-300, Nov. 1945.

REFUGEES

Hartridge, W.C. Refugees in Maryland from the St. Domingo slave revolt of 1793. MDH 38:103-22, June 1943.

Landon, F. Refugee Negroes from the United States in Ontario. DAL 5:523-31, Jan. 1926.

Landon, F. The work of the American Missionary Association among the Negro refugees in Canada West, 1848-64. OHS 21:198-205, 1924.

REGISTRATION

Russ, W.A., Jr. Registration and disfranchisement under radical Reconstruction. MVH 21:163-80, Sept. 1931.

Reid, R.L. How one slave became free: An episode in the old days of Victoria. BCH 6:251-6, Oct. 1942.

Reilley, E.C. Politico-economic considerations in Western Reserve's early slavery controversy. OAQ 52:141-57, Apr.-June 1943.

RELICS

Jackson, Mrs. F.N. Anti-slavery relics. CON 77:9-17, Jan. 1927.

RELIGIOUS EDUCATION

Lawrence, J.B. Religious education of Negroes in the colony of Georgia. GHQ 14:41-57, Mar. 1930.

REMINISCENCES

Cross, Cora M. Early days in Texas. Reminiscences by an old-time darky. TEX 4:380-93, Oct. 1929.

REPORT OF PRESIDENT'S COMMITTEE ON CIVIL RIGHTS

Wechsler, James A., and Nancy F. Wechsler. Report of President's Committee on Civil Rights: One year later. COM 6:297-304, Oct. 1948.

REPRESENTATION

Simpson, A.F. The political significance of slave representation, 1787-1821. JSH 7:315-42, Aug. 1941.

REPUBLIC OF TEXAS

Schoen, H. The free Negro in the Republic of Texas. SWH 39:292-308, Apr. 1936 and following issues.

REPUBLICAN PARTY

Halsell, Willie D., ed. Republican factionalism in Mississippi, 1882-4. JSH 7:84-101, Feb. 1941.

Holland, L.M. Republican primaries in Georgia. GHQ 30:212-7, Sept. 1946.

REPUBLICAN PARTY (cont'd)

Pendergraft, D. The political career of Thomas Corwin and the conservative Republican reaction, 1858-61. OAQ 57: 1-23, Jan. 1948.

Ward, J.C., Jr. The Republican party in Bourbon Georgia, 1872-1890. JSH 9:196-209, May 1943.

Williams, H. General Banks and the radical Republicans in the Civil War. NEQ 12:268-80, June 1939.

Williams, Helen, and H. Williams. Wisconsin Republicans and Reconstruction, 1865-70. WIM 23:17-39, Sept. 1939.

RE-SETTLEMENT

McGroarty, W.B. Settlement by colonies of emancipated Negroes in Brown Co., Ohio, 1818-46. WMQ 2d s. 21:208-26, July 1941.

RESIDENCE

Mitchell, J.B. An analysis of population by race, nativity and residence. ARK 8:115-32, Summer 1949.

RESTRICTIVE COVENANTS

Abrams, C. Homes for Aryans only: Restrictive covenant spreads legal racism in America. COM 3:421-7, May 1947.

Reuter, E.B. The personality of mixed bloods. ASS 22:52-9, 1928.

Rex, Millicent B. John Brown's life and burial at Lake Placid. AME 25:141-9, Apr. 1931.

Reynolds, John H. Presidential Reconstruction in Arkansas. ARA 1:352-61, 1906.

RHODE ISLAND, PROVIDENCE

Rammelkamp, J. The Negro community in Providence, R.I., 1820-42. RIH 7:20-33, Jan. 1948.

RHYMES

Perrow, E.C. Songs and rhymes of the South. JAF 26:123-73, Apr.-June 1913.

RICE

House, A.V., Jr. A Reconstruction share-cropper contract on a Georgia rice plantation. GHQ 26:156-65, June 1942.

House, A.V., Jr., ed. Deterioration of a Georgia rice plantation during the Civil War. JSH 9:98-113, Feb. 1943.

RICE, BEN

Tannar, A.H. Marais des Cygnes massacre and rescue of Ben Rice. KAN 14:224-34, 1915-8.

Rice, Eliza G. Louisiana planters' plea for self-government of slaves, 1849. JAH 3:621-6, Oct.-Dec. 1909.

Rice, M.M. Black Frank, a lovable character. WDT 53:434-6, Apr. 1929.

RICE, MADELEINE H.

Deye, A.H. Review of Madeleine H. Rice, American Catholic opinions in the slavery controversy. CHR 30:180-1, July 1944.

Lilly, E.P. Review of Madeleine H. Rice, American Catholic opinions in the slavery controversy. MVH 31:294-6, Sept. 1944.

Sydnor, C.S. Review of Madeleine H. Rice, American Catholic opinions in the slavery controversy. JSH 10: 492-3, Nov. 1944.

RICHARDSON, H.V.

Mokitimi, S. Review of H.V. Richardson, Dark glory: A picture of the church among the Negroes of the rural South. IRM 37:462-4, Oct. 1948.

Riddell, Justice. The story of Governor Sothel, one-time slave. DAL 9:475-80, Jan. 1930.

Riddell, W.R. A half-told story of real white slavery in the 17th century. NCH 9:299-303, July 1932.

Riddell, W.R. International complications between Illinois and Canada arising out of slavery. IHJ 25:123-6, Apr.-July 1932.

Riddell, W.R. Method of abolition of slavery in England, Scotland and Upper Canada compared. OHS 27:511-3, 1931.

Riddell, W.R. A Negro slave in Canadian Detroit, 1795. MHM 18:48-52, Winter 1934.

Riddell, W.R. An official record of slavery in Upper Canada. OHS 25:393-7, 1929.

Riddell, W.R. Slave trade in pre-Revolutionary Pennsylvania. PAM 52:1-28, Jan. 1928.

RIDDLES

Halpert, H. Some Negro riddles collected in New Jersey. JAF 56:200-2, July-Sept. 1943.

Perkins, A.E., comp. Riddles from Negro school children in New Orleans, La. JAF 35:105-15, Apr.-June 1922.

Ridgeway, William. Professor Ridgeway and racial origins. SCI 5:126-46, July 1910.

Riggs, J.B. Early Maryland landowners in the vicinity of Washington. CHS 48:249-63, 1949.

RIGHTS

Danziger, S. Courts and minority rights. PUB 16:866, Sept. 12, 1913.

RILEY, B.F.

Weatherhead, H.W. Review of B.F. Riley, Life and times of Booker T. Washington. IRM 7:125-7, Jan. 1918.

Riley, H.M. History of Negro elementary education in Indianapolis. INM 26:280-305, Sept. 1930.

RIOTS

Lestage, H.O., Jr. The White League in Louisiana and its participation in Reconstruction riots, 1866-74. LHQ 18:617-95, July 1935.

Robert, J.C. Review of R.A. Warner, New Haven Negroes: A social history. JSH 7:417-8, Aug. 1941.

ROBERT, J.C.

Morton, R.L. Review of J.C. Robert, The road from Monticello, a study of the Virginia slavery debate of 1832. WMQ 2d s. 22:70-5, Jan. 1942.

Robertson, J.A. Review of Mrs. N.W. Eppes, The Negro in the old South. NCH 3:380-3, Apr. 1926.

Robinson, J.T. History of suffrage in Arkansas. ARA 3:167-74, 1911.

ROBINSON, MARIUS RACINE

Nye, R.B. Marius Racine Robinson, his activities in the Ohio anti-slavery movement. OAQ 55:138-54, Apr.-June 1946.

Robison, Sophia M. Effects of the factors of race and nationality on the registration of behavior as delinquent in New York City in 1930. ASS 28:37-44, May 1934.

Rodabaugh, J.H. Miami University, Calvinism and the anti-slavery movement. OAQ 48:66-73, Jan. 1939.

RODMAN, S.

Washburn, G.B. Review of S. Rodman, Horace Pippin, a Negro painter in America. MAR 41:202, May 1948.

Rogers, W.M. Free Negro legislation in Georgia before 1865. GHQ 16:27-37, Mar. 1932.

ROLE

Lee, L.L. Role and status of the Negro in the Hawaiian community. ASR 13:419-37, Aug. 1948.

ROLFE, JOHN

Scisco, L.D. John Rolfe's story of first cargo of slaves, 1620. MAG 13:123-5, Mar. 1911.

ROMAN CATHOLIC CHURCH

Allen, C.E. The slavery question in Catholic newspapers, 1850-65. USC 26:99-169, 1936.

Butsch, J. Negro Catholics in U.S. CHR 3:33-51, Apr. 1917.

European Catholic opinions on slavery (reprint of an old and rare pamphlet). AMC 25:18-29, Mar. 1914.

Fisher, H.P. The Catholic Church in Liberia. AMC 40:249-310, Sept. 1929.

Meehan, T.F. Mission work among colored Catholics. USC 8:116-28, June 1915.

Murphy, Miriam T. Catholic missionary work among the colored people of the United States, 1776-1866. AMC 35:101-36, June 1924.

ROMAN CATHOLIC CHURCH (cont'd)

Nebbit, L. Letter of a colored child of the Sacred Heart. AMC 24:179-81, June 1913.

Russ, W.A., Jr. Anti-Catholic agitation. AMC 45:312-21, Dec. 1934.

Theobald, Stephen L. Catholic missionary work among the colored people of the United States (1776-1866). AMC 35:325-44, Dec. 1924.

Romero, F. The slave trade and the Negro in South America. HAH 24:368-86, Aug. 1944.

Roncal, J. The Negro race in Mexico: A statistical study. HAH 24:530-40, Aug. 1944.

ROOSEVELT, THEODORE

Link, A.S., ed. The Progressive party's lily-white policy in 1912: Correspondence between Theodore Roosevelt and Julian Harris. JSH 10:480-90, Nov. 1944.

ROSE, A.M.

Koenig, S. Review of A.M. Rose and Carolyn Rose, America divided: Minority group relations in the U.S. ASR 14: 435-7, June 1949.

Truman, D.B. Review of A.M. Rose and Caroline Rose, America divided: Minority group relations in the U.S. APS 43:821-3, Aug. 1949.

Rose, Carolyn. See ROSE, A.M.

Rose, J.C. Suffrage: Constitutional point of view. APS 1: 17-43, Nov. 1906.

Roseboom, E.H. Review of O. Crenshaw, The slave states in the presidential election of 1860. MVH 34:307+, Sept. 1947.

Ross, F.A. Urbanization and the Negro. ASS 26:115-28, 1932.

Ross, M. The 80th Congress and job discrimination: The outlook for a new F.E.P.C. COM 3:301-8, Apr. 1947.

Ross, M. They did it in St. Louis: One man against folklore. COM 4:9-15, July 1947.

Rothert, O.A. Two letters by Cassius Clay, 1862 and 1869. HIS 12:162-9, July 1938.

Roucek, J.S. Review of C.S. Johnson, Growing up in the black belt: Negro youth in the rural South. SOS 32:284, Oct. 1941.

RUNAWAY SLAVES

Landon, F. Anthony Burns in Canada. OHS 22:162-6, 1925.

Leslie, W.R. The constitutional significance of Indiana's statute of 1824 on fugitives from labor. JSH 13:338-53, Aug. 1947.

Sherwin, O. Boston: The case of Anthony Burns, Negro. NEQ 19:212-23, June 1946.

Smith, H.L. Aiding run-away slaves in Monroe Co. INM 13:288-97, Sept. 1917.

Trial and sentence of Biron, runaway Negro slave, 1728. LHQ 8:23-7, Jan. 1925.

Russ, W.A., Jr. Anti-Catholic agitation. AMC 45:312-21, Dec. 1934.

Russ, W.A., Jr. Disfranchisement in Louisiana, 1862-70. LHQ 18:557-80, July 1935.

Russ, W.A., Jr. Disfranchisement in Maryland, 1861-7. MDH 28:309-28, Dec. 1933.

Russ, W.A., Jr. Radical disfranchisement in Georgia, 1867-71. GHQ 19:175-209, Sept. 1935.

Russ, W.A., Jr. Radical disfranchisement in North Carolina, 1867-8. NCH 11:271-83, Oct. 1934.

Russ, W.A., Jr. Radical disfranchisement in Texas, 1867-70. SWH 38:40-52, July 1934.

Russ, W.A., Jr. Registration and disfranchisement under radical Reconstruction. MVH 21:163-80, Sept. 1931.

Russ, W.A., Jr. Review of Elsie Singmaster, I speak for Thaddeus Stevens. MVH 34:397-8, Dec. 1947.

Russ, W.A., Jr. Review of V.L. Wharton, The Negro in Mississippi. JSH 14:280-1, May 1948.

Russ, W.A., Jr. Was there danger of a second civil war during Reconstruction? MVH 25:39-58, June 1938.

RUSSELL, IRWIN

Webb, J.W. Irwin Russell and Negro folk literature. SFQ 12:137-49, June 1948.

Russell, R.R. The general effects of slavery upon Southern economic progress. JSH 4:34-54, Feb. 1938.

Ryan, J.H. Illinois anti-slavery struggle and its effect on the Methodist Church. IHL 19:67-76, 1913.

Ryan, J.H. Underground railroad incident in Illinois. IHJ 8:23-30, Apr. 1915.

Ryle, W.H. Slavery and party realignment in the Missouri state election of 1856. MOH 39:320-22, Apr. 1945.

S.P.G. See SOCIETY FOR THE PROPAGATION OF THE GOSPEL

SACO, JOSÉ ANTONIO

Notes on Saco's History of Negro slavery. HAH 24:452-7, Aug. 1944.

SACRED HEART

Nebbit, L. Letter of a colored child of the Sacred Heart. AMC 24:179-81, June 1913.

Saenger, G. Effect of the war on our minority groups. ASR 8:15-22, Feb. 1943.

SAID, OMAR IBN

Autobiography of Omar ibn Said, slave in North Carolina, 1831. AHR 30:787-95, July 1925.

St. Clair, K.E. Debtor relief in North Carolina during Reconstruction, 1865. NCH 18:215-35, July 1941.

ST. DOMINGO. See SANTO DOMINGO

ST. PHILIP'S CHURCH

Bishop, Shelton H. A history of St. Philip's Church: The first colored parish in the Diocese of New York. PEH 15:298-317, Dec. 1917.

Salmon, Andre. Negro art. BUR 36:164-72, Apr. 1920.

SALTER, REV. WILLIAM

Jordan, P.D. Rev. William Salter and the slavery controversy, 1837-64. IAJ 33:99-122, Apr. 1935.

Sampson, F.A., and W.C. Breckenridge. Bibliography of slavery in Missouri. MOH 2:233-44, Apr. 1908.

SAN DOMINGO. See SANTO DOMINGO

Sanders, A.G., tr. H.P. Dart, ed. Documents covering the beginning of the African slave trade in Louisiana, 1718. LHQ 14:103-77, Apr. 1931.

SANTO DOMINGO

Graham, H. Toussaint L'Ouverture, the Napoleon of San Domingo. DUB 153:86-110, July 1913.

Hartridge, W.C. Refugees in Maryland from the St. Domingo slave revolt of 1793. MDH 38:103-22, June 1943.

What U.S. is doing for Santo Domingo, Nicaragua and Haiti. NGE 30:143-77, Aug. 1916.

Sapir, E. Review of A book of American Negro spirituals. JAF 41:172-4, Jan.-Mar. 1928.

Savage, W.S. The origin of the Giddings Resolution, 1841. OAQ 47:20-39, Jan. 1938.

SCALAWAGS

Donald, D.H. The role of the scalawag in Mississippi Reconstruction. JSH 10:447-60, Nov. 1944.

Scelle, G. Slave-trade in Spanish colonies of America. AJI 4:612-61, July 1910.

Schafer, W. Fugitive slave act. Decision of the Booth Case. WIM 20:89-110, Sept. 1936.

Schmidt, H. Slavery and attitudes toward slavery in Hunterdon Co., N.J. NJS 58:151-69, July 1940 and following issue.

Schmidt, O.L. Illinois underground railroad. IHJ 18:703-17, Oct. 1925.

Schoen, H. The free Negro in the Republic of Texas. SWH 39: 292-308, Apr. 1936 and following issues.

SCHOOLS

Timberlake, Elsie. Did the Reconstruction give Mississippi new schools? MSS 12:72-93, 1912.

West Virginia Colored Institute. NAT 39:528-30, Dec. 1913.

SCHOOLS, ABOLITION

Ellsworth, C.S. Ohio legislative attack upon abolition schools. MVH 21:379-86, Dec. 1934.

Schuler, Kathryn R. Women in public affairs during Reconstruction. LHQ 19:668-750, July 1936.

SCIENTIFIC MANAGEMENT

Seal, A.G. John Carmichael Jenkins and his scientific management of his plantations. JMH 1:14-28, Jan. 1939.

Scisco, L.D. John Rolfe's story of first cargo of slaves, 1620. MAG 13:123-5, Mar. 1911.

SCOTLAND

Riddell, W.R. Method of abolition of slavery in England, Scotland, and Upper Canada compared. OHS 27:511-3, 1931.

Scott, Dred. See DRED SCOTT CASE

SCRIPTURE

Strong, J. Race question from the Scriptural side. HOM 58:123-9, Aug. 1909.

SCULPTURE

Szecsi, L. Negro sculpture in interior decoration. LST 7:326-7, June 1933.

Seal, A.G. John Carmichael Jenkins and his scientific management of his plantations. JMH 1:14-28, Jan. 1939.

Seal, A.G., ed. A Mississippian's defense of slavery. JMH 2:212-31, Oct. 1940.

Seale, Lee, and Marianna Seale. A Louisiana Negro ceremony: Easter Rock. JAF 55:212-8, Oct.-Dec. 1942.

Sears, L.M. Frederick Douglass: His career as U.S. minister to Haiti, 1889-91. HAH 21:222-38, May 1941.

SECESSION

Georgia Presbyterian Church on secession and slavery. GHQ 1:263-5, Sept. 1917.

John Q. Adams and secession, 1842. MAG 25:96-9, Sept.-Oct. 1917.

Shugg, R.W. A Louisiana co-operationist protest against secession. LHQ 19:199-203, Jan. 1936.

White, M.J. Louisiana and the secession movement of the early fifties. MIV 8:278-88, 1916.

SECONDARY GROUPS

Park, R.E. Assimilation in secondary groups with particular reference to the Negro. ASS 8:66-83, 1913.

SECRET SOCIETIES

Kennedy, Stetson. Nanigo in Florida. SFQ 4:153-6, Sept. 1940.

SECRETARY OF STATE

Letter from Secretary of State concerning John Brown. MAG 20:184, Mar.-Apr. 1915.

Seeman, M. Moral judgment: A study in racial frames of reference. ASR 12:404-11, Aug. 1947.

Seeman, M. Skin color values in three all-Negro school classes. ASR 11:315-21, June 1946.

SEGREGATION

Danziger, S. Segregation and land monopoly. PUB 19: 891-2, Sept. 22, 1916.

Davies, W.E. The problem of race segregation in the Grand Army of the Republic. JSH 13:354-72, Aug. 1947.

Dowd, J. Race segregation in a democracy. ASS 14:189-205, 1919.

Folmsbee, Stanley J. The origin of the first "Jim Crow" law. JSH 15:235-47, May 1949.

SEGREGATION (cont'd)

McLaughlin, James J. The black code. LHS 8:28-35, 1916; MIV 8:210-6, 1914-5.

Stephenson, G.T. Separation of the races in public conveyances. APS 3:180-204, May 1909.

Swann, T.W. Jim Crow laws threatened in Illinois. PUB 16:246, Mar. 14, 1913.

Selassie, Haile. See RAS TAFARI

SELF-DETERMINATION

Norton, H.K. Self-determination in the West Indies. The governments of the Caribbean. WDT 47:147-53, Jan. 1926.

SELF-GOVERNMENT

Rice, Eliza G. Louisiana planters' plea for self-government of slaves, 1849. JAH 3:621-6, Oct.-Dec. 1909.

SELF-LIBERATION

Braun, Robert. Man farthest down. PUB 16:152, Feb. 14, 1913.

SEMINOLE INDIANS

Porter, K.W. The Negro Abraham; his life among the Seminole Indians. FHS 25:1-43, July 1946.

SEMINOLE NEGROES

Porter, K.W. Notes on Seminole Negroes in the Bahamas. FHS 24:56-60, July 1945.

SENATE

McClendon, R. Earl. Status of the ex-Confederate states as seen in the readmission of U.S. senators. AHR 41:702-9, July 1936.

Senior, W. An episode in the slave trade. Great Britain. COR n.s. 54:561-6, May 1923.

SERMONS

Stidger, W.L. Negro spirituelles, a new idea in homiletics. HOM 90:26-9, July 1925.

SERVANTS

Smith, A.E. The indentured servant and land speculation in 17th century Maryland. AHR 40:467-72, Apr. 1935.

SERVITUDE. See also INDENTURED SERVANTS

Hoyt, W.D., Jr. White servitude in Northampton, Maryland, 1772-4. MDH 33:126-33, June 1938.

Patricia, Sr. Margaret. White servitude in the American colonies. AMC 42:12-53, Mar. 1931.

Siebert, W.H. Slavery and white servitude in East Florida, 1726 to 1776. FHS 10:3-23, July 1931.

Stuart, W. White servitude in New York and New Jersey. AME 15:19-37, Jan. 1921.

Settle, E. Ophelia. Social attitudes during the slave regime: Household servants versus field hands. ASS 28:95-8, May 1934.

SETTLEMENT

Taylor, G. Future white settlement: A rejoinder. GEO 13:130, Jan. 1923.

Sevier, M. Negro art. ATE 2:116-21, Aug. 1931.

SEX AND RACE

Black, Stephen. Black men and white women. ENG 29:352-7, Oct. 1919.

de Rivera, B. How women can halt "the great black plague." PRS 23:417-20, Mar. 1910.

SEX RATIO

Cox, O.C. Sex ratio and marital status among Negroes. ASR 5:937-47, Dec. 1940.

SHARECROPPERS

House, A.V., Jr. A Reconstruction share-sropper contract on a Georgia rice plantation. GHQ 26:156-65, June 1942.

SHARKEY, CLAY

Osborn, G.C. Life of a Southern plantation owner during Reconstruction, as revealed in the Clay Sharkey papers. JMH 6:103-12, Apr. 1944.

SHARKEY, CLAY (cont'd)

Osborn, G.C. Plantation life in central Mississippi as revealed in the Clay Sharkey papers. JMH 3:277-88, Oct. 1941.

SHARP, GRANVILLE

Granville Sharp, abolitionist. PCQ 16:22, Jan. 1929.

Sharpe, Esther E. Slavery in the territories under the Compromise of 1850. HIO 18:107-9, Mar. 1927.

SHAW, JOHN

Stevens, Wayne E. Shaw-Hansen election contest. IHJ 7: 389-401, Jan. 1915.

Sheppard, T.J. Putnam, Ohio, as an abolition centre. OAQ 19:266-9, July 1910.

SHERMAN, JOHN

Randall, J.G. Part played by Sen. John Sherman in financial legislation during Reconstruction. MVH 19:382-93, Dec. 1932.

Sherwin, O. The abolitionists and their fight against slavery. NEQ 18:70-82, Mar. 1945.

Sherwin, O. Boston: The case of Anthony Burns, Negro. NEQ 19:212-23, June 1946.

Sherwood, H.N. Colonization of manumitted slaves in Ohio. John Randolph's bequest. MVH 5:39-59, 1912.

Sherwood, H.N. Deportation projects. MVH 2:484-508, Mar. 1916.

Sherwood, H.N. Indiana and Negro deportation, 1817. MVH 9: 414-21, 1919.

Sherwood, H.N. Paul Cuffe and his contribution to the American Colonization Society. MVH 6:370-402, 1913.

Shillito, E. Samuel Chapman Armstrong. IRM 8:357-65, July 1919.

SHIPBUILDING

Northrup, H.R. Negroes in a war industry; the case of shipbuilding. JOB 16:160-72, July 1943.

SHIPS

View on board slave ship. HTM 3:188, Oct. 1912.

Shugg, R.W. A Louisiana co-operationist protest against secession. LHQ 19:199-203, Jan. 1936.

Shunk, E.W. "Ohio in Africa," a plan for a colony of Ohio free-Negro emigrants in Liberia, c. 1850. OAQ 51:70-87, Apr.-June 1942.

Siebert, W.H. Beginnings of the underground railroad in Ohio. OAQ 56:70-93, Jan. 1947.

Siebert, W.H. History of slavery in East Florida, 1776-1785. FHS 10:139-62, Jan. 1932 and previous issue.

Siebert, W.H. A Quaker section of the underground railroad in Northern Ohio. OAQ 39:429-502, July 1930.

Siebert, W.H. Slavery and white servitude in East Florida, 1726 to 1776. FHS 10:3-23, July 1931.

Siebert, W.H. The underground railroad in Massachusetts. NEQ 9:447-67, Sept. 1936.

Siebert, W.H. The underground railroad in Ohio. OAQ 4: 44-63, 1895.

SIEBERT, W.H.

Tuttle, C.E., Jr. Review of W.H. Siebert, Vermont's anti-slavery and underground railroad record. VHS n.s. 6: 3-11, Mar. 1938.

SIGNALS

Williams, Ora. Story of underground railway signals. ANN 27:297-303, Apr. 1946.

Sillen, S. The Negro's struggle for equal rights. WOR 6: 57-9, Feb. 1939.

SILVER

Linaker, R.H. A silver slave brand. CON 69:161-4, July 1924.

Simkins, F.B. Ben Tillman's view of the Negro and its reaction. JSH 3:161-74, May 1937.

Simkins, F.B. New viewpoints of Southern Reconstruction. JSH 5:49-61, Feb. 1939.

Simkins, F.S. White Methodism in South Carolina during Reconstruction. NCH 5:35-64, Jan. 1928.

SIMKINS, F.S.

Easterby, J.H. Review of F.S. Simkins and R.H. Woody, South Carolina during Reconstruction. NCH 10:85-7, Jan. 1933.

Stoney, S.G. Review of F.S. Simkins and R.H. Woody, South Carolina during Reconstruction. VQR 9:304-7, Apr. 1933.

Simms, H.H. Abolition literature, 1830-40, a critical analysis. JSH 6:368-82, Aug. 1940.

Simms, H.H. Review of F.W. Bond, The Negro and the drama. MVH 27:686, Mar. 1941.

Simms, Marion. Black magic in New Orleans yesterday and today. TRA 81:18-9, July 1943.

Simpson, A.F. The political significance of slave representation, 1787-1821. JSH 7:315-42, Aug. 1941.

Simpson, George E. Analysis of Haiti's social structure. ASR 6:640-9, Oct. 1941.

Simpson, George E. Four specialized ceremonies of the vodun cult in Northern Haiti. JAF 59:154-67, Apr.-June 1946.

Simpson, George E. Two vodun-related ceremonies from Haiti. JAF 61:49-52, Jan.-Mar. 1948.

Simpson, Lucretia C. Henry Clay and Liberia. JAH 16:237-45, July-Sept. 1922.

SIMPSON, BISHOP MATTHEW

Clark, R.D. Bishop Matthew Simpson and the Emancipation Proclamation. MVH 35:263-71, Sept. 1948.

SINGLETON, BENJAMIN "PAP"

Fleming, W.L. Moses of the colored exodus. AME 7:936-44, Oct. 1912.

SINGMASTER, ELSIE

Russ, W.A., Jr. Review of Elsie Singmaster, I speak for Thaddeus Stevens. MVH 34:397-8, Dec. 1947.

Weir, E. Review of Elsie Singmaster, I speak for Thaddeus Stevens. IHJ 40:351-2, Sept. 1947.

Sioussat, St. G.L. The Compromise of 1850 and the Nashville convention. THM 4:215-47, Dec. 1918.

Sitterson, J.C. Financing and marketing the sugar crop of the old South. JSH 10:188-99, May 1944.

Sitterson, J.C. Hired labor on sugar plantations of the ante-bellum South. JSH 14:192-205, May 1948.

Sitterson, J.C. The William J. Minor plantations: A study in ante-bellum absentee ownership. JSH 9:59-74, Feb. 1943.

SKIN COLOR

Seeman, M. Skin color values in three all-Negro school classes. ASR 11:315-21, June 1946.

SLATER FUND

Garrison, C.W., ed. Beginnings of Slater Fund for carrying education to the Negroes of the South. JSH 5:223-45, May 1939.

Slaughter, J.W. Our Caribbean policy. PUB 20:850-3, June 8, 1917.

SLAVE CODE

Taylor, R.H. Humanizing the slave code in North Carolina. NCH 2:323-31, July 1925.

SLAVE LABOR. See also SLAVERY

Bruce, Kathleen. Slave labor in Virginia iron industry. WMQ 2d s. 6:289-302, Oct. 1932 and following issues.

SLAVE NARRATIVES

Autobiography of Omar ibn Said, slave in North Carolina, 1831. AHR 30:787-95, July 1925.

SLAVE RESCUES

Fugitive or rescue case of 1857 in Ohio. OAQ 16:292-309, July 1907.

Galpin, W.F. Fugitive slave law of 1850. The Jerry Rescue precipitated a clash between the government and local abolitionists. NYH 26:19-33, Jan. 1945.

SLAVE REVOLTS

Hartridge, W.C. Refugees in Maryland from the St. Domingo slave revolt of 1793. MDH 38:103-22, June 1943.

SLAVE SHIPS

Hollis, D. In the track of slave ships. CHA 7th s. 17:721-3, Oct. 15, 1927.

SLAVE TRADE

Beltran, G.A. The slave trade in Mexico. HAH 24:412-31, Aug. 1944.

Carter, K. "The Cruz": An incident of the slave trade. CHA 19:177-80, Feb. 16, 1929 and following issue.

Catching slave-traders in Nigeria. WWL 19:331-6, Feb. 1912.

Clark, T.D. Slave trade between Kentucky and the cotton kingdom. MVH 21:331-42, Dec. 1934.

Cleven, N.A.N. Ministerial order of José de Galvez establishing a uniform duty on the importation of Negro slaves into the Indies. HAH 4:266-76, May 1921.

Coleman, J.W., Jr. Lexington, Ky., slave dealers and their Southern trade. HIS 12:1-23, Jan. 1938.

Corbitt, D.C. Shipments of slaves from the U.S. to Cuba, 1789-1807. JSH 7:540-9, Nov. 1949.

Creer, L.H. Spanish-American slave trade in the Great Basin, 1800-1853. NMH 24:171-83, July 1949.

Dodd, Dorothy. The schooner "Emperor" in the illegal slave trade in Florida. FHS 13:117-28, Jan. 1935.

Dounan, Elizabeth. The New England slave trade after the Revolution. NEQ 3:251-78, Apr. 1930.

Dounan, Elizabeth. Slave trade in South Carolina before the Revolution. AHR 33:804-28, July 1928.

Finley, Mrs. H.R. Measures against the American slave trade. AME 18:252-7, July 1924.

Georgia and the African slave trade. GHQ 2:87-113, June 1918.

Hastings, A.C.G. Slave traffickers. A capture thirty years ago. NAR 112:352-62, Mar. 1939.

Herron, Stella. The African apprentice bill, 1858. MIV 8:135-45, 1914-5.

Hill, L.F. The abolition of the African slave trade to Brazil. HAH 11:169-97, May 1931.

Hollis, D. In the track of slave ships. CHA 7th s. 17: 721-3, Oct. 15, 1927.

Howell, Isabel. Story of John Armfield, slave-trader. THQ 2:3-29, Mar. 1943.

King, J.F. Evolution of the free slave trade principle in Spanish colonial administration. HAH 22:34-56, Feb. 1942.

King, J.F. The suppression of the slave trade in the Latin American republics. HAH 24:387-411, Aug. 1944.

Phayre, I. The slave trade today. ENG 60:55-65, Jan. 1935.

Reminiscences of a slaving voyage. YHT 72:27-8, Sept. 1942.

Riddell, W.R. Slave trade in pre-Revolutionary Pennsylvania. PAM 52:1-28, Jan. 1928.

Romero, F. The slave trade and the Negro in South America. HAH 24:368-86, Aug. 1944.

Sanders, A.G., tr. H.P. Dart, ed. Documents covering the beginning of the African slave trade in Louisiana, 1718. LHQ 14:103-77, Apr. 1931.

Scelle, G. Slave-trade in Spanish colonies of America. AJI 4:612-61, July 1910.

SLAVE TRADE (cont'd)

Senior, W. An episode in the slave trade. Great Britain. COR n.s. 54:561-6, May 1923.

Stuart, W. Dutch and English importation to New Jersey and New York. AME 16:347-67, Oct. 1922.

View on board slave ship. HTM 3:188, Oct. 1912.

Wish, H. Revival of the African slave trade in the U.S., 1856-60. MVH 27:569-88, Mar. 1941.

SLAVE TRADERS

Howell, Isabel. Story of John Armfield, slave-trader. THQ 2:3-29, Mar. 1943.

SLAVEBREEDING

Wayland, Francis F. Slavebreeding in America: The Stevenson-O'Connell imbroglio of 1838. VAM 50:47-54, Jan. 1942.

SLAVEHOLDERS. See SLAVEOWNERS

SLAVEOWNERS

Carsel, W. The slaveholders' indictment of Northern wage slavery. JSH 6:504-20, Nov. 1940.

Haardt, Sara. The resulting enslavement of masters and mistresses of slaves in the old South. WDT 15:465-74, Apr. 1930.

Herndon, D.T. Nashville convention of 1850 to protest against exclusion of slave holders from territories. AHS 5:203-37, 1904.

Marshall, Ruth. Duane Mowry, ed. Property in Negroes: A Southern slaveholding woman's plea to Sen. J.R. Doolittle. AME 8:530-2, June 1913.

Slave owners, Spotsylvania Co., Va., 1783. VAM 4: 292-8, Jan. 1897.

Sydnor, C.S. The relation between a slave owner and his overseers. NCH 14:31-8, Jan. 1937.

SLAVERY. See also SLAVE LABOR

Aldrich, O.W. Illinois slavery. IHL 22:89-99, 1916.

Aldrich, O.W. Slavery or involuntary servitude in Illinois prior to and after admission as a state. IHJ 9:119-32, July 1916.

Alilunas, Leo. Fugitive slave cases in Ohio prior to 1850. OAQ 49:160-84, Apr.-June 1940.

Allen, C.E. The slavery question in Catholic newspapers, 1850-65. USC 26:99-169, 1936.

Allen, John W. Slavery and Negro servitude in Pope County, Illinois. IHJ 42:411-23, Dec. 1949.

Autobiography of Omar ibn Said, slave in North Carolina, 1831. AHR 30:787-95, July 1925.

Baker, Eugene C. The influence of slavery in the colonization of Texas. MVR 11:3-36, June 1924; and SWH 28:1-33, July 1924.

Bell, W.J., Jr. Relation of Herndon and Gibbon's exploration of the Amazon to North American slavery, 1850-5. HAH 19:494-503, Nov. 1939.

Beyer, R.L. Slavery in colonial New York. JAH 23:102-8, 1929.

Birkbeck, M. Slavery in U.S. IHL 10:147-63, 1905.

Buell, R.L. Conditions of slavery in Liberia. VQR 7:161-71, Apr. 1931.

Burroughs, W.G. Oberlin's part in the slavery conflict. OAQ 20:269-334, Apr.-July 1911.

Candler, M.A. Beginnings of slavery in Georgia. MAG 14:342-51, July 1911.

The case of Robin Holmes vs. Nathaniel Ford. ORE 23:111-37, June 1922.

Chester, S.H. African slavery as I knew it in Southern Arkansas. THM 9:178-84, Oct. 1925.

Clark, T.D. The slavery background of Foster's "My Old Kentucky Home." HIS 10:1-17, Jan. 1936.

Cocke, R.H. Sir Joseph de Courcy Laffan's views on slavery. WMQ 2d s. 19:42-8, Jan. 1939.

Cole, A.C. Lincoln's election an immediate menace to slavery in the states? AHR 36:740-67, July 1931.

Coles, H.L., Jr. Slaveownership and landownership in Louisiana, 1850-1860. JSH 9:381-94, Aug. 1943.

Connolly, J.C. Slavery and the causes operating against its extension in colonial New Jersey. NJS n.s. 14:181-202, Apr. 1929.

Corbitt, D.C. Notes on Saco's History of Negro slavery. HAH 24:452-7, Aug. 1944.

SLAVERY (cont'd)

Corwin, C.E. Efforts of Dutch colonial pastors for the conversion of the Negroes. PBY 12:425-35, Apr. 1927.

Crane, V.W. Benjamin Franklin on slavery and American liberties. PAM 62:1-11, Jan. 1938.

Curtis, Agnes B. A strange story of a Negro and his white deliverer. JAH 18:349-55, Oct.-Dec. 1924.

Davenport, T.W. Slavery in Oregon. ORE 9:309-73, Dec. 1908.

Davenport, T.W., and G.H. Williams. Oregon agitation up to 1801. ORE 8:189-273, Sept. 1908.

Dinkins, J. Negroes as slaves. SHS 35:60-8, Jan.-Dec. 1907.

Edward Coles, the man who saved Illinois from slavery. JAH 16:153-7, Apr.-June 1922.

Ellis, G.W. The new slavery in the South. JRD 7:467-88, Apr. 1917.

Emerson, F.V. Geographical influences in the distribution of slaves and slavery. AGS 43:13-26, June 1911 and following issues.

European Catholic opinions on slavery (reprint of an old and rare pamphlet). AMC 25:18-29, Mar. 1914.

Fleming, W.L. Kansas territory and the Buford expedition of 1856. AHS 4:167-92, 1904.

Folsom, J.F. A slave indenture of colonial days. NJS 3d s. 10:111-5, July-Oct. 1915.

Forbes, G. Part played by Indian slavery in removal of tribes to Oklahoma. OKC 16:163-70, June 1938.

Freidel, F. Francis Lieber, Charles Sumner, and slavery. JSH 9:75-93, Feb. 1943.

Fuller, J.D.P. Effect of the slavery issue on the movement to annex Mexico, 1846-48. MVH 21:31-48, June 1934.

Fuller, J.D.P. Slavery propaganda during the Mexican War. SWH 38:235-45, Apr. 1935.

Galbreath, C.B. Thomas Jefferson's views on slavery. OAQ 34:184-202, Apr. 1925.

Gehrke, W.H. Negro slavery among the Germans in North Carolina. NCH 14:307-24, Oct. 1937.

Georgia Presbyterian Church on secession and slavery. GHQ 1:263-5, Sept. 1917.

Giddings, F.H. Slavery and its abolition in the U.S. TIM 1:479-82, Mar. 1907.

Govan, T.P. Was plantation slavery profitable? JSH 8: 513-35, Nov. 1942.

Gregory, J.P., Jr. The question of slavery in the Kentucky constitutional convention of 1849. HIS 23:89-110, Apr. 1949.

Haardt, Sara. The resulting enslavement of masters and mistresses of slaves in the old South. WDT 15:465-74, Apr. 1930.

Hamilton, J.G. DeR. Lincoln's election an immediate menace to slavery in the states. AHR 37:700-11, July 1932.

Hammond, I.W. New Hampshire slaves. GSM 4:199-203, Nov. 1907.

Hand, J.P. Negro slavery in Illinois. IHL 15:42-50, 1910.

Harmon, G.D. Buchanan's attitude toward the admission of Kansas on the slavery question. PAM 53:51-91, Jan. 1929.

Harmon, G.D. Stephen A. Douglas--his leadership in Compromise of 1850, regarding government and question of slavery in territory acquired from Mexico. IHJ 21: 452-90, Jan. 1929.

Harris, N.D. Negro servitude in Illinois. IHL 11:49-56, 1906.

Hartwell, E.C. Economics of slavery. HTM 4:50, Feb. 1913.

Hawes, Lilla M. Amelia M. Murray on slavery; an unpublished letter. GHQ 33:314-7, Dec. 1949.

Hawley, C.A. Historical background of the Jasper Colony attitude toward slavery and the Civil War. IAJ 34:172-97, Apr. 1936.

Hawley, C.A. Whittier and Iowa. IAJ 34:115-43, Apr. 1936.

Haynes, N.S. Disciples of Christ and their attitude toward slavery. IHL 19:52-9, 1913.

Henry, H.M. Tennessee slave laws. THM 2:175-203, Sept. 1916.

SLAVERY (cont'd)

Hicks, Granville. Dr. Channing and the Creole case. AHR 37:516-25, Apr. 1932.

Historic account of slavery in Pennsylvania. AME 17:399-426, Oct. 1923.

Honeyman, A. Van D. A slave sale of 1827. NJS 53:250-1, Oct. 1935.

How Thomas Starr King saved California to the Union during the slavery discussion. CAL 3:10-5, Oct.-Nov. 1929.

Hubbart, H.C. Revisionist interpretations of Douglas and his doctrine of popular sovereignty. SOS 25:103-7, Mar. 1934.

Hunt, H.F. Slavery among the Indians of Northwestern America. WAS 9:277-83, Oct. 1918.

Jernegan, M.W. Slavery and the beginnings of industrialization in the colonies. AHR 25:220-40, Jan. 1920.

Jordan, P.D. Rev. William Salter and the slavery controversy, 1837-64. IAJ 33:99-122, Apr. 1935.

Keasbey, A.Q. Slavery in New Jersey. NJS 3d s. 4:90-6, Jan.-Apr. 1907 and following issues.

Kendall, J.S. Slavery in New Orleans. LHQ 23:864-86, July 1940.

Klem, Mary J. The Kansas-Nebraska slavery bill and Missouri's part in the conflict. MIV 9:393-413, 1919.

Kraus, M. Slavery reform in the 18th century. PAM 60:53-66, Jan. 1936.

Kull, I.S. Slavery in New Jersey. AME 24:443-72, Oct. 1930.

Leckie, J.D. Slavery in Mohammedan countries. CHA 7th s. 15:276-7, Apr. 4, 1925.

Leslie, W.R. The constitutional significance of Indiana's statute of 1824 on fugitives from labor. JSH 13:338-53, Aug. 1947.

Letters of S.P. Chase, Henry Clay, Henry George. INM 7:123-32, Sept. 1911.

Letters to Dr. William E. Channing on slavery and the annexation of Texas. NEQ 5:587-601, July 1932.

Levi, Kate E. The Wisconsin press and slavery. WIM 9:423-34, July 1926.

Lockley, Frederick. Oregon slavery documentary records. ORE 17:107-15, June 1916.

Lombard, Mildred E., ed. Contemporary opinions of Georgia. A journal of life on a slave-holding plantation. GHQ 14:335-43, Dec. 1930.

Lyons, John F. Attitude of Presbyterians in Ohio, Indiana and Illinois toward slavery. PBY 11:69-82, June 1921.

McCain, William D. The emancipation of Indiana Osborne. JMH 8:97-8, Apr. 1946.

McLean, Mrs. G.F. History of slaves and slavery. AMH 4:237-50, May 1909 and following issues; and AME 4: 531-41, Aug. 1909 and following issues.

Marshall, Ruth. Duane Mowry, ed. Property in Negroes: A Southern slaveholding woman's plea to Sen. J.R. Doolittle. AME 8:530-2, June 1913.

Martin, P.A. Slavery and abolition in Brazil. HAH 13: 151-96, May 1933.

Montgomery, Horace. A Georgia precedent for the Freeport question. JSH 10:200-7, May 1944.

Moody, V.A. Slavery on Louisiana sugar plantations. LHQ 7:191-303, Apr. 1924.

Mooney, C.C. Institutional and statistical aspects of slavery in Tennessee. THQ 1:195-228, Sept. 1942.

Morris, R.B. White bondage and compulsory labor in ante-bellum South Carolina. SOC 49:191-207, Oct. 1948.

Mowry, Duane. New York Democratic convention's "corner stone" resolution, 1847. IHJ 3:88-90, Oct. 1910.

Nelson, E.J. Missouri slavery, 1861-5. MOH 28:260-74, July 1934.

Osborne, D.F. The sectional struggle over rights of slavery in new territory added to U.S. GHQ 15:223-51, Sept. 1931.

Owen, D. Slavery in Indiana. Circumvention of Article VI, Ordinance of 1782. INM 36:110-6, June 1940.

Paquet, L.A. Slaves and slavery in Canada. RSC 3d s. 7:139-49, sec. 1, 1913.

Pelzer, L. Slavery and the Negro in Iowa. IAJ 2:471-84, Oct. 1904.

SLAVERY (cont'd)

Perry, C.E. The voice of New Hampshire in the slave controversy. NWH 61:63-6, Feb.-Mar. 1929.

Phelan, R.V. Slavery in central United States. WHP 252-64, 1905.

Phillips, U.B. Central theme of Southern history. AHR 34:30-43, Oct. 1928.

Phillips, U.B. Plantations with slave labor and free. AHR 30:738-53, July 1925.

Phillips, U.B. A slave plantation in 1792-6: The Worthy Park plantation, Jamaica. AHR 19:543-58, Apr. 1914.

Posey, W.B. Influence of slavery upon the Methodist Church in the early South and Southwest. MVH 17:530-42, Mar. 1931.

Posey, W.B. The slavery question in the Presbyterian Church in the old Southwest. JSH 15:311-24, Aug. 1949.

Potts, Alma G. Slavery in the old Northwest. SOS 33:70+, Feb. 1942.

Prichard, W. A Louisiana sugar plantation under the slavery regime. MVH 14:168-78, Sept. 1927.

Rammelkamp, C.H. Reverberations of the slavery conflict in Illinois College. MVH 14:447-61, Mar. 1928.

Ramsdell, C.W. The natural limits of the expansion of slavery. MVH 16:151-71, Sept. 1929; also SWH 33:91-111, Oct. 1929.

Ranck, J.B. The attitude of James Buchanan towards slavery. PAM 51:126-42, Apr. 1927.

Reat, J.L. Slavery in Douglas Co., Ill. IHJ 11:177-9, July 1918.

Reilley, E.C. Politico-economic considerations in Western Reserve's early slavery controversy. OAQ 52:141-57, Apr.-June 1943.

Rev. P.P. Alston's story of his rise up from slavery. SPM 73:375-8, May 1907.

Riddell, W.R. International complications between Illinois and Canada arising out of slavery. IHJ 25:123-6, Apr.-July 1932.

Riddell, W.R. Method of abolition of slavery in England, Scotland and Upper Canada compared. OHS 27:511-3, 1931.

Riddell, W.R. An official record of slavery in Upper Canada. OHS 25:393-7, 1929.

Russell, R.R. The general effects of slavery upon Southern economic progress. JSH 4:34-54, Feb. 1938.

Sampson, F.A., and W.C. Breckenridge. Bibliography of slavery in Missouri. MOH 2:233-44, Apr. 1908.

Schmidt, H. Slavery and attitudes toward slavery in Hunterdon Co., N.J. NJS 58:151-69, July 1940 and following issue.

Seal, A.G., ed. A Mississippian's defense of slavery. JMH 2:212-31, Oct. 1940.

Settle, E. Ophelia. Social attitudes during the slave regime: Household servants versus field hands. ASS 28:95-8, May 1934.

Sharpe, Esther E. Slavery in the territories under the Compromise of 1850. HIO 18:107-9, Mar. 1927.

Siebert, W.H. History of slavery in East Florida, 1776-1785. FHS 10:139-62, Jan. 1932 and previous issue.

Siebert, W.H. Slavery and white servitude in East Florida, 1726 to 1776. FHS 10:3-23, July 1931.

Slave auction, New Orleans. HTM 3:188, Oct. 1912.

Slave owners, Spotsylvania Co., Va., 1783. VAM 4:292-8, Jan. 1897.

Slavery agitation in Oregon up to 1861. ORE 8:189-273, Sept. 1908.

Slavery and Reconstruction. J.R. Doolittle correspondence, 1848-65. SHA 11:94-105, Mar. 1907.

Smith, M.H. Connecticut slave days. CNT 9:753-63, Oct. 1905.

Smith, M.H. Connecticut slaves in Revolutionary times. CNT 9:145-53, Jan. 1905.

Smith, M.H. Old slave days in Connecticut. CNT 10:113-28, Jan.-Mar. 1906 and following issue.

Spiller, R.E. Fenimore Cooper's defense of slaveowning America. AHR 35:575-82, Apr. 1930.

SLAVERY (cont'd)

Stenberg, R.R. The motivation of the Wilmot Proviso to a bill for purchase of Mexican territory, prohibiting slavery therein. MVH 18:535-40, Mar. 1932.

Stephen A. Douglas and his attempt to settle the slavery question in the territories, 1850-60. WAS 2:209-32, Apr. 1908 and following issues.

Stone, Lucie P. ed. Letter written in 1844 regarding slavery by a member of the Society of Friends. JAH 6: 613-5, July-Sept. 1912.

Stopford, P.G. An African coast experience. CHA 7:301-3, Apr. 7, 1917.

Stuart, W. Dutch and English importation to New Jersey and New York. AME 16:347-67, Oct. 1922.

Sydnor, C.S. The relation between a slave owner and his overseers. NCH 14:31-8, Jan. 1937.

Taylor, R.H. Humanizing the slave code in North Carolina. NCH 2:323-31, July 1925.

Todd, Willie G. North Carolina Baptists and slavery. NCH 24:135-59, Apr. 1947.

Trexler, H.A. Slavery in Missouri territory. MOH 3:179-97, Apr. 1909.

Turner, E.R. Abolition of slavery in Pennsylvania. PAM 36:129-42, Apr. 1912.

Turner, E.R. Slavery in colonial Pennsylvania. PAM 35: 141-51, 1911.

Views on slavery of Gov. Charles Goldsborough, 1834. MDH 39:332-4, Dec. 1944.

Washburne, E.B. Sketch of Edward Coles, second governor of Illinois and of slavery struggle of 1823-4. IHC 15: 1-135, 1920.

Waters, J.G. Kansas and the Wyandotte convention. KAN 11: 47-52, 1910.

Wayland, Francis F. Slavebreeding in America: The Stevenson-O'Connell imbroglio of 1838. VAM 50:47-54, Jan. 1942.

Westermann, W.L. Between slavery and freedom. AHR 50:213-27, Jan. 1945.

White, W.W. History of a slave plantation. SWH 26:79-127, Oct. 1922.

White, W.W. The Texas slave insurrection of 1860. SWH 52:259-85, Jan. 1949.

Wilkinson, N.B. The Philadelphia free produce attack on slavery. PAM 66:294-313, July 1942.

Williams, E.L., Jr. Negro slavery in Florida. FHS 28: 93-110, Oct. 1949 and following issue.

Winter, H. Early Methodism and slavery in Missouri, 1819-44; the division of Methodism in 1845. MOH 37:1-18, Oct. 1942.

Wish, H. The slave insurrection panic of 1856. JSH 5: 206-22, May 1939.

SLAVERY, WAGE

Carsel, W. The slaveholders' indictment of Northern wage slavery. JSH 6:504-20, Nov. 1940.

SLAVES. See also FUGITIVE SLAVES

Estimates of value of slaves, 1815. AHR 19:813-38, July 1914.

Gardner, D.H. The emancipation of slaves in New Jersey. NJS 9:1-21, Jan. 1924.

Gibb, H.L. Slaves in old Detroit, from a census of 1782. MHM 18:143-6, Spring 1934.

Hay, T.R. The question of arming the slaves. MVH 6:34-73, June 1919.

Kendall, J.S. Treatment of slaves in Louisiana. LHQ 22: 142-65, Jan. 1939.

Kendall, L.C. John McDonogh, his scheme for the liberation of his slaves and their exportation to Liberia. LHQ 15:646-54, Oct. 1932 and following issue.

Klingberg, F.J. Missionary activity of the S.P.G. among the African immigrants of colonial Pennsylvania and Delaware. PEH 11:126-53, June 1942.

Klingberg, F.J. The Society for the Propagation of the Gospel program for Negroes in colonial New York. PEH 8:306-71, Dec. 1939.

Landon, F. Anthony Burns in Canada. OHS 22:162-6, 1925.

Landon, F. Canada's part in freeing the slaves. OHS 17: 74-84, 1919.

SLAVES (cont'd)

Lewis, A.N. Amistad slave case, 1840. CNT 11:125-8, Jan. 1907.

Linaker, R.H. A silver slave brand. CON 69:161-4, July 1924.

McDonald, E.E. Disposal of Negro slaves by will in Knox Co., Indiana. INM 26:143-6, June 1930.

McGue, D.B. John Taylor, a slave-born pioneer. COL 18: 161-8, Sept. 1941.

McLean, Mrs. C.F. History of slaves and slavery. AMH 4: 237-50, May 1909 and following issues; and AME 4:531-41, Aug. 1909 and following issues.

Management of Negroes on Southern estates. THM 5:97-100, July 1919.

Milburn, P. Emancipation of slaves in the District of Columbia. CHS 16:96-119, 1913.

Norton, F.C. Negro slaves in Connecticut. CNT 5:320-8, June 1899.

Paquet, L.A. Slaves and slavery in Canada. RSC 3d s. 7: 139-49, sec. 1, 1913.

Phillips, D.E. Slaves who fought in the Revolution. JAH 5:143-6, Jan.-Mar. 1911.

Prichard, W., ed. Lease of a Louisiana plantation and slaves. LHQ 21:995-7, Oct. 1938.

Reid, R.L. How one slave became free: An episode in the old days of Victoria. BCH 6:251-6, Oct. 1942.

Rice, Eliza G. Louisiana planters' plea for self-government of slaves, 1849. JAH 3:621-6, Oct.-Dec. 1909.

Riddell, Justice. The story of Governor Sothel, one-time slave. DAL 9:475-80, Jan. 1930.

Riddell, W.R. A half-told story of real white slavery in the 17th century. NCH 9:299-303, July 1932.

Riddell, W.R. A Negro slave in Canadian Detroit, 1795. MHM 18:48-52, Winter 1934.

Scisco, L.D. John Rolfe's story of first cargo of slaves, 1620. MAG 13:123-5, Mar. 1911.

Settle, E. Ophelia. Social attitudes during the slave regime: Household servants versus field hands. ASS 28: 95-8, May 1934.

Sherwood, H.N. Colonization of manumitted slaves in Ohio. John Randolph's bequest. MVH 5:39-59, 1912.

Simpson, A.F. The political significance of slave representation, 1787-1821. JSH 7:315-42, Aug. 1941.

Slave auction, New Orleans. HTM 3:188, Oct. 1912.

Smith, H.L. Aiding run-away slaves in Monroe Co. INM 13:288-97, Sept. 1917.

Suit for damages for personal injuries to a slave, 1764. LHQ 5:58-62, Jan. 1922.

Sydnor, C.S. Life span of Mississippi slaves. AHR 35: 566-74, Apr. 1930.

Taylor, R.H. Slave conspiracies in North Carolina. NCH 5:20-34, June 1928.

Trabue, C.C. Voluntary emancipation of slaves in Tennessee. THM 4:50-68, Mar. 1918.

Trexler, H.A. The opposition of planters to employment of slaves as laborers by the Confederacy. MVH 27:211-24, Sept. 1940.

Trexler, H.A. The value and sale of the Missouri slave. MOH 8:69-85, Jan. 1914.

Trial and sentence of Biron, runaway Negro slave, 1728. LHQ 8:23-7, Jan. 1925.

Voss, L.D. Sally Mueller, the German slave. LHQ 12: 447-60, July 1929.

Wayland, Francis F. Slavebreeding in America: The Stevenson-O'Connell imbroglio of 1838. VAM 50:47-54, Jan. 1942.

Whittington, G.P., ed. Facts concerning the loyalty of slaves in Northern Louisiana in 1863 as shown in the letters of J.H. Ransdell to Gov. T.O. Moore. LHQ 14: 487-502, Oct. 1931.

Woolston, Florence. Slaves in U.S. TEC 16:135-44, Oct. 1911.

Work of Rev. Francis Le Jau in colonial South Carolina among Indians and Negro slaves. JSH 1:442-58, Nov. 1935.

SLAVES, DISTRIBUTION OF

Emerson, F.V. Geographical influences in the distribution of slaves and slavery. AGS 43:13-26, June 1911 and following issues.

SLAVOCRACY

Boucher, C.S. That aggressive slavocracy. MVH 8:13-79, June-Sept. 1921.

Small, E.W., and Miriam H. Small. Prudence Crandall, her efforts to promote Negro education, 1833-4. NEQ 17: 506-29, Dec. 1944.

Small, Miriam H. See Small, E.W.

Smelser, M. Housing in Creole St. Louis, 1764-1821: An example of cultural change. LHQ 21:337-48, Apr. 1938.

Smith, A.E. The indentured servant and land speculation in 17th century Maryland. AHR 40:467-72, Apr. 1935.

Smith, B. Negro in war-time. PUB 21:1110-3, Aug. 31, 1918.

Smith, G.W. Carpetbag imperialism in Florida, 1862-8. FHS 27:99-130, Oct. 1948 and following issue.

SMITH, GERRIT

Harlow, R.V. Gerrit Smith and the John Brown raid. AHR 38:32-60, Oct. 1932.

Smith, H.L. Aiding run-away slaves in Monroe Co. INM 13:288-97, Sept. 1917.

Smith, M.H. Connecticut slave days. CNT 9:753-63, Oct. 1905.

Smith, M.H. Connecticut slaves in Revolutionary times. CNT 9:145-53, Jan. 1905.

Smith, M.H. Old slave days in Connecticut. CNT 10:113-28, Jan.-Mar. 1906 and following issue.

Smith, R.M. Racial strains in Florida. FHS 11:16-32, July 1932.

Smith, R.W. Review of J.H. Franklin, From slavery to freedom. PHR 17:502-3, Nov. 1948.

Smith, W.H. Schuyler Colfax: His role in the development of Reconstruction policy. INM 39:323-44, Dec. 1943.

Smither, Harriet. Effect of English abolitionism on annexation of Texas. SWH 32:193-205, Jan. 1929.

SOCIAL ASSIMILATION

Weatherly, U.S. Racial elements in social assimilation. ASS 5:57-76, 1910.

SOCIAL ATTITUDES

Settle, E. Ophelia. Social attitudes during the slave regime: Household servants versus field hands. ASS 28:95-8, May 1934.

SOCIAL CONDITIONS

Landon, F. Social conditions among the Negroes in Upper Canada before 1865. OHS 22:144-61, 1925.

SOCIAL DIFFERENTIATION

Foreman, P.B. Negro lifeways in the rural South: A typological approach to social differentiation. ASR 13: 409-18, Aug. 1948.

SOCIAL PROGRESS

Osborn, H.F. Race progress and its relation to social progress. NIS 9:8-18, 1924.

SOCIAL SCIENTISTS

Glazer, N. The social scientists dissect prejudice. COM 1:79-85, May 1946.

SOCIAL SELECTION

Herskovits, M.J. Effect of social selection on the American Negro. ASS 20:77-82, 1926.

SOCIAL STRUCTURE

Frazier, E. Franklin. Negro-white contacts from the standpoint of the social structure of the Negro world. ASR 14:1-11, Feb. 1949.

Simpson, George E. Analysis of Haiti's social structure. ASR 6:640-9, Oct. 1941.

SOCIETY FOR THE PROPAGATION OF THE GOSPEL

Klingberg, F.J. Missionary activity of the S.P.G. among the African immigrants of colonial Pennsylvania and Delaware. PEH 11:126-53, June 1942.

Klingberg, F.J. The Society for the Propagation of the Gospel program for Negroes in colonial New York. PEH 8:306-71, Dec. 1939.

SOCIETY OF FRIENDS

King, Emma. Some aspects of the work of the Society of Friends for Negro education in North Carolina. NCH 1: 403-11, Oct. 1924.

Siebert, W.H. A Quaker section of the underground railroad in Northern Ohio. OAQ 39:429-502, July 1930.

Small, E.W., and Miriam H. Small. Prudence Crandall, her efforts to promote Negro education, 1833-4. NEQ 17: 506-29, Dec. 1944.

Stone, Lucie P., ed. Letter written in 1844 regarding slavery by a member of the Society of Friends. JAH 6: 613-5, July-Sept. 1912.

Tisler, C.C. Story of Prudence Crandall. IHJ 33:203-6, June 1940.

SOCIO-ECONOMIC STUDIES

Moses, E.R. Differentials in crime rates between Negroes and whites, based on comparisons of four socio-economically equated areas. ASR 12:411-20, Aug. 1947.

SOCIOLOGICAL ANALYSIS

Simpson, George E. Analysis of Haiti's social structure. ASR 6:640-9, Oct. 1941.

SOCIOLOGICAL METHODOLOGY

Cahnman, W.J. Attitudes of minority youth: A methodological introduction. ASR 14:543-8, Aug. 1949.

Ford, R.N. Study of white-Negro contacts. Scaling experience by a multiple response technique. ASR 6:9-23, Feb. 1941.

Foreman, P.B. Negro lifeways in the rural South: A typological approach to social differentiation. ASR 13: 409-18, Aug. 1948.

SOCIOLOGICAL RESEARCH

Bloom, Leonard. Concerning ethnic research: With discussion. ASR 13:171-82, Apr. 1948.

SOCIOLOGICAL THEORY

Frazier, E. Franklin. Sociological theory and race relations. ASR 12:261-71, June 1947.

SOCIOLOGY

Kephart, W.M. Is the American Negro becoming lighter? An analysis of the sociological and biological trends. ASR 13:437-43, Aug. 1948.
Comment by J.T. Blue, Jr., ASR 13:766-7, Dec. 1948.

SOLDIERS

Green, Ernest. Upper Canada's black defenders. OHS 27: 365-91, 1931.

Phillips, D.E. Slaves who fought in the Revolution. JAH 5:143-6, Jan.-Mar. 1911.

SOLIDARITY

Eno, J.N. Race in relation to solidarity, government. AME 27, 179-85, Apr. 1933.

SOLOMON, JOB BEN

Middleton, A.P. The strange story of Job Ben Solomon, the African, 1750. WMQ 3d s. 5:342-50, July 1948.

SONGS. See also FOLK SONGS, MUSIC, SPIRITUALS

Henry, M.E., ed. Negro songs from Georgia. JAF 44:437-47, Oct.-Dec. 1931.

Holzknecht, K.J. Negro song variants from Louisville. JAF 41:558-78, Oct.-Dec. 1928.

Perrow, E.C. Songs and rhymes of the South. JAF 26: 123-73, Apr.-June 1913.

SONGSTERS

Damon, S.F. The Negro in early American songsters. BSA 28:132-63, 1934.

SOTHEL, SETH

Riddell, Justice. The story of Governor Sothel, one-time slave. DAL 9:475-80, Jan. 1930.

Riddell, W.R. A half-told story of real white slavery in the 17th century. NCH 9:299-303, July 1932.

SOUTH

Boucher, C.S. That aggressive slavocracy. MVH 8:13-79, June-Sept. 1921.

SOUTH (cont'd)

Braun, Robert. Man farthest down. PUB 16:152, Feb. 14, 1913.

Brewer, W.M. Effects of the plantation system on the ante-bellum South. GHQ 11:250-73, Sept. 1927.

Buck, D.H. Poor whites of the ante-bellum South. AHR 31:41-54, Oct. 1925.

Davis, J. The South and British Africa. VQR 13:362-75, Summer 1937.

Dickson, Harris. The unknowable Negro. HAM 22:728-42, June 1909 and following issues.

Ellis, G.W. The new slavery in the South. JRD 7:467-88, Apr. 1917.

Emery, Julia C. How the church helps Southern Negro children. SPM 72:113-5, Feb. 1907.

Fleming, W.L. Plantation life in the South. JAH 3:233-46, Apr.-June 1909.

Foreman, P.B. Negro lifeways in the rural South: A typological approach to social differentiation. ASR 13: 409-18, Aug. 1948.

Garvie, C.F.C. South's problem. PUB 15:413-4, May 3, 1912.

Graves, John T. The Southern Negro and the war crisis. VQR 18:500-17, Autumn 1942.

Haardt, Sara. The resulting enslavement of masters and mistresses of slaves in the old South. WDT 15:465-74, Apr. 1930.

Harn, Julia E. Life and customs on plantations and in small communities of the ante-bellum South. GHQ 16: 47-55, Mar. 1932 and previous and following issues.

Jones, M.A. The Negro and the South. VQR 3:1-12, Jan. 1927.

N., V.E.P. The chief problem of the South. TIM 1:399-406, Mar. 1907.

Odum, H.W. Problems of the Southern states. JRD 6:185-91, Oct. 1915.

Perrow, E.C. Songs and rhymes of the South. JAF 26:123-73, Apr.-June 1913.

Phillips, U.B. Central theme of Southern history. AHR 34:30-43, Oct. 1928.

Posey, W.B. Influence of slavery upon the Methodist Church in the early South and Southwest. MVH 17:530-42, Mar. 1931.

Russell, R.R. The general effects of slavery upon Southern economic progress. JSH 4:34-54, Feb. 1938.

Stephenson, G.T. Racial distinctions in Southern law. APS 1:44-61, Nov. 1906.

Stone, A.H. Race problems in the South. SHA 11:20-37, Jan. 1907.

Valian, P. Internal migration and racial composition of the Southern population. ASR 13:294-8, June 1948.

Walker, H.J. Changes in the structure of race relations in the South. ASR 14:377-83, June 1949.

Williams, J.S. Negro and the South. MET 27:137-51, Nov. 1907.

Wright, R.C. The Southern white man and the Negro. VQR 9:175-94, Apr. 1933.

Young, J.H. Anna Elizabeth Dickinson--a woman abolitionist views the South in 1875. GHQ 32:241-51, Dec. 1948.

SOUTH AMERICA. See also LATIN AMERICA, SPANISH AMERICA

Bell, W.J., Jr. Relation of Herndon and Gibbon's exploration of the Amazon to North American slavery, 1850-5. HAH 19:494-503, Nov. 1939.

Romero, F. The slave trade and the Negro in South America. HAH 24:368-86, Aug. 1944.

SOUTH CAROLINA

Davis, H.C. Folk-lore in South Carolina. JAF 27:241-54, July-Sept. 1914.

Dounan, Elizabeth. Slave trade in South Carolina before the Revolution. AHR 33:804-28, July 1928.

Hamer, Marguerite B. South Carolina. A century before manumission. NCH 17:232-6, July 1940.

Jervey, T.D. White indentured servants in South Carolina. SOC 12:163-71, Oct. 1911.

Marshall, Ruth. Duane Mowry, ed. Property in Negroes: A Southern slaveholding woman's plea to Sen. J.R. Doolittle. AME 8:530-2, June 1913.

Morris, R.B. White bondage and compulsory labor in antebellum South Carolina. SOC 49:191-207, Oct. 1948.

SOUTH CAROLINA (cont'd)

Pennington, E.L. Work of Rev. Francis Le Jau in colonial South Carolina among Indians and Negro slaves. JSH 1: 442-58, Nov. 1935.

Simkins, F.S. White Methodism in South Carolina during Reconstruction. NCH 5:35-64, Jan. 1928.

Stoddard, A.H. Origin, dialect, beliefs and characteristics of the Negroes of the South Carolina and Georgia coasts. GHQ 28:186-95, Sept. 1944.

Tindall, George B. The campaign for the disfranchisement of Negroes in South Carolina. JSH 15:212-34, May 1949.

Woody, R.H. The labor and immigration problems of South Carolina during the Reconstruction period. MVH 18:195-212, Sept. 1931.

SOUTH CAROLINA, PEDEE COUNTRY

Bass, R.D. Negro songs from the Pedee country, South Carolina. JAF 44:418-36, Oct.-Dec. 1931.

SOUTH CAROLINA, ST. HELENA ISLAND

Telford, C.W. A race study of St. Helena Island Negroes with particular reference to what effect their isolation has had upon them. NDQ 21:126-35, Winter 1931.

SOUTHWEST

Posey, W.B. Influence of slavery upon the Methodist Church in the early South and Southwest. MVH 17:530-42, Mar. 1931.

Posey, W.B. The slavery question in the Presbyterian Church in the old Southwest. JSH 15:311-24, Aug, 1949.

SPANISH AMERICA. See also LATIN AMERICA, SOUTH AMERICA

A document (in Spanish) on the Negro in higher education in Spanish America: Case of José Ponseano de Ayarza, 1794-98. HAH 24:432-51, Aug. 1944.

King, J.F. Evolution of the free slave trade principle in Spanish colonial administration. HAH 22:34-56, Feb. 1942.

King, J.F. The Negro in continental Spanish America: A select bibliography. HAH 24:547-59, Aug. 1944.

SPANISH COLONIES

King, J.F. Evolution of the free slave trade principle in Spanish colonial administration. HAH 22:34-56, Feb. 1942.

Scelle, G. Slave-trade in Spanish colonies of America. AJI 4:612-61, July 1910.

Sparendam, W.F. The fraud of white civilization; a Negro's opinion. WOR 1:38-40, June 1936.

SPECULATION

Smith, A.E. The indentured servant and land speculation in 17th century Maryland. AHR 40:467-72, Apr. 1935.

SPEER, ROBERT E.

Linwood, F. Review of Robert E. Speer, Race and race relations. IRM 14:285-7, Apr. 1925.

Spiller, R.E. Fenimore Cooper's defense of slaveowning America. AHR 35:575-82, Apr. 1930.

SPIRITUALS. See also FOLK SONGS, MUSIC, SONGS

Crite, Alan R. Why I illustrate spirituals. WLD 1:44-5+, May 1938.

Gaul, H.B. Negro spirituals. MUS 17:147-52, Apr. 1918.

Harshaw, D.A. Philosophy of the Negro spiritual. HOM 95: 184-6, Mar. 1928.

Perkins, A.E. Negro spirituals from the far South. JAF 35:223-49, July-Sept. 1922.

Stidger, W.L. Negro spirituelles, a new idea in homiletics. HOM 90:26-9, July 1925.

Spraggins, T.L. Mobilization of Negro labor for the Department of Virginia and North Carolina, 1861-5. NCH 24: 160-97, Apr. 1947.

Spraggins, T.L. Review of V.L. Wharton, The Negro in Mississippi. NCH 25:272-4, Apr. 1948.

Stafford, W.P. Thaddeus Stevens. VHS 51-85, 1905-6.

Staiger, C.B. Abolitionism and the Presbyterian schism of 1837-8. MVH 36:391-414, Dec. 1949.

Stampp, K.M. Review of O. Crenshaw, The slave states in the presidential election of 1860. JSH 13:116-7, Feb. 1947.

Stampp, K.M. The Southern refutation of the pro-slavery argument. NCH 21:35-45, Jan. 1944.

STANDARDS

Odum, H.W. Standards of measurement in race development. JRD 5:364-83, Apr. 1915.

Starr, F. Review of R.B. Dixon, The racial history of mankind. APS 17:675-7, Nov. 1923.

STATES' RIGHTS

Stone, A.H. A Mississippian's view of civil rights, states rights, and the Reconstruction background. JMH 10:181-239, July 1948.

STATESMEN

Minor, R.C. The career of James Preston Poindexter, Negro statesman, in Columbus, Ohio. OAQ 56:266-86, July 1947.

STATISTICS

Mooney, C.C. Institutional and statistical aspects of slavery in Tennessee. THQ 1:195-228, Sept. 1942.

Roncal, J. The Negro race in Mexico: A statistical study. HAH 24:530-40, Aug. 1944.

STATUS

DuBois, W.E.B. Political and social status in European possessions in Africa. FOR 3:423-44, Apr. 1925.

Dunbar, R. Status of American Negroes. WOR 61-4, Mar. 1942.

Lee, L.L. Role and status of the Negro in the Hawaiian community. ASR 13:419-37, Aug. 1948.

Stavisky, L. Negro craftmanship in early America. AHR 54: 315-25, Jan. 1949.

Stavisky, L. Review of Herbert Aptheker, To be free: Studies in American Negro history. SOS 40:41, Jan. 1949.

Stenberg, R.R. The motivation of the Wilmot Proviso to a bill for purchase of Mexican territory, prohibiting slavery therein. MVH 18:535-40, Mar. 1932.

Stenberg, R.R. See McCormac, E.I.

Stephenson, G.M. Review of Louis Adamic, A nation of nations. MVH 32:598-9, Mar. 1946.

Stephenson, G.T. Racial distinctions in Southern law. APS 1:44-61, Nov. 1906.

Stephenson, G.T. Separation of the races in public conveyances. APS 3:180-204, May 1909.

Stephenson, W.H. The Negro in the thinking and writing of John Spencer Bassett, 1867-1928. NCH 25:427-41, Oct. 1948.

Stephenson, W.H. A quarter-century at Pleasant Hill. MVH 23: 355-74, Dec. 1936.

STEVENS, THADDEUS

Current, R.N. Love, hate and Thaddeus Stevens. PAH 14: 259-72, Oct. 1947.

Epstein, S. Thaddeus Stevens. NYH 29:72-4, Jan. 1948.

Padgett, J.A., ed. Letters to Thaddeus Stevens regarding Reconstruction. NCH 18:171-95, Apr. 1941, and following issues.

Stafford, W.P. Thaddeus Stevens. VHS 51-85, 1905-6.

Stevens, Wayne E. Shaw-Hansen election contest. IHJ 7:389-401, Jan. 1915.

STEVENSON, ANDREW

Wayland, Francis F. Slavebreeding in America: The Stevenson-O'Connell imbroglio of 1838. VAM 50:47-54, Jan. 1942.

Stidger, W.L. Negro spirituelles, a new idea in homiletics. HOM 90:26-9, July 1925.

Stoddard, A.H. Origin, dialect, beliefs and characteristics of the Negroes of the South Carolina and Georgia coasts. GHQ 28:186-95, Sept. 1944.

STODDARD, L.

Leys, N. Review of L. Stoddard, Rising tide of color against white supremacy. IRM 10:566-8, Oct. 1921.

STODDARD, L. (cont'd)

Review of L. Stoddard, Clashing tides of colour. GEJ 86: 377-9, Oct. 1935.

Stone, A.H. The basis of white political control in Mississippi. JMH 6:225-36, Oct. 1944.

Stone, A.H. Is race friction growing? ASS 2:69-110, 1907.

Stone, A.H. A Mississippian's view of civil rights, states rights, and the Reconstruction background. JMH 10: 181-239, July 1948.

Stone, A.H. Post bellum Reconstruction--an American experience. JMH 3:227-45, July 1945.

Stone, A.H. Race problem in the South. SHA 11:20-37, Jan. 1907.

Stone, Lucie P., ed. Letter written in 1844 regarding slavery by a member of the Society of Friends. JAH 6:613-5, July-Sept. 1912.

Stonequist, E.V. Review of R.A. Warner, New Haven Negroes: A social history. ASR 6:759, Oct. 1941.

Stoney, S.G. Review of F.S. Simkins and R.H. Woody, South Carolina during Reconstruction. VQR 9:304-7, Apr. 1933.

Stopford, P.G. An African coast experience. CHA 7th s. 7:301-3, Apr. 7, 1917.

STOREY, MOORFIELD

Morse, J.T., Jr. Moorfield Storey, 1845-1929. HGM 38: 291-302, Mar. 1930.

Stoutemyer, J.H. Certain experiments with backward races. JRD 5:438-66, Apr. 1916.

STOWE, HARRIET BEECHER

Hillis, N.D. Harriet Beecher Stowe and the Beecher family. MUN 46:191-201, Nov. 1911.

Jerrold, W. Centenary notes on Harriet Beecher Stowe. BKL 40:241-50, Sept. 1911.

Macer-Wright, P. "Uncle Tom's Cabin" and the "crusader in crinoline" who wrote it. WOR 59-62, July 1942.

Portrait. BKL 64:76, Apr. 1923.

"Uncle Tom's Cabin" written in Brunswick, Me. SJM 5:160, Aug.-Oct. 1917.

Strong, D.S. The poll tax: The case of Texas. APS 38:693-709, Aug. 1944.

Strong, D.S. Review of H.L. Moon, Balance of power, the Negro vote. APS 42:1220-1, Dec. 1948.

Strong, D.S. The rise of Negro voting in Texas. APS 42:510-22, June 1948.

Strong, J. Race question from the Scriptural side. HOM 58:123-9, Aug. 1909.

Strong, S.M. Review of St. Clair Drake and H.R. Cayton, Black metropolis: A study of Negro life in a Northern city. ASR 11:240-1, Apr. 1946.

Stuart, W. Dutch and English importation to New Jersey and New York. AME 16:347-67, Oct. 1922.

Stuart, W. White servitude in New York and New Jersey. AME 15:19-37, Jan. 1921.

STUDENTS

Folk-tales by Tuskegee students. JAF 32:397-401, July-Sept. 1919.

Johnson, C.S. Racial attitudes of college students. ASS 28:24-31, May 1934.

Studley, Marian H. An August First anti-slavery picnic. NEQ 16:567-77, Dec. 1943.

Stutler, B.B. The "originals" of John Brown's letter to the Rev. Luther Humphrey. WVA 9:1-25, Oct. 1947.

SUFFRAGE

Hart, A.B. Realities of suffrage. APP 2:149-70, 1905.

Kemmerer, D.L. The suffrage franchise in colonial New Jersey. NJS 52:166-73, July 1934.

SUFFRAGE (cont'd)

Mabry, W.A. Negro suffrage and fusion rule in North Carolina. NCH 12:79-102, Apr. 1935.

Mabry, W.A. The white supremacy campaign in suffrage amendment, 1900. NCH 13:1-24, Jan. 1936.

Robinson, J.T. History of suffrage in Arkansas. ARA 3: 167-74, 1911.

Rose, J.C. Suffrage: Constitutional point of view. APS 1:17-43, Nov. 1906.

SUGAR

Moody, V.A. Slavery on Louisiana sugar plantations. LHQ 7:191-303, Apr. 1924.

Prichard, W. A Louisiana sugar plantation under the slavery regime. MVH 14:168-78, Sept. 1927.

Sitterson, J.C. Financing and marketing the sugar crop of the old South. JSH 10:188-99, May 1944.

Sitterson, J.C. Hired labor on sugar plantations of the ante-bellum South. JSH 14:192-205, May 1948.

SUMNER, CHARLES

Campbell, J.E. Sumner--Brooks--Burlingame. The last of the great challenges. OAQ 34:435-73, Oct. 1925.

Freidel, F. Francis Lieber, Charles Sumner, and slavery. JSH 9:75-93, Feb. 1943.

Haynes, G.H. Biography of Charles Sumner. MAG 14:24-30, Aug. 1911 and following issues.

Wight, M. Portrait of Charles Sumner. MET 30:505, Aug. 1909.

SUPERNATURAL

Gittings, Victoria. What William saw; experiences of William Aquilla with the supernatural. JAF 58:135-7, Apr.-June 1945.

SUPERSTITIONS

Clark, J.H. West Indian superstitions. CHA 7th s. 8: 603-5, Aug. 17, 1918.

SUPREME COURT

Auchampaugh, P. Buchanan, the Court, and the Dred Scott case. THM 9:231-40, Jan. 1926.

Swann, T.W. Jom Crow laws threatened in Illinois. PUB 16: 246, Mar. 14, 1913.

Swayze, L.E. "Ossawattomie Brown," an old play on John Brown. KHQ 6:34-59, Feb. 1937.

Sweet, W.W. The Methodist Church and Reconstruction. IHL 20:83-94, 1914.

Sweet, W.W. Methodist Episcopal Church and Reconstruction. IHJ 7:147-65, Oct. 1914.

Swing, J.B. Thomas Morris, Ohio pioneer. OAQ 10:352-60, Jan. 1902.

Swint, H.L., ed. Reports from educational agents of Freedmen's Bureau in Tennessee, 1865-70. THQ 1:51-80, Mar. 1942 and following issue.

Swisher, C.B. Review of R.M. MacIver, The more perfect Union: A program for the control of inter-group discrimination in the U.S. APS 42:998-9, Oct. 1948.

Sydnor, C.S. The free Negro in Mississippi before the Civil War. AHR 32:769-88, July 1927.

Sydnor, C.S. Life span of Mississippi slaves. AHR 35: 566-74, Apr. 1930.

Sydnor, C.S. The relation between a slave owner and his overseers. NCH 14:31-8, Jan. 1937.

Sydnor, C.S. Review of A.Y. Lloyd, The slavery controversy, 1831-60. NCH 17:278-80, July 1940.

Sydnor, C.S. Review of Madeleine H. Rice, American Catholic opinions in the slavery controversy. JSH 10:492-3, Nov. 1944.

Synder, C.E. Dred Scott and his owner, Dr. John Emerson. ANN 3d s. 21:440-61, Oct. 1938.

Szecsi, L. Negro sculpture in interior decoration. LST 7: 326-7, June 1933.

Szecsi, L. Tr. by A.S. Riggs. Primitive Negro art. AAA 34: 130-6, May-June 1933.

TALLANT, R.

Hurston, Zora N. Review of R. Tallant, Voodoo in New Orleans. JAF 60:436-8, Sept.-Dec. 1947.

Johnson, A.K. Review of R. Tallant, Voodoo in New Orleans. SFQ 11:99-100, Mar. 1947.

TANEY, ROGER

Lee, T.Z. Chief Justice Taney and the Dred Scott decision. AIR 22:142-4, 1923.

Tannar, A.H. Marais des Cygnes massacre and rescue of Ben Rice. KAN 14:224-34, 1915-8.

TANNENBAUM, F.

Aptheker, Herbert. Review of F. Tannenbaum, Slave and citizen: The Negro in the Americas. AHR 52:755-7, July 1947.

Bernstein, D. Review of F. Tannenbaum, Slave and citizen: The Negro in the Americas. COM 3:399-400, Apr. 1947.

Cardozo, M. Review of F. Tannenbaum, Slave and citizen: The Negro in the Americas. CHR 33:66-7, Apr. 1947.

Franklin, J.H. Review of F. Tannenbaum, Slave and citizen: The Negro in the Americas. WMQ 3d s. 4:544-5, Oct. 1947.

Logan, R.W. Review of F. Tannenbaum, Slave and citizen: The Negro in the Americas. HAH 27:665-6, Nov. 1947.

Tapp, H. Conflict between Robert Wickliffe and Robert J. Breckinridge prior to the Civil War. HIS 19:156-70, July 1945.

Taylor, A.W. The church and the color line. HOM 92:479-81, Dec. 1926.

Taylor, E.G.R. Ideas current between 1580 and 1650 on influence of climate on racial characteristics. SGM 51: 1-6, Jan. 1935.

Taylor, Griffith. The distribution of future white settlement. GEO 12:375-402, July 1922.

Taylor, Griffith. Evolution and distribution of race, culture and language. GEO 11:54-119, Jan. 1921.

Taylor, Griffith. Future white settlement: A rejoinder. GEO 13:130, Jan. 1923.

Taylor, Helen L., ed. Negro beliefs and place legends from New Castle, Del. JAF 51:92-4, Jan.-Mar. 1938.

TAYLOR, JOHN

McGue, D.B. John Taylor, a slave-born pioneer. COL 18: 161-8, Sept. 1941.

Taylor, R.H. Humanizing the slave code in North Carolina. NCH 2:323-31, July 1925.

Taylor, R.H. Review of John S. Bassett, The plantation overseer. NCH 3:506-8, July 1926.

Taylor, R.H. Slave conspiracies in North Carolina. NCH 5: 20-34, June 1928.

TAYLOR, R.H.

Thompson, H. Review of R.H. Taylor, Slaveholding in North Carolina: An economic view. NCH 4:490-1, Oct. 1927.

TEACHERS

Baker, Emily V. Responsibility of the elementary teacher to overcome racial intolerance in future citizens. HIO 24:86-9, Feb. 1933.

Knight, E.W. Notes on career of John Chavis, Negro Presbyterian preacher and teacher, 1763(?)- , as a teacher of Southern white children and of his ministry. NCH 7:326-45, July 1930.

Phillips, Edna. A plan for cooperation between evening school teachers and librarians in the educational development of racial groups. ALA 26:29-30, Jan. 1932.

TEACHING

Israel, S. Teaching of Report of President's Committee on Civil Rights. SOS 39:102-4, Mar. 1948.

Wright, John C. Teaching English at Tuskegee Institute. EBM 3:26-30, Oct. 1908.

Teakle, T. Rendition of Barclay Coppoc. IAJ 10:503-66, Oct. 1912.

Tebeau, C.W. Visitors' views of politics and life, 1865-80. GHQ 26:1-15, Mar. 1942.

Telford, C.W. A race study of St. Helena Island Negroes with particular reference to what effect their isolation has had upon them. NDQ 21:126-35, Winter 1931.

TENANT FARMS

Tenant farms and landlords. PRS 25:801-8, June 1911.

TENNESSEE

Alexander, T.B. Kukluxism in Tennessee, 1865-69: A technique for the overthrow of radical Reconstruction. THQ 8:195-219, Sept. 1949.

Elliott, Helen. Frances Wright's experiment with Negro emancipation. INM 35:141-57, June 1939.

Emerson, O.B. Frances Wright and her Nashoba experiment. THQ 6:291-314, Dec. 1947.

England, J.M. The free Negro in ante-bellum Tennessee. JSH 9:37-58, Feb. 1943.

Henry, H.M. Tennessee slave laws. THM 2:175-203, Sept. 1916.

Martin, A.E. Tennessee anti-slavery societies. THM 1:261-81, Dec. 1915.

Mooney, C.C. Institutional and statistical aspects of slavery in Tennessee. THQ 1:195-228, Sept. 1942.

Odum, Anna K. Folk-songs from Tennessee. JAF 27:255-65, July-Sept. 1914.

Parks, J.H. The Tennessee Whigs and the Kansas-Nebraska bill, 1854. JSH 10:308-30, Aug. 1944.

Swint, H.L., ed. Reports from educational agents of Freedmen's Bureau in Tennessee, 1865-70. THQ 1:51-80, Mar. 1942 and following issue.

Trabue, C.C. Voluntary emancipation of slaves in Tennessee. THM 4:50-68, Mar. 1918.

TENNESSEE, KNOXVILLE

The colored library, Knoxville, Tenn. PLY 24:5-8, Jan. 1919.

TENNESSEE, NASHOBA

Parks, E.W. Frances Wright--founder of the emancipating labor society, Nashoba, Tenn. THM 2d s. 2:74-86, Jan. 1932.

TENNESSEE, NASHVILLE

Herndon, D.T. Nashville convention of 1850 to protest against exclusion of slave holders from territories. AHS 5:203-37, 1904.

Sioussat, St. G.L. The Compromise of 1850 and the Nashville convention. THM 4:215-47, Dec. 1918.

TERRITORIES

Herndon, D.T. Nashville convention of 1850 to protest against exclusion of slave holders from territories. AHS 5:203-37, 1904.

Sharpe, Esther E. Slavery in the territories under the Compromise of 1850. HIO 18:107-9, Mar. 1927.

Stephen A. Douglas and his attempt to settle the slavery question in the territories, 1850-60. WAS 2:209-32, Apr. 1908 and following issues.

Trexler, H.A. Slavery in Missouri territory. MOH 3: 179-97, Apr. 1909.

TEXAS

Baker, Eugene C. The influence of slavery in the colonization of Texas. MVR 11:3-36, June 1924; and SWH 28:1-33, July 1924.

Carroll, H.B. Nolan's "lost nigger" expedition of 1877. SWH 44:55-75, July 1940.

Cross, Cora M. Early days in Texas. Reminiscences by an old-time darky. TEX 4:380-93, Oct. 1929.

Letters to Dr. William E. Channing on slavery and the annexation of Texas. NEQ 5:587-601, July 1932.

Porter, K.W. Negroes and Indians on the Texas frontier, 1834-74. SWH 53:151-63, Oct. 1949.

Russ, W.A., Jr. Radical disfranchisement in Texas, 1867-70. SWH 38:40-52, July 1934.

Schoen, H. The free Negro in the Republic of Texas. SWH 39:292-308, Apr. 1936 and following issues.

TEXAS (cont'd)

Smither, Harriet. Effect of English abolitionism on annexation of Texas. SWH 32:193-205, Jan. 1929.

Strong, D.S. The poll tax: The case of Texas. APS 38: 693-709, Aug. 1944.

Strong, D.S. The rise of Negro voting in Texas. APS 42: 510-22, June 1948.

White, W.W. History of a slave plantation. SWH 26:79-127, Oct. 1922.

White, W.W. The Texas slave insurrection of 1860. SWH 52:259-85, Jan. 1949.

TEXAS, BROWNSVILLE

Paine, A.B. Truth about the Brownsville, Texas, affair, by Capt. "Bill" McDonald. PRS 20:221-35, Sept. 1908.

TEXAS, DALLAS

Edmiston, Dorothy. A ballet of the African Negro to be performed in Dallas, Texas. TEX 4:458-64, Nov. 1940.

TEXAS, FREESTONE COUNTY

Kirgan, Sadie E. Tales the darkies tell of ghosts that walk in Freestone County, Texas. TEX 5:385-91, May 1930.

TEXAS, HARRIS CO.

Muir, A.F. The free Negro in Harris Co., Texas. SWH 46:214-38, Jan. 1943.

TEXAS, MARION CO.

Moseley, J.A.R. The citizens white primary in Marion Co., Texas, of 1898. SWH 49:524-31, Apr. 1946.

THEATER

Swayze, L.E. "Ossawattomie Brown," an old play on John Brown. KHQ 6:34-59, Feb. 1937.

Theobald, Stephen L. Catholic missionary work among the colored people of the United States (1776-1866). AMC 35:325-44, Dec. 1924.

Thirsk, R. Obeah in the West Indies. CHA 7th s. 7:247-50, Mar. 17, 1917.

Thomas, K. Caribbean--America's "Mare Nostrum." JIR 11: 406-24, Jan. 1921.

Thompson, C. Mildred. The Freedmen's Bureau in Georgia in 1865-6. GHQ 5:40-9, Mar. 1921.

Thompson, E.B. Review of Richard Wright, Black boy: A record of childhood and youth. JMH 7:178-80, July 1945.

Thompson, E.T. Review of E. Franklin Frazier, The Negro in the U.S. ASR 14:813-4, Dec. 1949.

Thompson, E.W. White and black in the West Indies. IRM 19: 183-94, Apr. 1930.

Thompson, H. Review of R.H. Taylor, Slaveholding in North Carolina: An economic view. NCH 4:490-1, Oct. 1927.

Thompson, J.V. Pathways to prejudice. CJR 4:464-75, Oct. 1941.

THOREAU, HENRY DAVID

Ford, N.A. Henry David Thoreau's activities as an abolitionist. NEQ 19:359-71, Sept. 1946.

Thurston, Mrs. C.B. Letter of 1859. News of the John Brown raid on Harper's Ferry. MDH 39:162-3, June 1944.

TILLEY, J.S.

Mason, Frances. Review of J.S. Tilley, The coming of the glory. VAM 57:436-9, Oct. 1949.

Vandiver, F.E. Review of J.S. Tilley, The coming of the glory. MVH 36:531, Dec. 1949.

TILLMAN, BEN

Simkins, F.B. Ben Tillman's view of the Negro and its reaction. JSH 3:161-74, May 1937.

Timberlake, Elsie. Did the Reconstruction give Mississippi new schools? MSS 12:72-93, 1912.

Tindall, George B. The campaign for the disfranchisement of Negroes in South Carolina. JSH 15:212-34, May 1949.

Tisler, C.C. Story of Prudence Crandall. IHJ 33:203-6, June 1940.

Tison, Yvonne P. Review of H.L. Ballowe, The Lawd sayin' the same. LHQ 31:154-6, Jan. 1948.

Todd, Willie G. North Carolina Baptists and slavery. NCH 24:135-59, Apr. 1947.

Tors, M. The value of racial mingling. WDT 47:532-5, May 1926.

TOURGEE, ALBION W.

Nye, R.B. Albion W. Tourgee--his ideas concerning Reconstruction problems in the South. OAQ 50:101-14, Apr.-June 1941.

Trabue, C.C. Voluntary emancipation of slaves in Tennessee. THM 4:50-68, Mar. 1918.

TRADE UNIONS

Northrup, H.R. Race discrimination in trade unions. COM 2:124-31, Aug. 1946.

TREATIES

Treaty with the U.S. regarding the finances, economic development and tranquility of Haiti. (Text.) AJI Supp. 10:234-8, Oct. 1916.

Trexler, H.A. The opposition of planters to employment of slaves as laborers by the Confederacy. MVH 27:211-24, Sept. 1940.

Trexler, H.A. Slavery in Missouri territory. MOH 3:179-97, Apr. 1909.

Trexler, H.A. The value and sale of the Missouri slave. MOH 8:69-85, Jan. 1914.

TRIALS

McCarron, Anna T. Prudence Crandall's trial. CNT 12:225-32, Apr.-June 1908.

Trial and sentence of Biron, runaway Negro slave, 1728. LHQ 8:23-7, Jan. 1925.

Trieber, J. Legal status of Negroes in Arkansas before the Civil War. ARA 3:175-83, 1911.

"TRUE AMERICAN"

Craig, D.M. An old letter concerning Cassius M. Clay and the "True American," 1845, presented to the Filson Club. HIS 22:197-8, July 1948.

Harrison, L. Cassius M. Clay's anti-slavery newspaper, the "True American": Opposition in Kentucky to his struggle for emancipation of the Negro. HIS 22:30-49, Jan. 1948.

Trueblood, Lillie D. The story of John Williams, colored. INM 30:149-52, June 1934.

Truman, D.B. Review of L.C. Kesselman, The social politics of FEPC; a study in reform pressure movements. APS 43: 377-8, Apr. 1949.

Truman, D.B. Review of A.M. Rose and Caroline Rose, America divided: Minority group relations in the U.S. APS 43: 821-3, Aug. 1949.

Tumin, M.J. The idea of race dies hard: Current report on an old controversy. COM 8:80-5, July 1949.

Turner, E.R. Abolition of slavery in Pennsylvania. PAM 36: 129-42, Apr. 1912.

Turner, E.R. First abolition society. PAM 36:92-109, Jan. 1912.

Turner, E.R. Slavery in colonial Pennsylvania. PAM 35:141-51, Apr. 1911.

Turner, E.R. Underground railroad. PAM 36:309-18, July 1912.

Turner, L.D. Contrasts of Brazilian ex-slaves with Nigeria. VQR 27:55-67, Jan. 1942.

TUSKEGEE INSTITUTE

Chapple, J.M. Tuskegee Institute and its new work. NAT 33:617-24, Mar. 1911.

Folk-tales by Tuskegee students. JAF 32:397-401, July-Sept. 1919.

Goddard, A.E. Some lessons from Hampton and Tuskegee Institutes. NEW 18:86-102, Jan. 1911.

TUSKEGEE INSTITUTE (cont'd)

Haines, Marian G. Tuskegee Institute. GOV 2:96-115, Nov. 1907.

Park, R.M. Tuskegee international conference on the Negro. JRD 3:117-20, July 1912.

Washington, Booker T. Tuskegee Institute and its work. KID 20:153-5, Jan. 1908.

Wright, John C. Teaching English at Tuskegee Institute. EBM 3:26-30, Oct. 1908.

Tuttle, C.E., Jr. Review of W.H. Siebert, Vermont's anti-slavery and underground railroad record. VHS n.s. 6: 3-11, Mar. 1938.

U.A.W. See UNITED AUTO WORKERS

Udal, J.S. Obeah in the West Indies. FLL 26:255-95, Sept. 1915.

UNCLE REMUS

Wolfe, B. Uncle Remus and the malevolent rabbit: The Negro in popular American culture. COM 8:31-41, July 1949.

"UNCLE TOM'S CABIN"

Clarke, C.M. "Uncle Tom's Cabin"--how it reached the British public. CHA 7th s. 11:81-2, Jan. 8, 1921.

Dunn, J.P. Indiana's part in "Uncle Tom's Cabin." INM 7:112-8, Sept. 1911.

Macer-Wright, P. "Uncle Tom's Cabin" and the "crusader in crinoline" who wrote it. WOR 59-62, July 1942.

"Uncle Tom's Cabin" written in Brunswick, Me. SJM 5: 160, Aug.-Oct. 1917.

Ward, Aileen. Rev. Josiah Henson, the original Tom of "Uncle Tom's Cabin"; his story. DAL 20:335-8, Oct. 1940.

UNDERGROUND RAILROAD

Aiken, Martha D. The underground railroad. MHM 6:597-610, no. 4, 1922.

Bailey, William S. The underground railroad in southern Chautauqua County, N.Y. NYH 16:53-63, Jan. 1935.

Barnes, Charles E. Battlecreek as a station on the underground railway. MPC 38:279-85, 1912.

Blazer, D.N. Underground railroad in McDonough County, Ill. IHJ 15:579-91, Oct. 1922-Jan. 1923.

Coleman, J.W., Jr. Delia Webster and Calvin Fairbanks, underground railroad agents. HIS 17:129-42, July 1943.

Conklin, Julia S. Underground railroad in Indiana. INM 6:63-74, June 1910.

Cooley, Verna. Illinois and the underground railroad to Canada. IHL 23:76-98, 1917.

Garretson, O.A. Travelling on the underground railroad in Iowa. IAJ 22:418-53, July 1924.

Knabenshue, S.S. The underground railroad. OAQ 14:396-403, Oct. 1905.

Leak, R.R. Underground railroad in Hendricks Co., Indiana. INM 36:17-22, Mar. 1940.

Merkel, B.G. The underground railroad and the Missouri borders, 1840-60. MOH 37:271-85, Apr. 1943.

Ryan, J.H. Underground railroad incident in Illinois. IHJ 8:23-30, Apr. 1915.

Schmidt, O.L. Illinois underground railroad. IHJ 18:703-17, Oct. 1925.

Siebert, W.H. Beginnings of the underground railroad in Ohio. OAQ 56:70-93, Jan. 1947.

Siebert, W.H. A Quaker section of the underground railroad in Northern Ohio. OAQ 39:429-502, July 1930.

Siebert, W.H. The underground railroad in Massachusetts. NEQ 9:447-67, Sept. 1936.

Siebert, W.H. The underground railroad in Ohio. OAQ 4:44-63, 1895.

Turner, E.R. Underground railroad. PAM 36:309-18, July 1912.

Waldrip, W.D. Underground railroad station at Newport, Ind. INM 7:64-76, June 1911.

Watts, R.M. The underground railroad in Mechanicsburg, Ohio. OAQ 43:209-54, July 1934.

Wick, B.L. Delia Webster--her part in the underground railroad movement in Iowa. ANN 3d s. 18:228-31, Jan. 1932.

UNDERGROUND RAILROAD (cont'd)

Williams, Ora. Story of underground railway signals. ANN 27:297-303, Apr. 1946.

Wright, Mrs. F.B. The underground railroad. OAQ 14: 164-9, Apr. 1905.

UNDERGROUND RAILWAY. See UNDERGROUND RAILROAD

UNDERWOOD, JOSEPH ROGERS

Keith, E. Jean. Joseph Rogers Underwood of Kentucky and the American Colonization Society for the free people of color. HIS 22:117-32, Apr. 1938.

UNIFICATION MOVEMENT

Williams, T.H. Unification movement: Its influence on Louisiana's Reconstruction history. JSH 11:349-69, Aug. 1945.

UNION

How Thomas Starr King saved California to the union during the slavery discussion. CAL 3:10-5, Oct.-Nov. 1929.

UNIONISM

Bettersworth, J.K., ed. Mississippi unionism: The case of Mr. Lyon. JMH 1:37-52, Jan. 1939.

Klingberg, F.W. Operation Reconstruction: A report on Southern unionist planters. NCH 25:466-84, Oct. 1948.

UNIONS

Northrup, H.R. Race discrimination in trade unions. COM 2:124-31, Aug. 1946.

UNITED AUTO WORKERS

Howe, I., and B.J. Widick. The U.A.W. fights race prejudice; case history on the industrial front. COM 8:261-8, Sept. 1949.

UNIVERSAL RACES CONGRESS

Chamberlain, A.F. Universal Races Congress: Papers and proceedings. JRD 2:494-7, Apr. 1912.

UNIVERSITIES

Johnson, W.H. Lincoln University, the pioneer institution in the world for the education of the Negro. PBY 14:142-3, Sept. 1930.

Rodabaugh, J.H. Miami University, Calvinism and the anti-slavery movement. OAQ 48:66-73, Jan. 1939.

URBANIZATION

Frazier, E. Franklin. Impact of urban civilization on Negro family life. ASR 2:609-18, Oct. 1937.

Ross, F.A. Urbanization and the Negro. ASS 26:115-28, 1932.

UTOPIANISM

Emerson, O.B. Frances Wright and her Nashoba experiment. THQ 6:291-314, Dec. 1947.

Valian, P. Internal migration and racial composition of the Southern population. ASR 13:294-8, June 1948.

VALLANDIGHAM, CLEMENT L.

Coleman, C.H. Three Vallandigham letters, 1865. OAQ 43:461-4, Oct. 1934.

Van Fossan, W.H. Biography of Clement L. Vallandigham. OAQ 23:256-67, July 1914.

VALUES

Seeman, M. Skin color value in three all-Negro school classes. ASR 11:315-21, June 1946.

Vance, R.B. Review of E. Franklin Frazier, The Negro in the U.S. VQR 25:620-3, Autumn 1949.

Vance, R.B. Tragic dilemma: The Negro and the American dream. Review of recent books. VQR 20:435-45, Summer 1944.

Vandiver, F.E. Review of J.S. Tilley, The coming of the glory. MVH 36:531, Dec. 1949.

Van Fossan, W.H. Biography of Clement L. Vallandigham. OAQ 23:256-67, July 1914.

Van Loan, W.L. See Williams, Mildred.

VENEREAL DISEASE

de Rivera, B. How women can halt "the great black plague." PRS 23:417-20, Mar. 1910.

VILLARD, O.G.

Review of O.G. Villard, John Brown: A biography fifty years after. JRD 2:204-6, Oct. 1911.

Violette, E.M. Black code in Missouri. MIV 6:287-316, 1913.

VIRGINIA

Bruce, Kathleen. Slave labor in Virginia iron industry. WMQ 2d s. 6:289-302, Oct. 1932 and following issues.

Goodwin, Mary F. Christianizing and educating the Negro in colonial Virginia. PEH 1:143-52, Sept. 1932.

Hiden, Mrs. P.W. Inventory and appraisement of a Virginia well-to-do planter's estate, 1760. WMQ 2d s. 16:600-1, Oct. 1936.

Scisco, L.D. John Rolfe's story of first cargo of slaves, 1620. MAG 13:123-5, Mar. 1911.

VIRGINIA, FREDERICKSBURG

Adams, Fannie L.G. A childhood spent at Hayfield plantation near Fredericksburg, Va., during the Civil War. WMQ 2d s. 23:292-7, July 1948.

VIRGINIA, GREEN SPRING

Dimmick, J. Sir William Berkley's plantation at Green Spring, Va. WMQ 2d s. 9:129-30, Apr. 1929.

VIRGINIA, HARPER'S FERRY

Donovan, S.K. John Brown at Harper's Ferry and Charlestown. OAQ 30:300-36, July 1921.

England, G.A. Description of Harper's Ferry and incidents of John Brown's last days. TRA 50:28-32+, Mar. 1928.

Floyd, J.B. Official report of John Brown's raid upon Harper's Ferry. ORE 10:314-24, Sept. 1909.

Meader, J.R. Harper's Ferry raid. AME 7:29-36, Jan. 1912.

Thurston, Mrs. C.B. Letter of 1859. News of the John Brown raid on Harper's Ferry. MDH 39:162-3, June 1944.

VIRGINIA, RICHMOND

Eckenrode, H.J. Negroes in Richmond, Va., in 1864. VAM 46:193-200, July 1938.

VIRGINIA, SPOTSYLVANIA CO.

Slave owners, Spotsylvania Co., Va., 1783. VAM 4:292-8, Jan. 1897.

VODUN. See also BLACK MAGIC, HOODOO, OBEAH

Simpson, George E. Four specialized ceremonies of the vodun cult in Northern Haiti. JAF 59:154-67, Apr.-June 1946.

Simpson, George E. Two vodun-related ceremonies from Haiti. JAF 61:49-52, Jan.-Mar. 1948.

von Hornbostel, E.M. Review of Some American Negro songs. IRM 15:748-53, Oct. 1926.

VOODOO. See BLACK MAGIC, HOODOO, OBEAH, VODUN

Voss, L.D. Sally Mueller, the German slave. LHQ 12:447-60, July 1929.

VOTING

Moseley, J.A.R. The citizens white primary in Marion Co., Texas, of 1898. SWH 49:524-31, Apr. 1946.

Strong, D.S. The poll tax: The case of Texas. APS 38: 693-709, Aug. 1944.

Strong, D.S. The rise of Negro voting in Texas. APS 42:510-22, June 1948.

Weeks, O.D. The white primary: 1944-8. APS 42:500-10, June 1948.

W.P.A. WRITERS' PROGRAM

Armour, A.W. Review of W.P.A. Writers' Program, The Negro in Virginia. WMQ 2d s. 21:70-4, Jan. 1941.

W.P.A. WRITER'S PROJECT

Bascom, W.R. Review of Georgia W.P.A. Writer's Project, Drums and shadows: Survival studies among the Georgia coastal Negroes. JAF 55:262-3, Oct.-Dec. 1942.

WAGNER, RICHARD

Lockspeiser, E. Gobineau's friendship with Richard Wagner and the new racial cult. WOR 57-9, Feb. 1941.

Waldrip, W.D. Underground railroad station at Newport, Ind. INM 7:64-76, June 1911.

Walker, H.J. Changes in the structure of race relations in the South. ASR 14:377-83, June 1949.

WALKER, MARGARET

Williams, Mary L. Review of Margaret Walker, For my people. WVA 4:214-8, Apr. 1943.

Wallis, W.D. Moral and racial prejudice. JRD 5:212-29, Oct. 1914.

Walsh, Anetta C. Three anti-slavery newspapers published in Ohio prior to 1823. OAQ 31:171-212, Apr. 1922.

Walter, D.O. Proposals for a federal anti-lynching law. APS 28:436-42, June 1934.

WAR

Naruse, J. War and the concordia of race. JRD 5:268-75, Jan. 1915.

Ward, Aileen. Rev. Josiah Henson, the original Tom of "Uncle Tom's Cabin"; his story. DAL 20:335-8, Oct. 1940.

Ward, J.C., Jr. The Republican party in Bourbon Georgia, 1872-1890. JSH 9:196-209, May 1943.

WARMOTH, HENRY CLAY

Harris, F.B. Reconstruction period: The career of Henry Clay Warmoth, governor. LHQ 30:523-653, Apr. 1947.

Warner, C.D. Race and climate. OUT 44:38-9, Feb. 1917.

WARNER, R.A.

Johnson, C.S. Review of R.A. Warner, New Haven Negroes, a social history. NEQ 14:748-50, Dec. 1941.

Robert, J.C. Review of R.A. Warner, New Haven Negroes: A social history. JSH 7:417-8, Aug. 1941.

Stonequist, E.V. Review of R.A. Warner, New Haven Negroes: A social history. ASR 6:759, Oct. 1941.

WARREN, R.P.

Perkins, D. Review of R.P. Warren, John Brown, the making of a martyr. VQR 6:614-8, Oct. 1930.

WARTIME

Burma, J.H. Racial minorities in wartime. SOS 35:157-8, Apr. 1944.

Washburn, G.B. Review of S. Rodman, Horace Pippin, a Negro painter in America. MAR 41:202, May 1948.

Washburne, E.B. Sketch of Edward Coles, second governor of Illinois and of the slavery struggle of 1823-4. IHC 15: 1-135, 1920.

Washington, Booker T. Progress of the Negro race in Mississippi. WWL 13:409-13, Mar. 1909.

Washington, Booker T. Tuskegee Institute and its work. KID 20:153-5, Jan. 1908.

WASHINGTON, BOOKER T.

Braun, Robert. Man farthest down. PUB 16:152, Feb. 14, 1913.

Hollister, H.A. Booker T. Washington. An appreciation. SCH 35:144+, Jan. 1916.

What Booker T. Washington is doing for the Negroes in the U.S. WWL 16:464+, Oct. 1910.

WASHINGTON, D.C. See DISTRICT OF COLUMBIA, WASHINGTON

WASHINGTON, GEORGE

Hamilton, Oscar B. George Washington, colored, and the work of Silas Hamilton. IHJ 3:45-58, Oct. 1910.

Waters, J.G. Kansas and the Wyandotte convention. KAN 11: 47-52, 1910.

WATSON, G.

Lee, A. McC. Review of G. Watson, Action for unity. COM 3:497-8, May 1947.

WATSON, TOM

Woodward, C.V. Tom Watson and the Negro in agrarian politics. JSH 4:14-33, Feb. 1938.

Watts, R.M. The underground railroad in Mechanicsburg, Ohio. OAQ 43:209-54, July 1934.

Way, R.B. Was the fugitive slave clause in the constitution necessary? IAJ 5:326-36, July 1907.

Wayland, Francis F. Slavebreeding in America: The Stevenson-O'Connell imbroglio of 1838. VAM 50:47-54, Jan. 1942.

Weale, B.L.P. How color divides the world. WWL 14:598-604, Nov. 1909.

Weale, B.L.P. The position of the black man in the world today. WWL 15:237-43, Feb. 1910.

WEATHERFORD, W.D.

Gollock, G.A. Review of W.D. Weatherford, The Negro: From Africa to America. IRM 14:140-1, Jan. 1925.

Weatherhead, H.W. Review of B.F. Riley, Life and times of Booker T. Washington. IRM 7:125-7, Jan. 1918.

Weatherly, U.S. Racial elements in social assimilation. ASS 5:57-76, 1910.

Weatherly, U.S. Racial pessimism. ASS 18:1-17, 1923.

Weaver, H. Review of W.T. Jordan, Hugh Davis and his Alabama plantation. MVH 35:686, Mar. 1949.

WEAVER, R.

Alpert, H. Review of R. Weaver, The Negro ghetto. ASR 13:779-80, Dec. 1948.

WEBB, ARCHIE P.

Coffin, N.E. Case of Archie P. Webb. ANN 3rd s. 11:200-14, July-Oct. 1913.

Webb, J.L. Review of M.J. Herskovits and Frances S. Herskovits, Trinidad village: A study of a Protestant Negro culture. IRM 36:405-7, July 1947.

Webb, J.W. Irwin Russell and Negro folk literature. SFQ 12: 137-49, June 1948.

WEBSTER, DANIEL

McDowell, Tremaine. Webster's words on abolitionists. NEQ 7:315, June 1934.

WEBSTER, DELIA

Coleman, J.W., Jr. Delia Webster and Calvin Fairbanks, underground railroad agents. HIS 17:129-42, July 1943.

Wick, B.L. Delia Webster--her part in the underground railroad movement in Iowa. ANN 3d s. 18:228-31, Jan. 1932.

Wechsler, I.R. Review of F. Wilson, Crusader in crinoline: The life of Harriet Beecher Stowe. NEQ 15:161-3, Mar. 1942.

Wechsler, James A., and Nancy F. Wechsler. Report of President's Committee on Civil Rights: One year later. COM 6:297-304, Oct. 1948.

Wechsler, Nancy. See Wechsler, James A.

Weeks, O.D. The white primary: 1944-48. APS 42:500-10, June 1948.

Weir, E. Review of Elsie Singmaster, I speak for Thaddeus Stevens. IHJ 40:351-2, Sept. 1947.

Weir, Sally R. Reminiscences of the Ku Klux Klan. MET 26: 97-106, Apr. 1907.

Wells, L.G. Story of Myrtilla Miner. NYH 24:358-75, July 1943.

Wells, W.C. Reconstruction and its destruction in Hinds Co., Miss. MHS 9:85-108, 1906.

Welshans, Genevieve. Review of G.G. Brown, Law administration and Negro-white relations in Philadelphia; recreational facilities and Negro-white relations in Philadelphia. PAH 16:68-9, Jan. 1949.

Werner, A. Review of M.F. Ashley-Montague, Man's most dangerous myth: The fallacy of race. COM 1:91-9, Apr. 1946.

WEST

Hubbart, H.C. Pro-Southern influences in the free West, 1840-65. MVH 20:45-62, June 1932.

WEST INDIES. See also CARIBBEAN

Clark, J.H. West Indian superstitions. CHA 7th s. 8: 603-5, Aug. 17, 1918.

Cleven, N.A.N. Ministerial order of José de Galvez establishing a uniform duty on the importation of Negro slaves into the Indies. HAH 4:266-76, May 1921.

Norton, H.K. Self-determination in the West Indies. The governments of the Caribbean. WDT 47:147-53, Jan. 1926.

Studley, Marian H. An August First anti-slavery picnic. NEQ 16:567-77, Dec. 1943.

Thirsk, R. Obeah in the West Indies. CHA 7:247-50, Mar. 17, 1917.

Thompson, E.W. White and black in the West Indies. IRM 19:183-94, Apr. 1930.

Treaty with the U.S. regarding the finances, economic development and tranquility of Haiti. (Text.) AJI Supp. 10:234-8, Oct. 1916.

Udal, J.S. Obeah in the West Indies. FLL 26:255-95, Sept. 1915.

WEST VIRGINIA

Cox, J.H. Negro tales from West Virginia. JAF 47:341-57, Oct.-Dec. 1934.

West Virginia Colored Institute. NAT 39:528-30, Dec. 1913.

WEST VIRGINIA, CHARLESTOWN

Donovan, S.K. John Brown at Harper's Ferry and Charlestown. OAQ 30:300-36, July 1921.

WEST VIRGINIA, HARPER'S FERRY. See VIRGINIA, HARPER'S FERRY

WEST VIRGINIA COLORED INSTITUTE

West Virginia Colored Institute. NAT 39:528-30, Dec. 1913.

Westermann, W.L. Between slavery and freedom. AHR 50:213-27, Jan. 1945.

WESTERN RESERVE

Geiser, K.F. Anti-slavery movement, 1840-60, in the Western Reserve. MIV 5:73-98, 1912.

Reilley, E.C. Politico-economic considerations in Western Reserve's early slavery controversy. OAQ 52: 141-57, Apr.-June 1943.

Wharton, V.L. Review of Herbert Aptheker, Essays in the history of the American Negro. MVH 34:673-4, Mar. 1948.

Wharton, V.L. Review of E.M. Coulter, The South during Reconstruction. JMH 9:271-2, Oct. 1948.

Wharton, V.L. Review of B.J. Mathews, Booker T. Washington, educator and interracial interpreter. JSH 15:267-8, May 1949.

Wharton, V.L. Review of Bell I. Wiley, Southern Negroes, 1861-5. JMH 1:65-7, Jan. 1939.

WHARTON, V.L.

Moore, R.H. Review of V.L. Wharton, The Negro in Mississippi. JMH 9:268-9, Oct. 1947.

Murdock, R.K. Review of V.L. Wharton, The Negro in Mississippi. MDH 43:72, Mar. 1948.

Russ, W.A., Jr. Review of V.L. Wharton, The Negro in Mississippi. JSH 14:280-1, May 1948.

Spraggins, T.L. Review of V.L. Wharton, The Negro in Mississippi. NCH 25:272-4, Apr. 1948.

Wiley, B.I. Review of V.L. Wharton, The Negro in Mississippi. MVH 35:134-5, June 1948.

WHIGS

Parks, J.H. The Tennessee Whigs and the Kansas-Nebraska bill, 1854. JSH 10:308-30, Aug. 1944.

White, Alice P. The plantation experience of Joseph and Lavinia Erwin, 1807-36: Records and papers. LHQ 27: 343-478, Apr. 1944.

White, M.J. Louisiana and the secession movement of the early fifties. MIV 8:278-88, 1916.

White, W.W. History of a slave plantation. SWH 26:79-127, Oct. 1922.

White, W.W. The Texas slave insurrection of 1860. SWH 52: 259-85, Jan. 1949.

WHITE LEAGUE

Lestage, H.O., Jr. The White League in Louisiana and its participation in Reconstruction riots, 1866-74. LHQ 18:617-95, July 1935.

Pritchard, W., ed. Origin and activities of the "White League." LHQ 23:525-43, Apr. 1940.

WHITE PRIMARY

Moseley, J.A.R. The citizens white primary in Marion Co., Texas, of 1898. SWH 49:524-31, Apr. 1946.

Weeks, O.D. The white primary: 1944-48. APS 42:500-10, June 1948.

WHITE SUPREMACY

Burns, F.P. White supremacy in the South. The battle for constitutional government, 1866. LHQ 18:581-616, July 1935.

Mabry, W.A. The white supremacy campaign in suffrage amendment, 1900. NCH 13:1-24, Jan. 1936.

WHITES

Buck, D.H. Poor whites of the ante-bellum South. AHR 31: 41-54, Oct. 1925.

DuBois, W.E.B. Culture of white folk. JRD 7:434-47, Apr. 1917.

Haar, C.M. White indentured servants in colonial New York. AME 34:370-92, July 1940.

Hoyt, W.D., Jr. White servitude in Northampton, Maryland, 1772-4. MDH 33:126-33, June 1938.

Humphrey, G.D. Public education for whites. JMH 3:26-36, Jan. 1941.

Jervey, T.D. White indentured servants in South Carolina. SOC 12:163-71, Oct. 1911.

Knight, E.W. Notes on career of John Chavis, Negro Presbyterian preacher and teacher, 1763(?)- , as a teacher of Southern white children and of his ministry. NCH 7:326-45, July 1930.

Morris, R.B. White bondage and compulsory labor in ante-bellum South Carolina. SOC 49:191-207, Oct. 1948.

Moses, E.R. Differentials in crime rates between Negroes and whites, based on comparisons of four socio-economically equated areas. ASR 12:411-20, Aug. 1947.

Patricia, Sr. Margaret. White servitude in the American colonies. AMC 42:12-53, Mar. 1931.

Riddell, W.R. A half-told story of real white slavery in the 17th century. NCH 9:299-303, July 1932.

Siebert, W.H. Slavery and white servitude in East Florida, 1726 to 1776. FHS 10:3-23, July 1931.

Simkins, F.S. White Methodism in South Carolina during Reconstruction. NCH 5:35-64, Jan. 1928.

Sparendam, W.F. The fraud of white civilization; a Negro's opinion. WOR 1:38-40, June 1936.

Stone, A.H. The basis of white political control in Mississippi. JMH 6:225-36, Oct. 1944.

Stuart, W. White servitude in New York and New Jersey. AME 15:19-27, Jan. 1921.

Taylor, Griffith. The distribution of future white settlement. GEO 12:375-402, July 1922.

Taylor, Griffith. Future white settlement: A rejoinder. GEO 13:130, Jan. 1923.

Voss, L.D. Sally Mueller, the German slave. LHQ 12: 447-60, July 1929.

White is the finest race? STR 43:148-55, Feb. 1912.

Willcox, W.F. On the future distribution of white settlement. GEO 12:646-7, Oct. 1922.

Wilson, L., and H. Gilmore. White employers and Negro workers. ASR 8:698-705, Dec. 1943.

Wright, R.C. The Southern white man and the Negro. VQR 9:175-94, Apr. 1933.

WHITTIER, JOHN GREENLEAF

Hawley, C.A. Whittier and Iowa. IAJ 34:115-43, Apr. 1936.

WHITTIER, JOHN GREENLEAF (cont'd)

Higginson, Thomas W. John Greenleaf Whittier as abolitionist. BKN 26:259-62, Dec. 1907.

Whittington, G.P., ed. Facts concerning the loyalty of slaves in Northern Louisiana in 1863 as shown in the letters of J.H. Ransdell to Gov. T.O. Moore. LHQ 14:487-502, Oct. 1931.

Wick, B.L. Delia Webster--her part in the underground railroad movement in Iowa. ANN 3d s. 18:228-31, Jan. 1932.

WICKLIFFE, ROBERT

Tapp, H. Conflict between Robert Wickliffe and Robert J. Breckinridge prior to the Civil War. HIS 19:156-70, July 1945.

Widick, B.J. See Howe, I.

Wight, M. Portrait of Charles Sumner. MET 30:505, Aug. 1909.

WILBERFORCE, WILLIAM

Haseltine, G.C. Biographical sketch of William Wilberforce. ENG 57:59-65, July 1933.

Wiley, B.I. Review of H. Crum, Gullah: Negro life in the Caroline Sea Islands. AHR 46:933-4, July 1941.

Wiley, B.I. Review of J.H. Franklin, From slavery to freedom. JSH 14:264-5, May 1948.

Wiley, B.I. Review of V.L. Wharton, The Negro in Mississippi. MVH 35:134-5, June 1948.

WILEY, BELL I.

Wharton V.L. Review of Bell I. Wiley, Southern Negroes, 1861-5. JMH 1:65-7, Jan. 1939.

Wilkins, Mary, ed. The American Cotton Planters' Ass'n: Papers, 1865-6. THQ 7:335-61, Dec. 1948 and following issue.

Wilkinson, N.B. The Philadelphia free produce attack on slavery. PAM 66:294-313, July 1942.

Willcox, W.F. On the future distribution of white settlement. GEO 12:646-7, Oct. 1922.

WILLES, THOMAS

Buried at master's feet. AME 6:814-5, Aug. 1911.

Williams, E.L., Jr. Negro slavery in Florida. FHS 28:93-110, Oct. 1949 and following issue.

Williams, G.H. See Davenport, T.W.

Williams, H. General Banks and the radical Republicans in the Civil War. NEQ 12:268-80, June 1939.

Williams, H. See Williams, Helen.

Williams, Helen, and H. Williams. Wisconsin Republicans and Reconstruction, 1865-70. WIM 23:17-39, Sept. 1939.

Williams, J.S. Negro and the South. MET 27:137-51, Nov. 1907.

WILLIAMS, JOHN

Trueblood, Lillie D. The story of John Williams, colored. INM 30:149-52, June 1934.

Williams, Mary L. Review of Margaret Walker, For my people. WVA 4:214-8, Apr. 1943.

Williams, Mildred, and W.L. Van Loan. Education for racial equality. SOS 34:308-11, Nov. 1943.

Williams, Ora. Story of underground railway signals. ANN 27:297-303, Apr. 1946.

Williams, T.H. Reconstruction. An analysis of some attitudes. JSH 12:469-86, Nov. 1946.

Williams, T.H. Review of J.W. DeForest, A Union officer in the Reconstruction. JSH 14:560-1, Nov. 1948.

Williams, T.H. Unification movement: Its influence on Louisiana's Reconstruction history. JSH 11:349-69, Aug. 1945.

WILLS

McDonald, E.E. Disposal of Negro slaves by will in Knox Co., Indiana. INM 26:143-6, June 1930.

WILMOT PROVISO

Mowry, Duane. New York Democratic convention's "corner stone" resolution, 1847. IHJ 3:88-90, Oct. 1910.

Stenberg, R.R. The motivation of the Wilmot Proviso to a bill for purchase of Mexican territory, prohibiting slavery therein. MVH 18:535-40, Mar. 1932.

Wilson, C.J. People's attitude toward the Negro in early Ohio. OAQ 39:717-68, Oct. 1930.

WILSON, F.

Review of F. Wilson, Crusader in crinoline: The life of Harriet Beecher Stowe. NAR 119:86-8, July 1942.

Wechsler, I.R. Review of F. Wilson, Crusader in crinoline: The life of Harriet Beecher Stowe. NEQ 15:161-3, Mar. 1942.

WILSON, H.P.

Ramsdell, C.W. Review of H.P. Wilson, John Brown. SWH 17:318-20, Jan. 1914.

Wilson, L., and H. Gilmore. White employers and Negro workers. ASR 8:698-705, Dec. 1943.

Winston, S. Negro bootleggers in Eastern North Carolina. ASR 8:692-7, Dec. 1943.

Winter, H. Early Methodism and slavery in Missouri, 1819-44; the division of Methodism in 1845. MOH 37:1-18, Oct. 1942.

WISCONSIN

Levi, Kate E. The Wisconsin press and slavery. WIM 9:423-34, July 1926.

Marshall, Ruth. Duane Mowry, ed. Property in Negroes: A Southern slaveholding woman's plea to Sen. J.R. Doolittle. AME 8:530-2, June 1913.

Schafer, W. Fugitive slave act. Decision of the Booth case. WIM 20:89-110, Sept. 1936.

Williams, Helen, and H. Williams. Wisconsin Republicans and Reconstruction, 1865-70. WIM 23:17-39, Sept. 1939.

WISCONSIN, MADISON

McCormick, T.C., and R.A. Hornseth. The Negro in Madison, Wisconsin. ASR 12:519-25, Oct. 1947.

Wish, H. Revival of the African slave trade in the U.S., 1856-60. MVH 27:569-88, Mar. 1941.

Wish, H. The slave insurrection panic of 1856. JSH 5:206-22, May 1939.

Wolf, Hazel C. See Hesseltine, W.B.

Wolfe, B. Uncle Remus and the malevolent rabbit: The Negro in popular American culture. COM 8:31-41, July 1949.

WOMEN

Marshall, Ruth. Duane Mowry, ed. Property in Negroes: A Southern slaveholding woman's plea to Sen. J.R. Doolittle. AME 8:530-2, June 1913.

Mulcaster, J.G. A quadroon girl of Southern Illinois. IHJ 28:214-7, Oct. 1935.

Schuler, Kathryn R. Women in public affairs during Reconstruction. LHQ 19:668-750, July 1936.

Young, J.H. Anna Elizabeth Dickinson--a woman abolitionist views the South in 1875. GHQ 32:241-51, Dec. 1948.

WOODBURN, J.A.

Ramsdell, C.W. Review of J.A. Woodburn, The Life of Thaddeus Stevens. SWH 17:93-5, July 1913.

Woodruff, C.E. Laws of racial and intellectual development. JRD 3:156-75, Oct. 1912.

WOODSON, CARTER G.

Moroney, T.B. Review of Carter G. Woodson, A century of Negro migration. CHR 6:527-9, Jan. 1921.

Woodward, C.V. Tom Watson and the Negro in agrarian politics. JSH 4:14-33, Feb. 1938.

Woodward, J.W. Some implications from our present knowledge concerning prejudice. ASR 11:344-56, June 1946.

Woody, R.H. The labor and immigration problems of South Carolina during the Reconstruction period. MVH 18:195-212, Sept. 1931.

Woody, R.H. See SIMKINS, F.S.

WOOL TRADE

Letter from John Brown on the wool trade, 1849. MAG 16: 36-8, Jan. 1913.

Woolley, R.W. Fight for race purity. PRS 23:3-11, Jan. 1910 and following issues.

Woolston, Florence. Slaves in U.S. TEC 16:135-44, Oct. 1911.

Work, John W. Changing patterns in Negro folk songs. JAF 62: 136-44, Apr.-June 1949.

Work, M.N. Aspects and tendencies of the race problem. ASS 19:191-6, 1925.

Work, M.N. Review of J. Dowd, The Negro in American life. IRM 16:298-9, Apr. 1927.

WORKERS

Powell, Dorothy M. The Negro worker in Chicago industry. JOB 20:21-32, Jan. 1947.

Wilson, L., and H. Gilmore. White employers and Negro workers. ASR 8:698-705, Dec. 1943.

WORKS PROGRESS ADMINISTRATION. See W.P.A.

WORLD WAR I

Ellis, G.W. The Negro and the war for democracy. JRD 8:439-53, Apr. 1918.

Haynes, George E. Effect of war conditions on Negro labor. ACA s. 8:299-312, Feb. 1919.

Jacob Lawrence, his pictures of the South-to-North migration of Negroes that began during the First World War. FOR 24:102-9, Nov. 1941.

Johnson, J.W. Negro in war-time. PUB 21:1218-9, Sept. 21, 1918.

Pendleton, Helen B. Negro in war-time. PUB 21:1290, Oct. 12, 1918.

Smith, B. Negro in war-time. PUB 21:1110-3, Aug. 31, 1918.

WORLD WAR II

Bernanos, Georges. Nation against race. DUB 209:1-6, July 1941.

Graves, John T. The Southern Negro and the war crisis. VQR 18:500-17, Autumn 1942.

The Negro's problem in the present emergency. FTE 25:76+, June 1942.

Northrup, H.R. Negroes in a war industry; the case of shipbuilding. JOB 16:160-72, July 1943.

Saenger, G. Effect of the war on our minority groups. ASR 8:15-22, Feb. 1943.

WORTH, DANIEL

Clarke, Grace J. Anti-slavery letter of Daniel Worth to George W. Julian, and other documents. INM 26:152-7, June 1930.

Wright, Mrs. F.B. The underground railroad. OAQ 14:164-9, Apr. 1905.

WRIGHT, FRANCES

Elliott, Helen. Frances Wright's experiment with Negro emancipation. INM 35:141-57, June 1939.

Emerson, O.B. Frances Wright and her Nashoba experiment. THQ 6:291-314, Dec. 1947.

Wright, John C. Teaching English at Tuskegee Institute. EBM 3:26-30, Oct. 1908.

Wright, R.C. The Southern white man and the Negro. VQR 9: 175-94, Apr. 1933.

WRIGHT, RICHARD

Thompson, E.B. Review of Richard Wright, Black boy: A record of childhood and youth. JMH 7:178-80, July 1945.

WRITINGS

Porter, Dorothy B. Early American Negro writings: A bibliographical study with a preliminary check list of the published writings of American Negroes, 1760-1835. BSA 39:192-268, Third Quarter, 1945.

WYANDOTTE CONVENTION

Waters, J.G. Kansas and the Wyandotte convention. KAN 11:47-52, 1910.

WYNDHAM, H.A.

Review of H.A. Wyndham, The Atlantic and slavery. GEJ 86:291-2, Sept. 1935.

Yost, Genevieve. History of lynchings in Kansas. KHQ 2: 182-219, May 1933.

YOUNG, D.

Gibson, B.D. Review of D. Young, The American Negro. IRM 19:306-7, Apr. 1930.

Young, J.H. Anna Elizabeth Dickinson--a woman abolitionist views the South in 1875. GHQ 32:241-51, Dec. 1948.

Young, J.H. Anna Elizabeth Dickinson--her campaign during the Civil War period for and against Lincoln. MVH 31: 59-80, June 1944.

Young, K. Review of G. Myrdal, An American dilemma. ASR 9: 326-30, June 1944.
Comment: G. Nettler, ASR 9:686-8, Dec. 1944.

YOUTH

Cahnman, W.J. Attitudes of minority youth: A methodological introduction. ASR 14:543-8, Aug. 1949.

Zorn, R.C. Review of E.M. Coulter, The South during Reconstruction. ARK 7:153-4, Summer 1948.

Zornow, William F. Judicial modifications of the Maryland black code in the District of Columbia. MDH 44:18-32, Mar. 1949.